Cracks in the Outfield Wall

Cracks in the Outfield Wall

The History of Baseball Integration in the Carolinas

CHRIS HOLADAY

THE UNIVERSITY OF NORTH CAROLINA PRESS Chapel Hill

*This book was published
with the assistance of the Z. Smith Reynolds Fund
of the University of North Carolina Press.*

© 2024 James C. Holaday
All rights reserved

Designed by Richard Hendel
Set in Utopia, Transat, and Bordonaro types
by codeMantra
Manufactured in the United States of America

Cover art: *Left to right:* Bubba Morton, Ted Richardson, and Wendell Antoine of the 1957 Durham Bulls. Courtesy of the *Durham Herald* Newspaper Photograph Collection, Wilson Special Collections Library, UNC-Chapel Hill Library, Chapel Hill.

Library of Congress Cataloging-in-Publication Data
Names: Holaday, J. Chris, 1966– author.
Title: Cracks in the outfield wall : the history of baseball integration in the Carolinas / Chris Holaday.
Description: Chapel Hill : The University of North Carolina Press, 2024. | Includes bibliographical references and index.
Identifiers: LCCN 2023047466 | ISBN 9781469678849 (cloth ; alk. paper) | ISBN 9781469678856 (paperback ; alk. paper) | ISBN 9781469678863 (epub) | ISBN 9798890887245 (pdf)
Subjects: LCSH: Carolina League (Baseball league)—History. | Discrimination in sports—United States—History—20th century. | Baseball—United States—History—20th century. | African American baseball players—North Carolina—History. | African American baseball players—South Carolina—History. | BISAC: SPORTS & RECREATION / Baseball / History | HISTORY / United States / State & Local / South (AL, AR, FL, GA, KY, LA, MS, NC, SC, TN, VA, WV)
Classification: LCC GV875.C37 H65 2024 | DDC 796.357089/960730756—dc23/eng/20231117
LC record available at https://lccn.loc.gov/2023047466

Contents

Illustrations

Author's Note

The story of baseball in the Carolinas has long intrigued me. From the small towns that proudly fielded professional teams, to employees of textile mills who turned to baseball to temporarily escape from horrendous working conditions, to kids hoping to—and sometimes succeeding in—making a career out of being a baseball player, it is a rich history. It is also a story of racial segregation. Black and white were kept apart for decades, and the end of that segregation did not come about suddenly. It was a long process filled with steps forward and setbacks. It also involved little kids and professional athletes, many of them no more than teenagers themselves.

In one of the seminal works on baseball integration, historian Jules Tygiel wrote in 1983, "The acceptance of blacks in interracial competition dented Jim Crow's armor, and in many instances, caused people, particularly business owners, to re-evaluate the efficacy and wisdom of southern racial policies. Even as resistance to integration escalated, the baseball diamond remained an oasis of relative enlightenment amidst an increasingly hostile environment."[1] This was true in North and South Carolina, and I wanted to examine the issue more closely and understand how it took place.

As to why integration happened when it did, the answer is not simple. At the professional level there were so many other factors at play, including the ever-increasing influence of the major leagues and the 1950s demise of many minor league teams due to societal changes. In the middle of it all was a bunch of guys brave enough to ignore Jim Crow laws who just wanted to make a living playing the game they loved. Though they may not have been marching in protests or participating in sit-ins, all these men played a role in the civil rights struggle just by doing their jobs. Some of those involved with integration of the professional game in the Carolinas went on to great fame. So many others, however, faded into obscurity. Perhaps the pressure of being some of the first to cross the color line was too much for them. Perhaps an injury forced them to give up on baseball dreams, or perhaps they just got homesick and returned to Cuba or California or a small southern town. Regardless, all Black players in the 1950s and '60s had a role in baseball integration, and all of them have a story. Part of what I wanted to do is share those stories.

Eventual acceptance of desegregation in professional baseball did not carry over to the game at the grassroots level. Perhaps it was too close to the incendiary education issue, but it was also not as subject to outside control. Proponents of segregated baseball may have felt they had little control if a major league club assigned Black prospects to their town's team, but they could control who their kids played with and against. The youth game has never had the media attention of the professional game, but I wanted to include it because it is an important part of the overall story.

I chose to focus on three decades, from early incidents of racial conflict on the baseball diamond in American Legion baseball to the Civil Rights Act of 1964. The Civil Rights Act certainly did not end the struggles of Black players in the game of baseball, but it at least marked an end to Jim Crow.

Introduction

Separate but equal. That is the myth by which society in the American South operated for much of a century. Black and white were kept apart, a situation that was enforced by so-called Jim Crow laws from Reconstruction to the mid-1960s. The Code of Laws of South Carolina, in reference to travelers, once stated, "No persons . . . shall furnish meals to white and colored passengers in the same room, or at the same table, or at the same counter." Another law addressed the work environment: "It shall be unlawful for any person, firm or corporation . . . to allow . . . different races to labor and work together within the same room, or to use the same doors of entrance and exit at the same time . . . or to use the same stairway and windows at the same time, or to use at any time the same lavatories, toilets, drinking water buckets, pails, cups, dippers or glasses."[1] In neighboring Georgia, a law was even on the books that specifically addressed amateur baseball: "It shall be unlawful for any amateur white baseball team to play baseball on any vacant lot or baseball diamond within two blocks of a playground devoted to the Negro race, and it shall be unlawful for any amateur colored baseball team to play baseball in any vacant lot or baseball diamond within two blocks of any playground devoted to the white race."[2]

The separate part of Jim Crow was definite. George Altman, who was a major league all-star for the Chicago Cubs, wrote of growing up in segregated Goldsboro, North Carolina, in the 1940s:

> All of the schools were segregated and the town was divided. I never played with white kids on the playground. I never knew them at all. I never crossed paths with them. We didn't live far away from the white high school, but I never knew exactly where it was. I never saw them in the streets and my family didn't take a newspaper, so I didn't even keep up with what they were doing. At the same time I never felt any discrimination. We stayed in our area. The only time I might run into white people was when I had a paper route and delivered

the newspaper in the morning. It was sort of like having two worlds with them never overlapping.

The whole time I was in high school, all the competition was segregated. We never played against white schools at all. My teammates were all black. . . . We very much would have liked to have played against the white high school in our town or other white high schools in our area. In the years since I have often thought about how strange the world was back then when everything was segregated. We live in a very different society now.[3]

When it came to equal, one of the few things that might have been the same for both Black and white was a love for the game of baseball. The Carolinas have always been a baseball hotbed, and throughout the first half of the twentieth century, teams of Black and white players—though segregated—could be found playing on the diamonds of most towns and cities in the states. Every spring, baseball became the center of discussion everywhere, from tobacco warehouses to big-city banks to Black barbershops. It was truly the national pastime and king of the sports scene, as college football and basketball were still secondary sports.

The shared love of baseball and the special place the game has in the American psyche make the story of its integration so important. If baseball could be integrated, then America could be integrated. In the early 1960s, former Negro league and major league star Monte Irvin said, "Baseball has done more to move America in the right direction than all the professional patriots with their billions of cheap words. Baseball has proved it can be done."[4] That is a profound statement, considering he was referring to what is essentially a fun game for children played with a stick and a ball. But baseball did push the country forward with regard to racial integration. It was already a sport where the playing field was equal regardless of economic background; poor mill worker or rich college kid, the only thing that mattered was skill. Once race was eliminated as an obstacle to equality, baseball truly offered all its players a chance for virtually unlimited opportunities. Baseball can also be a business. To make money, all one needs is a winning team to bring in the paying fans. Winning requires talented players, and sometimes those players happen to be Black.

Eventually, Black and white did come together on the baseball field in the Carolinas. It was a slow process, but white baseball fans grew to accept talented Black players sharing the field with white players well

Children play baseball on the playground of Allen-Benedict Court, a Columbia public housing complex, in 1955. Courtesy of *The State* Newspaper Photograph Archive, Richland Library, Columbia, SC.

before they accepted integration in other circumstances. The story involves local residents who were not opposed to integration, but more importantly it involves national organizations. Some, such as the American Legion, often looked the other way and did not directly address the issue. Little League Inc., on the other hand, was staunchly against discrimination. It paid the price as a mass exodus of youth teams in the South resulted. The most important national group with regard to integration, however, was professional baseball, particularly the major leagues. With their influence and economic power, they played a huge role in integration.

To understand baseball integration in the Carolinas (as well as in the entire South), the (white) professional baseball system and the paternal relationship between the major and minor leagues that grew in the 1950s must be examined. At the turn of the twentieth century, professional baseball outside the major leagues was not united, and leagues operated independently of each other. There were no shared structures or rules, and leagues frequently came and went. To stabilize the system (which, they hoped, could lead to growth), representatives of the minor leagues met in the fall of 1901. They created the National Association of Professional Baseball Leagues, which put into place a plan to organize and classify all professional baseball in the country below the level of the major leagues. Beginning with the 1902 season, the organization operated with a hierarchical system that essentially placed the larger cities at the top and smaller ones at the bottom. The plan designated league classifications such as A, B, C, and D. Each level had guidelines that member clubs were required to follow for salaries, roster sizes, rules on the field of play, and more, and players signed binding contracts. Member teams, which comprised only players who could be considered "white" by the social mores of the day, were located across the United States and Canada. This entire professional baseball system—the major leagues and the associated minor leagues—became officially known as Organized Baseball.[5]

Initially, the minor leagues operated independently of the major leagues. To survive financially, they relied upon ticket sales as well as the selling of promising players—whom they had under contract—to interested higher-level teams. The early 1920s saw the first appearance of the "farm system" in professional baseball. Created by Branch Rickey of the St. Louis Cardinals, it was the alignment of minor league clubs with specific major league teams. Players under contract to the major league club (sometimes a full roster, sometimes just a few) were assigned to an affiliated minor league club at a skill-appropriate level. Major league clubs increasingly were in favor of the system because it allowed them to sign talented young players to low-paying contracts and develop them into major league players. This was often much more cost-effective than purchasing the contract of a star minor leaguer. And minor league teams were happy to sign with a major league organization because the farm system relieved them of the burden of having to pay player salaries. Some independent teams remained in operation for years, but the influence of the major leagues over the minor leagues increased until it became almost total in the 1950s.

In the 1940s, the top of the minor league ladder, essentially one step below the major leagues, was designated AA. This is the level (now called AAA) at which the Durham and Charlotte teams play today. Most of the larger cities in North and South Carolina at that time were at the levels of A or B. This list, which sometimes fluctuated, included Columbia, Greenville, and Charleston at the A level and Durham, Raleigh, Greensboro, Charlotte, Spartanburg, and Asheville (among others) at the B level. The most common level of professional baseball in the states, however, was Class D, the bottom rung of the ladder. In 1948, the high point of minor league baseball in North Carolina, forty-four towns had professional teams; thirty-five of them were Class D. It is still essentially the same system in place today, though the current classifications of AAA, AA, and A were implemented in 1963.[6]

In the third quarter of the nineteenth century, there were a few Black professional baseball players in both the major and minor leagues. Instead of their numbers increasing, however, they were forced out of the game in the 1890s by a "gentleman's agreement." Without any formal rule or announcement, white team owners decided that, going forward, no teams would sign Black players. No one would seriously challenge this unwritten rule until 1946.

By no means, though, did exclusion from the white professional baseball system stop African Americans from playing the game. In fact, said the *Negro Digest* in 1943, "baseball to a Negro . . . either player or fan . . . is just as much the All-American game as it is to members of other races." The difference was that Black baseball players who wanted to pursue a professional career (or even to play the game at the amateur level) but did not qualify as white were resigned to play in leagues for players of African descent. Called the Negro leagues, they were similar to the leagues of Organized Baseball, though much less formal in the way they operated. Like white professional baseball, the major league Black teams were located in the big cities of the North and Midwest. Top Black players strove to make it in the game and play for the likes of the Kansas City Monarchs or Pittsburgh's Homestead Grays. As with white players, most Black players labored on smaller teams in smaller towns, hoping to make a few dollars and perhaps earn a chance to move up the ladder. For any player and in any time period, it has been extremely difficult to make a career out of professional sports. It was not unheard of, however, and even African Americans from the Carolinas did find success on the baseball diamond. One example is that of the four Taylor brothers. C. I., "Candy" Jim, "Steel Arm" Johnny, and Ben Taylor were born in Anderson, South Carolina, in the last quarter of the nineteenth century. C. I. was the oldest, and his baseball skills took him to Birmingham, Alabama. The other brothers eventually followed, and all went on to long careers as players, coaches, managers, and team owners outside the South in cities including Indianapolis, St. Paul, Chicago, and Baltimore. Ben Taylor, the youngest of the four, was elected to the Baseball Hall of Fame in 2006.[7]

What appears to have been the first attempt to organize a professional league for Black players in the United Stated actually took place in the South. The short-lived Southern League of Colored Base Ballists was founded in 1886, and its members included the Charleston Fultons. With other teams located as far away as New Orleans and Memphis, travel was undoubtedly difficult—not to mention costly. Later attempts at forming leagues for Black players in the North were more successful because populations were larger and travel easier.[8]

In the 1940s South, the Black baseball system was not as structured as that of the white minor leagues. Most towns in the Carolinas had a Black team, but these played sporadically and were often not in organized leagues. Notable exceptions were the Asheville Blues, who played in the Negro Southern League for three seasons (1945–47), and the Charlotte Black Hornets (1946) and Raleigh Tigers (1947), who were members of the same league for a single year. A Negro American Association was formed in 1948 but lasted less than two years. Published records are scarce, but its members included Asheville, Raleigh, Greensboro, Winston-Salem, and Durham in North Carolina as well as Orangeburg, South Carolina. Otherwise, most Black teams operated in the semipro category. There was money involved, but teams did not follow strict rules with regard to operations.[9]

Often, Black teams "barnstormed" and played games in various towns around the area or country, with the players' only payment perhaps a share of the gate proceeds. Local Black teams, such as the Greenville Black Spinners or the Raleigh Tigers, might play traveling clubs like the Jacksonville Eagles. Other times, two traveling Black teams might face each other in an exhibition in a city that was home to neither. Even in the waning years of the Negro leagues such events continued; as a late as 1952, the Indianapolis Clowns played the Philadelphia Stars in Spartanburg's Duncan Park.[10] Sometimes, usually in the spring before the season began, Black teams even played against white minor league teams. There was usually no issue with this so long as everything was segregated. Author and baseball historian L. M. Sutter identified barnstorming as a key factor in integration. "White fans became more comfortable and realized it was OK to watch Black teams and players," she said, "especially if players were talented and the level of play was very high."[11]

The National Association of Professional Baseball Leagues (that is, the white minor leagues) officially desegregated in 1946 when Jackie Robinson, Johnny Wright, and Roy Partlow signed with the Brooklyn Dodgers organization and were assigned to Montreal.[12] In addition to this being a monumental event in the civil rights struggle, it opened a door of opportunity for talented Black athletes. The introduction of baseball integration was not without detriment, however. Wrote Wendell Smith in the *Pittsburg Courier*, one of the leading Black-owned newspapers in the United States, "Before Negro players were accepted in organized baseball, Negro baseball was a thriving business. . . . The golden era died, however, when Jackie Robinson joined the Brooklyn Dodgers in 1947. That was the opening wedge and after Robinson made good there was a wild scramble for Negro talent."[13]

Despite a new group of athletically gifted players becoming available, the complete integration of the baseball system was slow in coming. In the minor leagues, the first years' efforts were spent on the northern fringes of the system. By coincidence, the Brooklyn Dodgers' top minor league club, the Montreal Royals, was located in Canada, far from the Jim Crow South. The farthest south the Royals' schedule took the team (and Jackie Robinson) was Baltimore. By the end of the 1950 season, Black players had yet to take the field for a professional team below the Mason-Dixon Line.[14] The only exceptions were major league spring training games in Florida, though Black players still faced restrictions even then; Jackie Robinson was not allowed to play outside the Dodgers' facility in Daytona Beach in his first spring training.[15]

Though the number of teams in the South was much higher, major league clubs often chose to start their African American players off with a farm team in the North or the West. Many southern team owners were afraid to sign Black players due to fears of being boycotted by fans or having opponents cancel games. In some places there were even ordinances that prohibited Black and white interaction. With team finances often so tight, any loss of revenue could be disastrous. There were also logistical complications involved with having Black players; they were not allowed to stay in the same lodgings as their teammates when on the road, nor could they eat in the same restaurants. From the major league team standpoint, it was not good business sense to throw prospects into a hostile atmosphere where they might face constant harassment. Players were an investment, and if they were to contribute to the success of the big-league ball club one day, they needed to focus on sharpening their skills rather than worry about threats from racist fans.

As other major league organizations began to follow the Brooklyn Dodgers' lead and hire Black players, they maintained the same strategy of keeping their Black athletes away from the South. Dave Hoskins, who would later play for the Cleveland Indians, made his debut in professional baseball in 1948 with the Grand Rapids Jets in Michigan. It was not until 1952 that he played in the South. That season, Hoskins integrated the Texas League and starred for the Dallas Eagles.[16] Other African American stars of the 1950s also began their careers in Organized Baseball far outside the South. Hank Aaron made his minor league debut in Eau Claire, Wisconsin, while fellow Alabama native Willie Mays played in Trenton and Minneapolis before his big-league debut. Pitcher Don Newcombe played for Nashua, New Hampshire, and Montreal, and Frank Robinson, who would eventually become the first Black manager of a major league team, began his playing career in Ogden, Utah.[17]

As the number of Black players in the minor league system increased, it became inevitable that many would play for teams in the South. How they dealt with it depended on their state of origin. For players actually from the South, Jim Crow was nothing new. They understood the situation and how to navigate within its limitations. Players from northern or western states often had the most difficult time. They had faced discrimination, but it was nothing like the oppressive laws of the South. "Yeah, it was like going to another world," said California native Aaron Pointer, when he was sent to Salisbury, North Carolina, in 1961. Black players from Cuba and other Spanish-speaking countries likely found the situation baffling. In addition to being discriminated against for not speaking English, they were also subject to Jim Crow laws—but at the same time, they were often viewed differently from Black Americans. Said Cuban pitcher Luis Tiant, "It was tough for all the black players, but at least the American blacks spoke English."[18]

The career of Marvin Williams began in the early 1940s, and by the time integration was underway he was too old to be considered a major league prospect. Still, he continued to play, joining the Columbia Reds in May 1955. In his long career, Williams played in the Negro National League for Philadelphia as well as for teams in Mexico, Cuba, Venezuela, Canada, and numerous other places in the United States. Courtesy of *The State* Newspaper Photograph Archive, Richland Library, Columbia, SC.

The stories told by early Black players are similar. Obviously there were racial taunts from fans, but they often ceased (or greatly decreased) at home if a player excelled on the field and was an asset to the team. It was on the road that Black players suffered the most harassment. Though it is rarely heard today, heckling has long been a part of baseball. White players were no stranger to verbal abuse from fans, but the taunts usually had to do with perceived lack of skill. Race gave hecklers new—and much more vicious—ammunition. Still, most Black players who wrote of experiencing racial insults from the stands learned to ignore them. Black players unused to the Jim Crow South (for instance, Bill White from Ohio and Frank Robinson from California) were primarily the ones who reacted.

Many white players from other parts of the country were also shocked by the South when the game took them there. They were from places where few African Americans lived, were used to the milder discrimination that existed in many places, or perhaps were just oblivious to how Black Americans were treated. These were, after all, often teenagers and young adults who were focused on baseball above all else.

Pennsylvania native Russell Buhite played for Rutherford County in the Western Carolina League in 1960. Later a distinguished university history professor, he wrote of his first experience with the Jim Crow South. "I could hardly believe my eyes at the 'white' and 'colored' drinking fountains, and I could not contain my revulsion at the whites-only cafés run by low-life proprietors who refused service to our black players," he recalled.

> Then there were the sideline trips to the all-black sections of town, where we put our black players up in rooming houses. Nothing brought racism to my consciousness quite so directly, however, as an experience with a black teammate and friend with whom I swapped sports coats for an evening out. I learned from southern teammates that this was "unacceptable" behavior—and dangerous! Why did black fans sit in the left-field bleachers, always the left-field bleachers, by themselves? No one could answer that one. Nor could anyone tell me why the "nigra" high schools were such ramshackle edifices.[19]

Haven Schmidt, who played for High Point–Thomasville in 1956 and Columbia in 1960, shared similar sentiments in a 2019 interview.

> Being from Iowa, I never realized what those guys went through in the South. I spent almost all of my career down there and I saw how hard it was on the Black players. I think organizations sent the better prospects to teams in the South because they felt good players would take less abuse. Maybe, but they still had to go through a lot. Most of it was on the road, but even at home I heard comments. As a catcher I was closer to the stands, and I heard the names. I can't imagine going through what some of them did.[20]

In the world of professional baseball, acceptance by the fans has always depended upon success on the field. A player of any ethnicity quickly found himself booed if he failed to perform and soon out of a job. But white players were given a chance while Black players were automatically suspect solely due to race. Recalled Bill Bethea, one of the first two Black athletes with the Lexington, North Carolina, team in 1960,

> I had to do one thing when I first played in Lexington. We nearly had a little riot there. They were calling me names and things my first time to pitch there, so when I went out I just pulled my shirt up to make sure that I had "Lexington Indians" on my shirt. I said, "I'm supposed to be with you all. This is the home team and I'm with the home team." But the police came and they got quieted down. . . . I had made up my mind I was gonna win 'em over. I'm not gonna come out and be vicious and nasty. That wouldn't solve anything. That first time I pitched in Lexington, by the seventh inning I think I had struck out 15 and I heard one person in the stands—a white gentleman—say, "Come on, Bill," like that. Things had quieted down since the police had to talk to 'em. After that, I didn't have a problem.[21]

The experiences of Bethea are similar to those of many others in the early years of baseball integration in the South. Athletes had to prove themselves on the field of play, but once they did so, they gained a level of acceptance from white fans, at least at home. There was some hypocrisy in that, however. Fans might accept a Black player on the home team but then taunt one on an opposing team with racial slurs. "It doesn't make sense that these bigots cheer a Negro athlete and accept him as an equal as long as he wears the hometown uniform," said Black Hall of Famer Monte Irvin. Still, it was progress and showed that for many of those fans, skill on the field was a factor that could transcend race. If a Black player could hit a home run or strike out an opposing batter and help the team win, then he was just as good as any white player. Often, the difficulty for Black players in the early years of baseball integration in the Carolinas was finding that chance to prove themselves. Thanks to the influence of Major League Baseball and its farm system, Black players slowly became more and more common—and accepted—as the 1960s progressed.[22]

Chapter 1

AMERICAN LEGION, EPISODE I

In the summer of 1934, six teams of high school–age boys met in Gastonia, North Carolina, for a three-day tournament to decide the Eastern Sectional Champion of American Legion baseball. The winner would advance to Chicago and face the top team from the West to determine the overall national champion. The six teams meeting in Gastonia originated from Cincinnati; Charlotte; Tampa; Springfield, Massachusetts; Trenton, New Jersey; and Cumberland, Maryland. "Very little is known of the teams to play here except for Charlotte," wrote the reporter for the *Charlotte Observer* in a tournament preview. Truer words could not have been spoken, because when the Springfield team arrived, it had a Black member.[1]

American Legion baseball was sponsored by a nonprofit service organization for the veterans of World War I. In 1919, American veterans in Paris founded a group that was open to any soldier, sailor, or marine who had served between April 6, 1917, and November 11, 1918.[2] They named it the American Legion, and posts, as they were called, of the organization soon spread across the United States. The American Legion National Convention passed a resolution in 1923 expressing firm support of equal rights and opportunities "without distinction as to race, color, creed or class." Separate posts were established for Black and white members, however, primarily because the armed forces were segregated—and Jim Crows laws in the South would not have allowed anything other.[3]

The goal of the American Legion was to focus on benefits and support for veterans as well as programs for children. The organization soon identified athletic competition as a way to promote health, sportsmanship, and active citizenship. Based upon those ideals, the first American Legion baseball program for high school–age boys was founded in South Dakota in 1925. Legion posts around the country began to adopt similar programs, and tournaments featuring post teams soon followed. The program rapidly expanded, and teams representing Legion posts began to play tournaments to determine state and regional champions.

The Legion's first national baseball tournament for teenagers was held in Philadelphia in 1926. While the vast majority of participants in these tournaments were white, it was not unheard of for a team to have a Black member in areas of the country where racial interaction was permissible.[4]

The atmosphere surrounding the 1934 tournament in Gastonia was festive. A parade was scheduled on August 23 before the opening game at the stadium of Gastonia High School. That evening, a banquet for all teams and Legion officials, including C. M. "Chuck" Wilson from the national headquarters, was planned at Gastonia's Armington Hotel. Bands played to welcome the teams as they disembarked from their trains. But band members reportedly stopped mid-note when the star pitcher for Springfield Post 21 from Massachusetts, Ernest "Bunny" Taliaferro, stepped off the train.[5]

When the Springfield players went to their hotel, complications immediately arose. Coach Syd Harris was informed that, per local ordinances (in other words, Jim Crow laws), Taliaferro would not be allowed to stay in the hotel with his teammates. The only exception would be if the coach listed Taliaferro as his valet. Then, in a back room, the player could be given a cot—not a bed, however, because those were for white people. When the team protested this arrangement, tournament officials attempted to find a solution. What they proposed was that Taliaferro stay in the home of a local Black doctor while in town. In this scenario, though, not only would the teenager be staying with a stranger in a strange town but he would not be able to dine or even socialize with his teammates.[6]

On that first day in Gastonia, Springfield Post 21 was scheduled to have a practice session. By that time, word had spread that the team had a Black member. A crowd showed up at the practice and booed Taliaferro when he came up to bat. Soon onlookers began assaulting the team with thrown objects. The situation deteriorated rapidly from that: Coach Harris received a threatening phone call at the hotel, and the Cumberland and Tampa teams stated that they refused to play against a Black athlete. Springfield Post 21 was essentially left with the only option of removing Taliaferro from its roster if it wanted to participate in the tournament.

Being first told that Taliaferro was not allowed to stay with them and now that he couldn't play was too much for the rest of the Springfield squad. Team captain Tony King refused to take the field without Taliaferro, and the rest of the team agreed. Syd Harris decided it was time to leave Gastonia. He sent a telegram back to his Legion post: "Situation too dangerous. Boys threatened. Bringing team home." The team boarded a train and headed north. The athletes arrived in Springfield to a very supportive crowd.[7]

The treatment of the Springfield team was met with outrage in Massachusetts and made national news. A telegraph from Springfield mayor Henry Martens to Frank Samuels, national adjutant of the American Legion at the organization's headquarters in Indianapolis, stated, "Public indignation here at the treatment accorded Springfield post junior baseball team at Gastonia, N.C. leads me to urge your organization to accede request for participation of Springfield team in Chicago playoff." Commander William Connelly of the Springfield Legion post commented that the national Legion "is faced with the clear question of whether it will choose to stand by the principles it professes, or whether it will permit intimidation by a group apparently uninterested in fair play of the spirit of a free America." In the *Boston Globe*, sportswriter Jerry Nason said, "A brace of Southern teams, or the officials thereof, refused to plant a foot on a field where a Negro boy stood, glove in hand, waiting to oppose them."[8]

Though the Associated Press indicated that Tampa and Cumberland had actually refused to play, the *Charlotte Observer* reported that the two teams had merely stated that they did not like the idea of playing but did not refuse, as it would have meant forfeiture. Somewhat surprisingly, the Charlotte team in the tournament did not refuse to play Springfield. The *Boston Globe* reported that Charlotte "adapted itself to the ticklish situation, displaying excellent sportsmanship in stating that it would play regardless of the setting as it was 'the Legionaire thing to do.'"[9]

The treatment of the Springfield team drew general condemnation in the newspapers of the North. Many articles even expressed surprise at the discrimination that Bunny Taliaferro faced. It is understandable that a bunch of high school kids from Massachusetts were not familiar with the South and its laws, but most adults, especially newspaper reporters, should have had knowledge of the discriminatory treatment of Black citizens in all aspects of life in the South. And racial discrimination was certainly not limited to the South; it was just more obvious and supported by laws. In the South, the common sentiment regarding the incident was more "That's just the way it is here and those guys should have known better." Charlotte sports columnist Wade Ison wrote, "It is no fault of the American Legion that the state of North Carolina laws prohibit a negro from stopping at a hotel for white people. It appears that the Springfield delegation acted a bit hasty, for had they stayed the darkie boy could have put up with the Gastonia doctor and other teams would have either played the Springfield team or would have withdrawn from the tournament. It's a pretty good rule to act like Romans when in Rome."[10]

The Springfield incident may have been the first time that the issue of race was ever addressed on a baseball field in the Carolinas. It was an issue that no one, particularly white baseball officials, wanted to address. Doing so would mean they would have to confront the larger issue of Jim Crow laws. The general feeling was that white people had their baseball and Black people had their baseball, and that was how things were supposed to remain.

More than eight decades later, when the mayor of Gastonia learned of the events surrounding the 1934 Legion tournament, he sent a letter of apology to the mayor of Springfield. The two mayors then arranged a weekend of "friendship baseball" for which the team from Gastonia Post 23 traveled to Massachusetts for a series of three games against Springfield-area Legion teams.[11]

Chapter 2
ONLY AN ISSUE FOR THE AMERICANS

While American Legion baseball had (and still has) a big following, the world of professional baseball is on another level. Player skill, fan interest, and media attention are greatly amplified. Many of the top youth players of American Legion baseball advance—or hope to do so—to a situation where they are paid to play the game as professionals.

In Organized Baseball—the name for the white major leagues and their affiliated professional minor leagues—the story of integration in the Carolinas essentially begins with a story of "passing." In 1937, a stocky, 5′8″ outfielder named Bobby Estalella joined the Charlotte Hornets of the Class B Piedmont League. A promising prospect from Cuba, he had been signed by Washington Senators scout Joe Cambria in 1934, had his name anglicized from Roberto to Bobby, and had been brought to the United States. While playing for the Senators' minor league affiliate in Albany, New York, Estalella had earned brief "cups of coffee" with the big-league club in 1935 and 1936. Assigned to Charlotte in 1937, Estalella hit .349 with 33 home runs. He was even better the next season and won the Triple Crown for the Hornets with a .378 batting average, 38 home runs, and 123 RBIs.[1] There was no denying that Bobby Estalella had baseball ability. There was also no denying that he had some African ancestry and, according to rules of the time, should have been barred from Organized Baseball. For a player of his skill level, however, the Senators organization was obviously willing to overlook any ambiguity regarding racial heritage.

During his time in Charlotte, Estalella was a fan and sportswriter favorite. Newspapers sang his praises, though they did mention his physical appearance. Late in the 1938 season, *Charlotte Observer* sports columnists Jake Wade wrote of "the little bow-legged dark-skinned chap": "Although he has been with the club only about half the season he has kissed some 18 home runs and has been, in every way, an amazing, spectacular performer."[2] Opposing players in the Piedmont League also had great respect for Estalella's talents. "That Bobby Estalella was

Bobby Estalella with the team in Mariano, Cuba, during the winter of 1947. Collection of the author.

one good hitter," recalled Durham Bulls outfielder Norman Small years later. "One game, in Durham, he hit a ball that went just over my head. It rolled up the hill in centerfield into the corner against the fence. By the time I got to it and threw it back to home, Estalella was back in the dug-out havin' a drink of water."[3]

On November 15, 1938, sportswriters voted Estalella the Most Valuable Player in the Piedmont League from a list of twenty-five candidates. With three first-place votes and two second, Estalella edged out Norfolk shortstop (and future Hall of Famer) Phil Rizzuto by one point. The committee that made the selection for the *Sporting News* comprised Charlotte's Jake Wade as well as sportswriters from Durham, Asheville, Winston-Salem, Rocky Mount, Portsmouth, Norfolk, and Richmond.[4]

Estalella was recalled to Washington in 1939 and spent the entire season with the Senators. The team tactfully mentioned to the press that he was "born of Spanish parents in Havana."[5] He was eventually traded to the Athletics organization and became an above-average player for Philadelphia during the war years. Estalella went on to spend a few seasons playing in Mexico before making a brief return to the Athletics in 1949. In 1951, at age forty, "the swarthy little man with the cannon bat" returned to Charlotte.[6] Before knee surgery forced him to retire from the game, Estalella batted .310 in 18 games for the Hornets that season, including away contests in Anderson, Rock Hill, and Greenwood.[7]

Cuban baseball historian Roberto González Echevarría wrote that Estalella was "a very light mulatto . . . white enough to play in the American League and in Organized Baseball."[8] Wrote baseball historian Joanne Hulbert, "Questions about his ancestry were a shadow behind the headlines" because of his excellence on the field.[9] Hulbert also noted that Estalella was considered Black by many of his teammates and even a few prominent sportswriters of the time. But because he was listed as "Cuban," that descriptive term was enough for most.[10] F. Lennox Campello wrote, "Certainly in the Deep South, no one was fooled by the owners' claim that Estalella was not black but Cuban. But the spectacular deception worked, at least on paper, and this talented athlete thus became the first man of recognizable African ancestry to play Major League baseball."[11] Many years later, Estalella was asked to comment about the racial question. He answered simply, "It was only an issue for the Americans."[12] Estalella proved that race made no difference in terms of success on the baseball field and exposed a double standard in which ambiguous racial heritage could be ignored. Regardless, it was an issue no one in professional baseball in the Carolinas or the South wanted to openly confront until 1951.[13]

Chapter 3

AMERICAN LEGION, EPISODE II

The events in Gastonia in 1934 had been something of an embarrassment for American Legion baseball. To prevent similar situations from arising in the future, one solution would have been to mandate that tournaments involving teams from outside the South never be held in that region. The Legion took no such action, however, and just four years later the specter of Jim Crow appeared again. In 1938, San Diego Post 6 advanced to the national semifinals in Charlotte. As in Springfield, Massachusetts, having an integrated Legion team was not an issue in San Diego; the Post 6 squad had two Black members: catcher John Ritchey and third baseman Nelson Manuel.

Ritchey and Manuel played regularly as their team won tournaments in California and North Dakota and advanced toward the championship. When they arrived in North Carolina, however, Coach Mike Morrow was told that the players would not be allowed to take the field. The boys, two of the younger members of San Diego Post 6, were forced to watch as their teammates claimed victory over Detroit in Charlotte. The team then advanced to the national finals in Spartanburg, South Carolina, to face Spartanburg Post 28, the 1936 National Champion. Again, Ritchey and Manuel were forced to sit out. Despite being short two players on the roster, San Diego prevailed and won the deciding game in front of 9,000 fans.[1]

Two years later, the San Diego Post 6 team, with John Ritchey and Nelson Manuel as starting members, advanced through the different levels of competition. Again the team reached the semifinals, which—again—was to be played in North Carolina. This time the two-out-of-three series was to be played in the town of Shelby and the opponent was St. Louis's Aubuchon-Dennison Post. Coach Morrow fully expected that Ritchey and Manuel would not be allowed to play, but no one from the host Shelby Legion protested. Wrote J. Cullen Fentress of the *San Diego Evening Tribune*,

The 1938 San Diego Post 6 American Legion team, with Nelson Manuel (*front row, third from left*) and John Ritchey (*front row, right end*). Collection of the author.

> Out of a clear sky yesterday came word from Shelby, N.C. that officials in charge of the American Legion Junior Baseball championship competition there ruled that John Ritchey and Nelson Manuel, Negro members of the team representing Post Six of San Diego would be permitted to take part in the semi-finals. It will mark a new era in the South, for never before has the "color line" been crossed in that section in these competitions. Two years ago Mike Morrow, coach of the San Diego team, headed into the final phases of play without the services of outstanding Negro players. That his team was able to win the title under such a handicap was considered all the more remarkable.[2]

On August 28, 1940, Ritchey and Manuel made history. They became the first African Americans to ever play with and against white players in Legion baseball in the South. In front of 3,000 fans in the first game of the series, San Diego beat St. Louis 5–4. In his column "Talking It Over," Tom Akers of the *San Diego Evening Tribune* reported that "no hint of objection was heard from any quarter. In fact, the spectators showed a generous, sportsmanlike spirit that was both gratifying and surprising. . . . It is related that each time the boys came to bat, the assembled thousands cheered lustily." San Diego went on to easily defeat St. Louis in the second game, 13–4. In that game, Ritchey, the team's leadoff hitter, was 3-for-5 at the plate with 3 runs batted in and 2 stolen bases. Manuel was 1-for-5 with 3 runs scored.[3]

News that the two Black players actually participated in two games in the South quickly spread in newspapers. The *California Eagle*, a Black-owned newspaper, said that the "Gibraltar Rock of prejudice [has] been penetrated in the South." In his column, sportswriter J. Cullen Fentress wrote, "There is one thing about this series that makes it history-making, aside from the fact, of course, that on the California team are two Negro lads—Nelson Manuel and John Ritchey—both of whom are stars. The important thing is that they are playing on the team before southern spectators—in Dixie!" Fentress went on to call attention to some larger implications of the event. "One of the arguments advanced against the Negro ballplayer in the major leagues is that most of the clubs train in the South and it is felt that the natives thereof just wouldn't allow the big leaguers to bring Negro players in their personnel," he wrote. "And, if a Negro major leaguer can't work out with his club he might as well not be on the team. The American Legion's San Diego club, however, is showing the fallacy of such an argument." It was even reported that messages were sent by San Diego Legionnaires to Shelby congratulating that city on its unexpected attitude toward permitting the boys to play.[4]

Though there was now a precedent, not all newspapers were so sure that the foray into integration would continue. After the semifinal series it was reported in the *Charlotte News* that "the two Negro stars with the Westerners may or may not play" in the final. The newspaper suggested that, in the spirit of sportsmanship, Albemarle "may insist they play their full strength." The Black-owned *Carolina Times* stated, "The south's age old 'custom' of racial discrimination has again flared up as a threat to upset the success of a well-planned and otherwise smooth running national sports classic." Indeed, as the opening game approached, there were rumblings that Ritchey and Manuel would not be allowed to play in Albemarle. Unsure of the situation, Mike Morrow kept the boys on the bench for the first game. "They've played for me all the way across the country," he said. "They are good boys and good ballplayers. They are two of my best players. They played in Shelby, N.C. last week. I didn't see any riots. This is the first game they've missed."[5]

With no protest officially filed, Morrow stated he planned to use his two Black players in the second game. It wasn't to be, however. Charlotte sportswriter Jake Wade wrote that he was handed a communiqué by Chuck Wilson, national director of the Legion baseball program, that clarified the organization's position. Reported Wade, "The colored boys were out because the Legion decided to abide by southern customs when playing in the South."[6]

San Diego won the first 2 games of the best-of-5 series but lost the next 3. A reported 13,500 people watched (including Ritchey and Manuel from the bench) as Albemarle defeated San Diego, 9–8, in the deciding game. Afterward, "Legion officials feted the San Diego and Albemarle teams with a nice banquet." Undoubtedly this would have been held in a segregated facility, and it is unknown whether Ritchey and Manuel participated.[7]

Before the deciding fifth game, Manuel and Ritchey had actually "warmed up in infield practice, causing the grandstands to speculate," reported the *Charlotte News*. "But Coach Mike Morrow was not rebellious, gave in to [Legion director] Homer Chaillaux's statement that it was not the thing to do and kept two of his best players on the bench while his club went down in defeat. He could have used one as a pinch-hitter in the ninth but he resisted temptation . . . but in batting practice, Ritchey parked a ball on the powerline support outside the park." We cannot know for certain why Morrow did not put his Black players in the important game. Perhaps he was afraid of the actions the Legion would take if he disobeyed, or perhaps he feared for the safety of his players. Whatever the reason, the odds are good that the contributions of players as talented as Ritchey and Manuel could have led to a different result in the series.[8]

Once again, the American Legion received a flood of negative press from across the country for its actions (or lack thereof). Wendell Smith, the country's top African American sportswriter, wrote in the *Pittsburgh Courier*, "The American Legion bowed to un-Americanism again last week by permitting the Legion of Albemarle, N.C., to bar San Diego's two colored stars, Johnny Ritchey and Nelson Manuel. Playing down in Albemarle, N.C., the two colored kids were benched because the Southerners didn't want to play against them. The San Diego Legion submitted to Albemarle's demands." In the *Oakland Tribune*, columnist Art Cohn wrote, "Once below the Mason and Dixon, the most un-American of prejudices, racial discrimination, reared its ugly head, and as a result, two regulars on the San Diego team were ruled ineligible. It seems that John Ri[t]chey and Nelson Manuel, the two boys involved, had been found guilty . . . of being Negroes."[9]

It can only be speculated as to why Ritchey and Manuel were allowed to play in Shelby but not Albemarle. Perhaps Legion officials in Shelby had a more progressive view on racial matters. A more likely reason would be that those who would be most opposed to breaking racial barriers did not give much attention to a series of games between teams from San Diego and St. Louis. It was a different story, however, when it came to a series against a team with a strong local following. All anyone had to do to get rid of two of the best players on the visiting team was point out that their participation should not be allowed.

Nelson Manuel was eligible for one more season of American Legion baseball. In 1941, he and future major leaguer Bob Usher led Post 6 to the national championship. Fortunately, the final that year was at home against a team from Illinois, so it was free from controversy. Other than Manuel's prowess as a high school football star, little else is known of his life.

The story of John Ritchey is much more well known. After high school he enrolled at San Diego State and joined the baseball team. The military draft interrupted Ritchey's college career, but he returned to school after serving in Europe during World War II. In 1947, he signed with the Chicago American Giants of the Negro American League. A successful season there earned him a tryout for the Chicago Cubs. No contract emerged, so Ritchey returned to San Diego. He signed with the Padres of the Pacific Coast League and became that league's first Black player (its only one in 1948). Though he never made it to the major leagues, Ritchey had a successful baseball career on the West Coast. In addition to San Diego, he played for Portland, Sacramento, and San Francisco in the Pacific Coast League and spent two seasons with Vancouver in the Class B Western International League. Ritchey also played winter baseball in Venezuela and Mexico. He retired from the game at age thirty-three after spending part of the 1956 season with Syracuse in the Class A Eastern League. Today a bronze bust of John Ritchey is on display in San Diego's Petco Park to honor his contributions to baseball in the city. On April 15, 2019, Jackie Robinson Day in Major League Baseball, the San Diego Padres created a $20,000 John Ritchey San Diego State University Scholarship for a graduating high school senior who "breaks barriers."[10]

Chapter 4
EXHIBITIONISTS AND BARNSTORMERS

Before minor league teams were integrated in the South, major league clubs helped prepare fans for what was to come. It had long been a tradition for big-league teams to put on preseason exhibition games as they traveled to their home cities after spring training. Leaving Florida and heading north, teams passed through South and North Carolina. Stopping along the way for a game gave them extra practice and, as these games usually drew large crowds, the chance to make a few dollars. Sometimes major league teams traveled together and played each other, though often the opponent was the local minor league team. The early Black players in the major leagues inevitably became part of these exhibition games, at least in cities where it was allowed. Suddenly, African Americans were able to come out and cheer for one of their own in a major league uniform. Uncomfortable though it may have been for some of them, white fans were shown that the two races could successfully interact, despite what Jim Crow laws said.

The first major league team to integrate, the Brooklyn Dodgers, was also the first to field an integrated team in an exhibition game in the Carolinas. The Dodgers made several stops in the region in the years before local professional teams were integrated. On April 8 and 9, 1948, more than 9,000 fans packed Asheville's McCormick Field to watch 2 games between the Asheville Tourists and the Dodgers. In 1950, the Dodgers made an exhibition stop in Greensboro. The next day, a report on the game against the Greensboro Patriots in the *Brooklyn Daily Eagle* was headlined "Carolina Slaughter!" Jackie Robinson went 3-for-7 with 3 RBIs, and every Dodger got at least one hit as the defending National League champions walloped their Carolina League opponents, 22–0. The *New York Daily News* reported that the reason the Dodgers added Greensboro to the exhibition schedule was that Jackie Robinson's barnstorming team had drawn 8,000 fans the previous fall. That total was surpassed by the Dodgers. Stated the *Daily News*, "Today's roped-off mob, predominately Negro, totaled 8,433."[1]

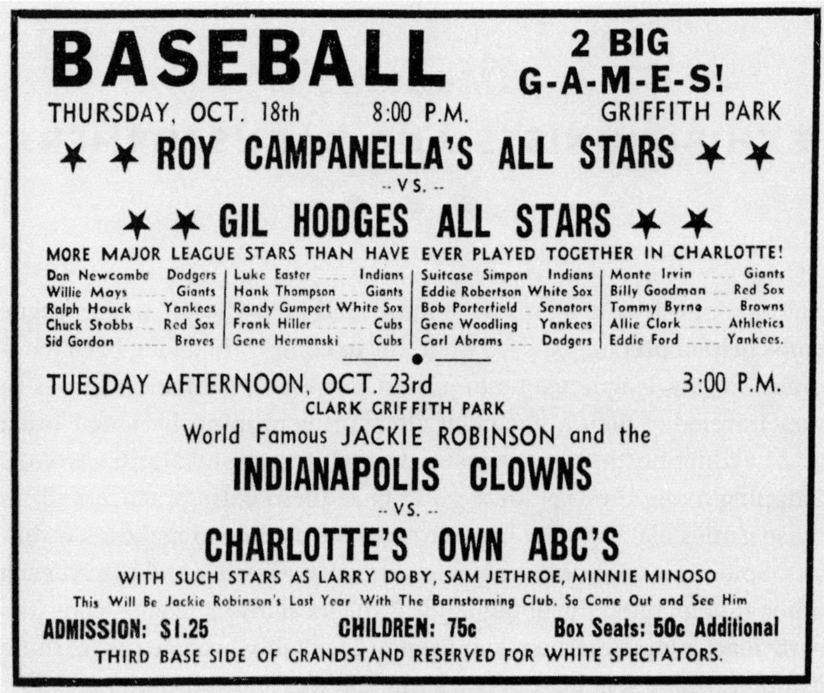

An advertisement for two Charlotte exhibition games in the fall of 1951. The first game featured two teams of major leaguers facing each other, one with Black members and one with white. The second game was between two teams of Black players that included Jackie Robinson and a few other major league stars. Collection of the author.

On April 9, 1951, the Dodgers returned to Asheville. The game drew a record crowd of 6,479, more than 2,000 over McCormick Field's official capacity. The *Daily News* noted, "Standees crowded both foul lines along the outfield, and fringed the distant hip-high fence at the base of the high hill that bounds the beautiful field." The throng of fans was treated to an exciting game: Jackie Robinson hit an inside-the-park homer, and Brooklyn came from behind to take a 9–8 victory over the Tourists. The star of the game was catcher Roy Campanella, who hit 2 home runs and drove in 4 runs. Just a few seasons before, Campanella had been barnstorming with the Baltimore Elite Giants of the Negro National League.[2]

In the fall, after the regular season was over, it was common for big-league ballplayers to assemble traveling "all-star" teams to play exhibition games as a source of off-season income. These barnstorming tours usually focused on the southern half of the United States, where they gave fans in towns far from the major leagues a chance to see top-level players. After his rise to stardom, Jackie Robinson followed this tradition and assembled a traveling team known as the Jackie Robinson All-Stars. Unlike his Brooklyn Dodgers squad, this team did not have a mixed-race roster. Instead, Robinson recruited other Black major leaguers—including Larry Doby, Don Newcombe, and Roy Campanella—to join him. The roster was filled out with top stars of the Negro leagues, often including such greats as North Carolina's own Buck Leonard. These teams would face off against other barnstorming Black teams or assembled teams of talented local players.

In 1949, Jackie Robinson brought his team to the Carolinas. The tour began in Newport News, Virginia, on October 11 and then had stops in Greensboro and Charlotte (where the players faced the South Carolina All-Stars, a Black team assembled for the event) before more dates in Tennessee and Arkansas. After going as far as Houston, Jackie Robinson's All-Stars worked their way back through the Deep South and played mid-November games in Charleston and Columbia (where their opponent was the Jacksonville Eagles). Robinson's team returned in 1950 and was in the Carolinas for four days, October 12–15. The athletes played games in Durham, Raleigh, Charlotte, Charleston, and Columbia. Roy Campanella also led his own Black barnstorming team at times. His team never played in South Carolina, but they did make several North Carolina appearances: Winston-Salem, Goldsboro, Durham, Charlotte, and Salisbury in 1951 and Charlotte in 1952.[3]

After the 1953 season, Jackie Robinson embarked on what would be his final tour with an all-star team. Interestingly, Robinson included four white players on his roster for the first time: Brooklyn teammate Gil Hodges, Ralph Branca of Detroit, Cleveland's Al Rosen, and Bobby Young of the St. Louis Browns (Rosen suffered an injury early in the tour and returned home). The tour, which began in Baltimore and headed south, made North Carolina stops in Charlotte, Asheville, and Conover. As mixed-race contests were slowly becoming more accepted, even in parts of the South, no problems resulted from the appearance of Robinson's All-Stars in those towns. This was not true in Birmingham, Alabama, however. There, a scheduled game was almost canceled due to city rules that prohibited Black and white players from sharing the field. Instead, Robinson and tour promoter Ted Worner decided to sit the three white players in the stands rather than risk their arrest. They were criticized by civil rights activists for the decision to continue the game, who saw it as a concession to segregationists. In hindsight, however, if the game had been canceled, it would have been a forgotten incident. Instead, it drew nationwide attention to the issue.[4]

Chapter 5
TRUE BEGINNINGS

By 1951, the professional minor leagues were struggling. For all of baseball's previous history, games in smaller towns and cities had been as much about serving as a communal gathering as they were about a sporting event. In the early 1950s, however, this dramatically changed.

The spread of television, which offered in-home entertainment, including major league games, greatly contributed to minor league baseball's demise. In 1950, only 9 percent of homes in the United States owned a television. By 1953 that percentage was nearly 45 percent, and it reached nearly 90 percent by the end of the decade. Baseball historian Steve Treder firmly placed the blame for the decline of the minor leagues on the rise of television. "The implications of this can hardly be overstated in terms of revenue generation and marketing opportunities for the sport, and in many other ways as well," he wrote. "Perhaps none of the many impacts of TV on baseball was bigger than what it meant for the minor leagues and semi-pro baseball. In 1950 there were 58 minor leagues in organized baseball, and countless more semi-pro operations. By 1960 there were only 22 minor leagues, and semi-pro baseball had largely become extinct."[1] With television as a new entertainment option, the decision of fans to spend evenings at a local baseball game became a far less easy one to make. While television indelibly changed baseball, it had an effect that went beyond sport. Wrote Treder, "Among the many ways television transformed small town American life in the 1950s was the shift away from communal gatherings at events such as minor league and semi-pro baseball games."[2]

In the early 1950s, "the minor leagues were buffeted by a variety of factors," wrote economist David Surdam. He pointed out that, while the rapid spread of television played a substantial role, the South still lagged behind other parts of the country in terms of television ownership. In fact, in 1950, less than 2.5 percent of homes in North Carolina owned televisions (the state's first commercial television stations, WBTV in Charlotte and WFMY in Greensboro, went on the air in 1949). That number was even lower in South Carolina, as the state had no television stations until 1953 (WCOS in Columbia was the first).[3] Surdam called out several additional factors for minor league baseball's decline, including overexpansion of the minor leagues in the late 1940s, a shrinking pool of potential players (partly due to the Korean War), and changes in American patterns of leisure spending. Another factor was the spread of home air conditioning. The window unit had been developed in 1945, and by 1947, 43,000 units had been sold.[4] Residents could stay comfortable in their homes on a warm summer evening instead of seeking cooling breezes at the baseball park. But it was the broadcast of major league games, Surdam stated, that "may have delivered the coup de grace for many weak minor league teams."[5]

As attendance numbers dropped across the country, teams were forced to fold. In North Carolina, the Class D Blue Ridge and Tobacco State Leagues both ceased operation after the 1950 season due to financial difficulties.[6] With more and more teams and leagues declaring bankruptcy, it became increasingly apparent that if they wanted to survive, southern team owners were going to need new ways to achieve financial stability. In the short term, winning games would certainly help draw fair-weather fans and increase attendance. An obvious way that could be accomplished was by turning to the large talent pool made up of African American players.

As the 1951 season approached, the growing number of Black players in other parts of the country—many of whom were very successful on the field—made it apparent to southern team owners that they would soon have to consider having Black players on their previously all-white teams. As with the minor league system as a whole, those first attempts at integration took place on the fringe of the South in areas where few African Americans lived and Jim Crow laws were perhaps not so rigorously enforced.

In far west Texas, team owner and manager Jay Haney of the Class C Lamesa Lobos announced in early March that he was holding a tryout specifically for African American players. Stating he had served with Black soldiers in the army with no problem and that there was currently a shortage of players due to the Korean War, Haney solicited input from fans on the move. He argued his reasoning behind the move in a letter to the *Amarillo Times* on March 4. "Personally, I feel that if we are able to obtain two far above average Negro men who can really play ball it would be a credit to the league as well as to our town," Haney wrote.

"Since the American Negro works in our factories, helps harvest our crops, cans our food, cooks our meals, takes care of our children and above all fights overseas beside our white boys we feel baseball has every right to employ them."[7] In an interview with the *Abilene Reporter-News,* Haney was quoted as saying, "We are not trying to rearrange the laws of the South. The fact that he is a ball player will not give him special privileges. He will be warned in advance of the abuse he must expect from opposing teams and fans. So, if he wants to play ball under those conditions, we should be big enough to give him that opportunity."[8]

Haney held his tryout for Black players on March 19. From twenty participants he identified Connie Heard of Texas City and J. W. Wingate of Beaumont, both twenty-three years old, as legitimate candidates. Heard had played for Nashua in the New England League in 1949, and Wingate had reportedly played in Canada. The pair were invited to spring training with the rest of the team, but both were released just before the season began. Perhaps Haney decided he didn't want to challenge the racial status quo after all, or perhaps he felt the players' skills were not at the level of his team. Haney changed his mind at the last minute, however, and brought Wingate back.[9] Wingate started the season with strong performances in the field, but his performance at the plate soon lagged. Citing a business decision to bring in a better player but undoubtedly facing pressure from segregationists, Haney released Wingate a month into the season. In the end, Wingate appeared in 27 games in the Class C West Texas–New Mexico League, which helped open the door for players like Dave Hoskins the next season in the Texas League, the state's most prominent association.[10]

Far to the east, the Class D Mountain States League also played in an area of the South that was marginal in terms of population and political importance. Located in the coal region of the Appalachian Mountains, the eight-team circuit was made up of four members in Kentucky, one in Tennessee, and three in Virginia. In that league, the Middlesboro (Kentucky) Athletics hired an established African American pitcher from the area named Bob Bowman. With a career that dated back to the 1930s, Bowman had pitched for the traveling Ethiopia Clowns as well as the Asheville Blues of the Negro Southern League. In his forties by the 1951 season, Bowman was still impressive on the mound. He made his debut May 8, stayed with the team for the entire season, and turned in a 17–6 record.[11]

Class D teams such as those in the remote Mountain States League drew little attention, but in the Class B Carolina League, the cities were much larger. In 1951 the league comprised the North Carolina cities of Durham, Winston-Salem, Raleigh, Greensboro, Fayetteville, Burlington, and Reidsville, as well as Danville, Virginia. The ballparks were bigger, the crowds larger, and the level of play much higher. Not only were top prospects among the players, but former major leaguers looking to continue earning a paycheck by playing the game were common. In 1951, the roster for the Raleigh Capitals included playing manager Joe "Ducky" Medwick (who was inducted into the Baseball Hall of Fame in 1968) and Lawrence "Crash" Davis, a former Duke University star who had played for the Philadelphia Athletics. Durham's playing manager was former major leaguer Clarence "Ace" Parker, while Winston-Salem featured third baseman Ray Jablonski, who was on his way to an eight-year career in the big leagues.[12] It was into this intimidating environment that a recent high school graduate was thrust to become the first African American to integrate professional baseball in North Carolina.

Located just above the North Carolina line, Danville, Virginia had a population of 35,066 in the 1950 census.[13] The town's professional baseball history dated back to the 1920s, and since 1945 Danville had fielded a team in the Carolina League.[14] In early August 1951, the independent Danville Leafs were near the bottom of the league standings. Fan interest had waned, and without a major league working agreement to offset costs, the team was struggling financially. Desperately hoping to increase attendance, the owners listened to a solution proposed by local Black leaders: sign Percy Miller Jr. The talented Miller, who had recently graduated from Danville's Langston High, had been playing with a local Black team, the Danville All-Stars. In a game against the barnstorming Jacksonville Eagles, his talents had impressed the visiting team and he was offered a job. At age seventeen he spent what would be the first of two summers traveling around the United States and Canada playing baseball.[15]

At first, Miller did not want to sign with the Danville Leafs, stating he planned to report to football practice at West Virginia State, but his father convinced him.[16] The Carolina League was consulted on the signing and saw no legal problem with it. According to league president Ted Mann, "There's nothing in the league constitution to prevent any club from using a colored player and as far as I'm concerned, it's perfectly legal."[17]

When news of the signing hit the news, the *Danville Bee* reported that the reactions of the other members of the Leafs were "mixed." Some only said, "No comment." A few remarks concerned only Miller's performance on the field. “I never played with a Negro before,” teammate Roy Peterson said. “But, I see nothing wrong with it, especially if this boy Miller can help us win ball games.”[18] Leafs manager Bob Latshaw, a native of Colorado who had attended the University of Southern California, had no problem with the move. “I didn’t see anything wrong with signing the Negro,” he said. “I had three on a team of mine in Canada, and they were easy to handle.”[19]

Miller recalled later that when he reported to his first practice with the team, he was essentially ignored, and no one would play catch with him. But then, he said, pitcher Al Ronay came over and suggested a game of “pepper.” He tossed the ball to Miller, who tapped it back to him. “You’re pretty good with the bat,” Ronay remarked. Other members of the team soon joined in. “From then on,” Miller said, “everybody was all right.”[20]

On August 9, 1951, the integration of professional baseball officially made inroads much deeper into the South. On that date, Percy Miller Jr. made his debut with the Danville Leafs in a game against the visiting Durham Bulls. As he ran out to his position in right field, Miller recalled he could hear kids heckling him from the fence along the first baseline. Most fans in League Park, however, gave him loud applause.[21] At the plate, Miller struck out in his first at bat, but on his second trip to the plate, he hit a single that drove in 2 runs. The Leafs went on take a 5–4 win over the eventual league champs. The next day, the *Danville Bee*’s headline read, “Negro Gets 2-Run Single in Debut.”[22] More importantly for the team owners, finances improved. Leafs officials said some fans had vowed not to attend any game while Miller was on the roster, but despite that, the paid attendance in his first game was 1,718, double the normal. That included about 600 Black spectators (ten times more than usual) packed into the segregated section down the third baseline.[23]

The Leafs’ first road trip with Miller as a member was to Raleigh, North Carolina. When the bus arrived at the Sir Walter Hotel, his teammates started entering, but different arrangements had been made for Miller. “My manager took me by the arm,” he recalled in a 1998 interview. “‘Wait a minute,’ he said. ‘Go to this address. There’s a cab waiting for you right there.’ He gave me eight dollars and an address.” Segregation required Miller to stay at a boardinghouse owned by an African American. “I had no idea it was going to take place. That was a shock to me. If they had told me before we left Danville, I would have been more prepared.”[24]

On the field in Raleigh, Miller recalled he had no problems. Joe Medwick, a New Jersey native who had played for the Cardinals was player/manager of the Capitals. "During the game, he ran by, smiled, and said, 'Keep plugging away. You'll be alright.' I thought that was pretty nice," Miller recalled in 1998. "Raleigh was okay to play in. People just went about their business." Miller had worse experiences on the next trip. "Winston-Salem was the worst place in the league. I came into one game as a pinch hitter," he said in 1998. "They really booed me. I tried to think I was in my own backyard in Danville. I thought, 'If I could take it there, I could take it here.'"[25]

The next road trip on the schedule for the Leafs was to Durham. The Bulls manager was Ace Parker. A native of Virginia and a graduate of Duke University, Parker had played both Major League Baseball and in the National Football League. He did not express concern about Miller. Said Parker in a quote that appeared in several area newspapers, "I think it is alright to play Negroes. I played with them in professional football and once the game is underway you don't realize that you have them on the team. Just another ballplayer as far as I am concerned."[26] Miller did not make the trip to Durham in mid-August, however. The reason was given that "he will be kept at home for intensive batting and fielding practice."[27]

On August 27, the Leafs traveled to Burlington. There Don Labbruzzo, business manager of the Burlington Bees, announced that "a portion of the left field bleachers will be reserved for colored fans who are expected to turn out to see Danville's Percy Miller in action."[28] Unfortunately for those fans, Miller was benched for 6 games and did not play in Burlington. He did see action again on August 30, when he had 1 of the 2 hits his team could manage against the Greensboro Patriots. In a doubleheader against the Reidsville Luckies on September 3, the last day of the season, Miller went 1-for-3 in the nightcap. Overall, he had appeared in 19 games for the Leafs and managed 7 hits in 38 at bats for a .187 average. Despite obvious talent, he probably was in over his head in terms of experience. In addition to having to deal with racism, the nineteen-year-old Miller was on a team with an average age of almost twenty-eight.[29]

The challenges facing Miller on the field had been predicted by "several veteran baseballers around Durham," according to the *Carolina Times*, the city's Black newspaper. Some even felt that the road ahead for Miller would be tougher than it had been for Jackie Robinson, since he had played in the North rather than in the South. One of those interviewed, Elbert "Pops" Turner, had played for several top Negro league teams in the 1920s and '30s before becoming baseball coach at North

Carolina College in Durham. Turner pointed to the fact that Miller just had been playing high school baseball, and in terms of skill, the jump from that level to Class B ball "is a long one." Turner also stated that late August was a difficult time for any rookie to break into a team, since pressure was on from pennant contenders. "The fact that Miller must win over not only fans and players, but his own teammates makes the pressure on him doubly great," he added.[30]

As the 1952 season approached, Miller was still under contract to the Leafs. In February, however, the team announced it was releasing him. Joe Mehaffey, president of the Danville Leafs, stated that "the young Negro simply is not ready for Class B and therefore the Washington Senators have no plans for him on the 1952 team."[31] Certainly, Miller was not given much of a chance to prove himself, and the club could have faced pressure by those against integration, but in fairness he was not the only player released. The Leafs had managed to sign a working agreement with the Senators, so the big-league club dictated much of the lineup. In fact, the Senators did assign three Black players from Cuba to the Leafs in 1952, including Juan Delis, who would make it up to Washington in 1955.[32]

Chapter 6

ON THE ROCKS IN GRANITE FALLS

When the color line was officially broken by a baseball team based in North Carolina a few weeks after Percy Miller's signing, it was done quietly and with little fanfare. It happened in the small Caldwell County town of Granite Falls. In 1950, 90 percent of the town's 2,286-person population was white.[1] Built around seven cotton mills, Granite Falls was located less than ten miles northwest of the much larger town of Hickory (population 4,755 in 1950).[2] Baseball had long been popular in the town, and Granite Falls had won the area textile league championship the three previous seasons. The world of professional baseball proved to be much more challenging both on and off the field, however.

The Class D Western Carolina League—two levels below the Carolina League—had been formed in 1948 at the peak of minor league baseball's popularity in the country. It brought professional baseball to some of the medium-sized towns of North Carolina's foothills and mountains. Members that first year included Shelby, Morganton, Marion, and Hendersonville. As the 1951 baseball season approached, word spread that Gastonia, the Western Carolina League's last-place club in 1950, had failed to come up with its $800 entrance fee. If the team withdrew, it left the league in the awkward situation of trying to create a schedule with only seven members.[3]

In Granite Falls, six local businessmen—Finley German, Tode Yount, Harvey Winn, John Warlick, J. S. Rayfield, and M. B. Killian—hastily formed a plan and raised the money to put forth a last-minute bid to field a team. Nearby league member Hickory agreed to waive its territorial rights (ten miles to the nearest team), and the bid was accepted. The late entry into the league gave Granite Falls' owners only two weeks to hire a manager and find players.[4]

In the eight-team Western Carolina League, only two of the eight members (Lenoir and Rutherford County) were affiliated with major league clubs. This was not uncommon, but it did change the economics of running a club. With a major league "working agreement," many players were provided by the parent organization. The plan was that they would hone their skills at a lower level and eventually be promoted up the ladder. With an unaffiliated club, the hope was to find a rising star player and sell his contract to a higher-level club or major league organization while still maintaining a team that could win on the field.[5]

In North Carolina, thirty-five teams across the state opened the 1951 season, but before long some of them began to struggle financially. In early June, both Greenville and Tarboro—towns well-established in professional baseball and with much larger populations than Granite Falls—dropped out of the Coastal Plain League in the eastern part of the state. In the neighboring North Carolina State League, the Landis club moved to Elkin in July in search of better attendance figures. The Granite Falls Rocks faced similar financial struggles, and their lack of success on the field achieved record-setting levels. In a small town, the losses on the field did not help increase attendance where the fan base was already limited. Players were frequently dealt to other teams in hopes of raising funds, but with little money left to spend, it became difficult to find new players. As the team owners struggled to complete the season with few player options, they found a solution that was obvious though unconventional: the hiring of talented African American players from the area.[6]

In late August, Granite Falls hired Frank "Boney" Flemming, a pitcher from Morganton; catcher Bill Smith from Conover; and three players from Hickory: pitcher Christopher Rankin, catcher Russell Shuford, and outfielder Eugene Abernathy. Flemming (also spelled Fleming) was the most accomplished of the group and had pitched for the Asheville Blues of the Negro Southern League. The Hickory players were from the Black Ridgeview section of that town. Finley German, one of the six owners of the Granite Falls team, said in a 1992 interview, "I have forgotten how we got them, how much they cost us or what the details were. But I do remember they accepted our offer graciously and the town graciously accepted them. I just didn't want to make an issue out of it. I wasn't interested in that. We just did it more or less to fill out the roster so we could finish the season."[7]

On Saturday, August 25, history was made in a doubleheader between the Granite Falls Rocks and the Newton-Conover Twins. Pitcher Leo Kantorski was on the mound for both games and led Newton-Conover to 9–5 and 6–2 victories. A native of Pennsylvania, Kantorski had pitched for Lenoir-Rhyne College in Hickory and graduated in May 1951.[8] The *Hickory Daily Record* reported the result on August 27 with headlines that read "Leo Kantorski Pulls Iron Man Stunt with Two Wins; Negroes Make Debut." The first paragraph of the article was about Kantorski, with his pitching perhaps the biggest news. The second paragraph read,

> The first Negro players to see action in the Class D Western Carolina league played for Granite Falls. All three of the colored men to play hail from Ridgeview at Hickory. Russell Shuford worked behind the plate the major portion of both games for the Rocks. Christopher Rankin pitched two innings of the first game and two and two-thirds innings of the second game. Gene Abernathy, one of Ridgeview's top all-around athletes, went in as a pinch-hitter in the first game and played center field in the second game. None of the trio got a hit and Shuford was charged with two errors.[9]

When interviewed in 1992, Kantorski was asked about the significance of the event.

> It's funny, I don't even recall that at all. I don't remember those games being historically important. I do remember that I pitched both games of a double-header. . . . But the blacks? I just don't remember that at all and maybe there's a reason for that. To me, playing with and against black athletes was never anything unusual. I grew up in New Kensington [Pennsylvania] and from the time I made the high school baseball team, I had teammates who were black. . . . So, I guess I never was the kind of person who would have thought that was anything but the way it ought to be. It just didn't seem remarkable to me and I suppose that's why it apparently hasn't stuck in my memory.

At least to a white player from an area without Jim Crow laws, having Black players on the field was no big deal.[10]

On August 29, the *Daily Record* had another game report from Granite Falls, this time against Marion: "With four negroes in the lineup, the first to play on a white team in North Carolina, the Granite Falls Rocks went down in favor of Marion's Marauders, 10–3 The negroes were Bill Smith of Newton, a catcher; Boney Flemming of Asheville, formerly a pitcher for the Negro Asheville Blues; Christopher Rankin of Hickory, a right-handed pitcher; and Gene Abernathy of Hickory, an outfielder. Another negro, Russell Shuford, a catcher, is also with the club, but not in action after suffering a broken finger."[11]

The *Asheville Citizen-Times* reported the signing in its August 29 edition: "Danville in the Carolina League broke the ice in signing Negro players in the state when they signed Percy Miller some weeks ago, but Granite Falls of the Class D Western Carolina League has gone whole hog by signing five of them." After a report on the game against Marion, the article continued, "Reaction among fans in Granite Falls to the signing of the Negro players is practically nil. They just seem to accept that they are there and so long as they play good ball there is no criticism."[12]

Saturday, September 1, was the final game of the season. It proved to be another loss for the Rocks as they fell to the Morganton Aggies, 5–4. Jack Clark of Morganton batted against pitcher Boney Flemming in that final game. In a 1992 interview he recalled the game:

> I had batted against Boney Flemming before that. The Asheville Blues used to play exhibition games around North Carolina and they'd come play against our Piedmont League team. But that was a black team playing against a white team. They weren't mixed. Yet those games really drew the fans because the Blues were really good. They could have won the Western Carolina League championship in 1951. No question about it. I remember Boney, and somewhere I remember watching Russell Shuford play because how strong his arm was and how he'd throw people out without ever coming out from behind the plate.[13]

In the end, the aptly named Rocks went through five managers and finished with a 14–96 record for a winning percentage of .127, the lowest in the history of professional baseball.[14] That unenviable record (which still stands today) unfortunately overshadowed the team's positive accomplishments in the realm of integration.

Another unfortunate fact also obscured the accomplishments of the team and its players. The *1952 Official Baseball Guide* indicates that at least 16 games are missing from the complete record for the 1951 Western Carolina League.[15] All were from games involving Granite Falls, where, due to what was apparently loss of interest in the dismal season, the official scorer for the team failed to send in the box scores (apathy that began before the Black players were signed). The result was that the five Black players were never officially given credit for their barrier-breaking appearances. This was certainly an unusual occurrence in a sport that is so carefully documented with statistics.

In a 2018 interview, David Yount, the son of Rocks co-owner Tode Yount, remembered the season. A high school senior when the season began, he worked in the concession stand and—as a former high school player—was even recruited to play a few games in the outfield at the end of the season (stats that were also lost). Recalled Yount,

> Granite Falls was a town that thrived on its cotton mills, but we stretched to field a team that season. Some of our players worked in the mills and were given time off to play. Most of the rest were local from within driving distance. We did hire a Cuban shortstop, though. Antonio Campos. He was kind of our star. I do remember when we hired the Black players. Nobody made a big deal about it. I think everyone realized there was a lot of athleticism that had been kept down and that's what we needed. Somehow, we had seen those players before, I think in a game in Lenoir, which is just thirteen miles away. Maybe a town game before the season. Anyway, when we needed players, we contacted them. I remember everyone got along with them and there was a lot of laughter in the dugout. I still marvel how good their spirits were. I recall the whole thing with pride.[16]

None of the five players who appeared for Granite Falls (nor Percy Miller, nor even J. W. Wingate or Bob Bowman) ever advanced up the baseball ladder toward the major leagues. Their willingness to play on previously all-white teams—and endure any harassment and frustration that went with that—did, however, inspire other African American athletes to take a chance on playing for teams in the South. The gains were minuscule in North Carolina in 1951, but important small steps were taken and a few first hurdles had been overcome.

Chapter 7
ALONG THE COASTAL PLAIN

When the 1952 baseball season opened, only six out of sixteen major league teams had integrated.[1] In North Carolina there was not a Black player on the roster of any of the thirty professional teams playing in five different minor leagues in the state. That would change in early June, however. The Class D Coastal Plain League had operated as a professional circuit since 1937. League members in 1952 were the eastern North Carolina towns of Wilson, Goldsboro, Tarboro, Kinston, Rocky Mount, New Bern, Edenton, and Roanoke Rapids. Only three clubs had major league working agreements: Kinston (Detroit Tigers), Goldsboro (St. Louis Cardinals), and Roanoke Rapids (Washington Senators). As was the case with minor leagues across the country, continually declining attendance numbers were a threat to the Coastal Plain League's survival.[2]

A month into the season, the last-place New Bern Bears were struggling to win games. Not unexpectedly, the poor results on the field led to a decrease in fan interest, which in turn hurt team finances. The seasonal attendance total for 1951 had been 45,388, an average of 720 per game. Without a drastic change, it would be even lower in 1952. With a situation much like what had been faced by Granite Falls the previous August, team owner Mark Skinner of New Bern attempted a similar remedy: he turned to the virtually untapped talent pool of African American ballplayers. A talented Black player could attract Black fans, but he could also help the team win. That, in turn, would lead to an increase in white fans as well. As long as fans would accept the hiring of a Black player, there was essentially no risk to the team.[3]

New Bern, located in Craven County at the confluence of the Neuse and Trent Rivers, is one of North Carolina's oldest towns. In 1950 it had a population of 15,812, 42 percent of whom were African American.[4] Like most small southern towns, New Bern was very segregated and undoubtedly had its share of racial strife. It would not be until 1964 that the New Bern schools were desegregated and 1968 that the town hired its first Black policeman.[5] But owner Mark Skinner, a baseball-loving

Before he joined the New Bern Bears, Charlie Roach (*back row, second from left*) played for the semipro Goshen Red Wings from Greensboro, pictured here in 1948. *Front row, left to right:* Clemente Verona, Joe Siddle, William Davis, Spud Chandler, Ed Ledwell, and John Tonkins. *Back row:* Charles Parks, Charlie Roach, Hubert Simmons, Benny Harrison, Herman Taylor, (first name unknown) Johnson, Scooter Watkins, and Brian Morris (business manager). Pitcher William Davis had previously played for Negro big-league teams in Washington and Philadelphia. Collection of the author.

building contractor, took a chance on integration in 1952 with hopes of increasing attendance as well as performance on the field. "He wasn't scared to do anything," his son Richard said in a 2012 interview. "If it was for baseball, he would do it."[6]

The New Bern Bears' Black trainer and bus driver played an important role in the club's integration. Phillip "Rabbit" Martin was a native of Leaksville, North Carolina, and from his hometown he knew a talented player named Charlie Roach. A twenty-two-year-old third baseman who was playing for the Durham Eagles, a Black semipro team, Roach had graduated from Winston-Salem Teachers College. He had also had success playing with the Goshen Red Wings, a Black team based in Greensboro. Martin recommended Roach to Skinner, and the Bears' owner made an offer that was accepted. Roach was set to make his debut with the Bears on June 9, though the team decided to move him from third base to the outfield, farther from the fans, in case anyone threw things at him (which they did not).[7]

Roach did not disappoint in his first game at New Bern's Kafer Park, and in two trips to the plate, he grounded out and hit a single. He advanced to score the run that would tie Tarboro at 2–2, just before the game was called in the fifth inning on account of rain.[8] Perhaps showing the cultural importance placed on baseball, the Black-owned *Carolina Times* from Durham proudly reported on Roach's debut on its front page (an article on the first Black graduate of the University of North Carolina's law school was on page 2). Though not quite correct in its statement about his being the first African American player in a white league in the state, the article read, "The first Negro ball player ever to be hired by a white league in North Carolina . . . drew a round of applause [from Black and white fans] when he stepped up to bat."[9] In other league towns, newspapers also reported Roach's debut. In the *Rocky Mount Evening Times*, Roach was quoted as saying that he was grateful to team owner Mark Skinner for the "opportunity given to me" and that he was "particularly grateful for the way the fans received me." The article also indicated that much was expected from Roach in terms of offensive production, since he came to New Bern "with a reputation as a heavy hitter."[10]

Two days later, in his third game, Roach took the field before a reported 1,000 spectators for a home game against Kinston (the seasonal per-game average was only 472).[11] Unfortunately for the New Bern fans, the eventual league champs took an 8–2 win, partially thanks to five errors committed by the Bears. One of the most costly was committed by Charlie Roach. Reported the *New Bern Sun Journal*, Kinston's "Joe Cauci led off the inning with a single and scored when Charlie Roach, new Negro outfielder, miscued on Al Benza's fly to leftfield for a three-base error."[12] In a 2012 interview with *Sun Journal* sportswriter Bill Hand, Richard Skinner, the club owner's son who was working the ticket booth for the game, recalled fans reacting with something "worse than the boos!" In his article, Hand speculated that perhaps the crowd was willing to forgive errors by four white players—outfielders, the shortstop, and the pitcher—but not the Black player.[13] Roach was also hitless in the game and was 1-for-9 overall.[14]

Surprisingly, Roach's appearance with New Bern did not draw big attention across the league. It is possible some sportswriters saw the spread of integrated teams in the South as inevitable and so thought there was no point in making a big deal about it. Perhaps more plausible, however, is simply that no one noticed. Players were frequently given brief trials with low-level professional clubs, so a new name on the roster was common. These players were often ignored until they proved themselves on the field (or failed attempting to do so), and their photos were not printed. Whatever the reason, the *Wilson Daily Times* did not even mention Roach's appearance. On June 12, the newspaper's sports column that often focused on the Coastal Plain League commented only on New Bern's slump in the league standings. Bernard West wrote that the Bears "were looking like the class of the league" until they "took a nose dive" at the beginning of June. He called them "the mystery club of the circuit right now" and thought they could recover with some significant roster moves.[15]

On June 13, the *New Bern Sun Journal* mentioned Roach's name for the final time: "Charlie Roach, Negro outfielder with the New Bern Bears for several days, was sold outright to the Danville Leafs of the Class B Carolina League for an undisclosed price, according to Mark Skinner, club president. The sale was consummated on Wednesday after Roach had been with the club for only three days."[16] In a 1996 interview, Roach stated that he had worked out with the Danville club but did not sign with them. He returned to semipro baseball and pursued a teaching career in Durham.[17]

The next league member to make an attempt at integration was Rocky Mount. Coincidentally, Rocky Mount (population 27,697 in 1950)[18] had produced one of the greatest African American baseball players ever. Walter "Buck" Leonard had been born in town and began his career playing for the Rocky Mount Black Swans, a semipro team. He signed with Pittsburgh's Homestead Grays in 1934 and spent fifteen seasons in the Negro National League as a star first baseman. In 1952, when baseball integration finally came to his hometown, the forty-four-year-old Leonard was wrapping up his career in Mexico. He would make what was essentially an encore appearance with the Portsmouth (Virginia) Merrimacs of the Piedmont League in 1953. The 10 games Leonard played with that team were his only ones in Organized Baseball, the previously all-white baseball system. In 1962 he did help integrate baseball in another way when he was hired by Frank Walker as vice president of the Rocky Mount Leafs, most likely the first African American front office executive in minor league baseball in the state. He held the position until 1975. Buck Leonard was elected to the National Baseball Hall of Fame in 1972.[19]

Four days after Charlie Roach was sent to Danville, sportswriter Howard Criswell addressed the signing of a Black player, Charlie England, by the Rocky Mount Leafs in his June 17 column in the *Rocky Mount Evening Telegram*. He wrote that team owner (and former major leaguer) Frank Walker had said he would not be averse to hiring a Black player, but the challenge was finding one who could "take the proper attitude in playing and have the ability." Walker apparently wanted an outstanding athlete but also one with the mental toughness to ignore potential racial taunts. Criswell stated that the second part of Walker's quote was perhaps the most important. In his column, he claimed that "people inherently respect ability" in others regardless of factors such as color of skin. With regard to the player the Leafs did sign, it would be an issue "to be reckoned with since Charlie England's skin is brown."[20] The ability of the fans to overlook race and focus on skill would be tested.

A graduate of Shaw University in Raleigh, England was a right-handed pitcher who played baseball in the military before accepting a job as a coach at Black Pattillo High School in Tarboro, North Carolina, in 1949.[21] Perhaps referring to behaving as a professional and representative of the town, England said when asked about his signing, "I'm going to try to live up to the code of the club and the league. It's a great honor and I'm going to do my best." Sportswriter Criswell said this kind of effort was all anyone could ask for, but he closed his article with "especially if he delivers the goods."[22]

England got his first chance on June 18, 1952, in a home game against Kinston. A reported 3,100 spectators turned out for the game, the Leafs' largest crowd since 1947 (the per-game average that season was less than 700).[23] The segregated section for Black fans was "overflowing out onto the field, and all the way out to the left-field wall."[24] England took the mound to start the game and promptly struck out Kinston's Wayne Blackburn, the league's leader in hitting. Unfortunately, it was downhill from there, and England gave up 6 hits and 7 runs in three innings before being replaced. Despite the poor outing, the *Rocky Mount Evening Telegram* reported that "everyone in the stands, white and Negro, was solidly behind him. There were only a few minor boos, no insults, only an undercurrent of feeling for Charlie England."[25]

A few days later, England was given another start but was hit hard and had to be replaced in the fourth inning. That game proved to be the end of England's short stay with the Rocky Mount Leafs. On June 27, Howard Criswell reported that Frank Walker felt that "England is a fine young man but doesn't have the stuff" to play in the league, so he was given his release.[26]

England returned to Tarboro and resumed his coaching job. He remained at Pattillo though 1957, leading the school to a state football championship in 1953. He then moved to Black Dunbar High School in Lexington, North Carolina, and won three more state titles (1958, 1959, and 1963). When the school system in that town was desegregated, England joined the coaching staff at Lexington Senior High School. There, as assistant coach, he helped the team take consecutive state titles in 1985 and 1986. According to the *Dispatch*, Lexington's newspaper, England's "willingness to move to the formerly all-white school has been heralded as part of the reason for a smooth transition during desegregation." In 1999, the Lexington school board voted unanimously to change the name of Dunbar Intermediate School, formerly Dunbar High School, to Charles England Intermediate School. England was named to the North Carolina High School Athletic Association Hall of Fame in 2000 and was a charter member of the Davidson County Sports Hall of Fame in 2002.[27]

Though Charlie England's trial did not turn out as Frank Walker had hoped, he continued to search for pitching help from talented Black players. His next target was a 6′3″ right-hander named Lafayette Stallings, a local star. Wrote Criswell, "The big Negro pitcher and first baseman has played ball with pro teams in Baltimore and Philadelphia."[28] On June 29, 1952, Walker signed Stallings to a contract with the Leafs and promptly gave him the starting assignment for the team on July 1 against Kinston at home. The headlines read "Second Negro Pitcher to Start for Leafs Here Tonight." Stallings had been working out with the club at the same time as Charlie England, during which time he threw batting practice and worked on running to get in shape.[29]

In his debut, Stallings gave up 2 runs in the first inning but maintained his composure. Stallings struck out two and gave up 9 hits in eight innings. When he left the game in the ninth, the Leafs were trailing 5–3.[30] The headlines on the sports page of the *Rocky Mount Telegram* covered the game the next day. The article read, "A revised line-up which included Manager Turkey Tyson at first, a Negro pitcher and a new outfielder was not enough to stop Kinston last night." It later added, "The two newcomers to the teams, pitcher Lafayette Stallings and outfielder Pete Hall, performed well, and the team looked better than it has for the past two weeks."[31] After the game, manager Cecil "Turkey" Tyson stated that Stallings "was a better pitcher than England."[32] In his "News about Negroes" column in the *Rocky Mount Evening Telegram*, R. D. Armstrong reported on Stallings: "One of the proudest fans at the game Tuesday night was Stallings' father, who put aside his chores early in the day and made the trip to Rocky Mount to see his son go against the Eagles. He, along with approximately 800 other Negro fans, were pulling for the big righthander on every pitch."[33]

Despite the promise that many saw in Stallings, the trial did not work out. On July 7, Frank Walker announced that the pitcher was placed on the voluntarily retired list. In most situations, players who voluntarily retired asked for their release rather than essentially be cut by the team. Perhaps Stallings was not comfortable or perhaps he wanted to pursue other opportunities, but the reason for his departure was not given. Another possible reason might be injury. Armstrong's column did mention that Stallings relied on his curveball instead of his fastball due to a sore arm.[34] Walker did not completely discount Stallings's potential and even stated he might be brought back the following spring.[35]

Less than two weeks later, it was the Wilson Tobs' turn to attempt integration in the league. Like every other team in the league, they were struggling to bring fans to the park. Located twenty miles south of Rocky Mount, Wilson in 1950 had a population of just over 23,000 total residents, 9,716 of them African American. In 1947, the Tobs had a seasonal attendance of 138,00 fans, with a per-game average of just under 2,000. These numbers were helped by the fact that the Tobs were league champs in 1947, but by 1951, seasonal attendance had dropped to 54,753. An average of only 869 fans per game came to see the fourth-place team (which would make it to the finals of the playoffs). In an attempt to lure a new group of fans—African Americans—the club signed Rich Square native Ernest Canada on July 20, 1952. A double threat who could both pitch and hit, Canada lettered all four years at North Carolina A&T in Greensboro. On the mound in college he lost only one conference game, averaged 15 strikeouts per game his senior year, and was named All-Central Intercollegiate Athletic Association in 1949, 1950, and 1951.[36]

L. C. "Slim" Boykin, owner of the Tobs, reported he had called a team meeting before signing Canada, and he felt certain that there was 100 percent support "if he helps the ballclub." In an attempt to allay any fears Wilson fans might have, he further stated that Canada "was a perfect gentleman who doesn't drink or smoke, and who wants to advance in the baseball world."[37] He also made it clear that the new team member was aware of the expectations, stating, "If he caused trouble at all, or if he didn't continue to play as well as he had been playing, he would have to be released." Unlike New Bern and Rocky Mount, the Wilson team was challenging for first place, and any player—Black or white—who couldn't help the team continue winning would be replaced. The *Rocky Mount Evening Telegram* reported that "the fourth Negro player signed in the league," a "center fielder," would appear at the town's Municipal Stadium with the visiting Wilson Tobs in his first game and that "owner Slim Boykin has announced that he will be played regularly." Canada did indeed start at center field in his first game and went 2-for-4 at the plate.[38]

The *Wilson Daily Times* hailed the signing of Canada. After his first game, the sports headlines read, "Wilson Signs Colored Player" with a subheading of "Ernest Canada Has Brilliant Debut with Locals; Gets 3 Hits." The article indicated that the "colored centerfielder, signed by the Tobs late Saturday, was a big success. The 21-year-old from Rich Square got a hit in each of the two games Saturday night and played brilliantly afield." In his July 22 column, Wilson sportswriter Bernard West commented, "We have talked to lots of people about the situation and we've found the majority of fans seem to be in favor of Canada remaining here as long as he plays as well as he did on Saturday night." Few subsequent newspaper reports that referenced Canada even mentioned his race, and his name was prefaced only by his position. On July 26, part of West's column carried the subheading of "Report on Canada." He wrote that Canada was batting .346 through 7 games. He added, "Probably the most important fact to report on Canada, however, is that the fans are accepting him. He is getting a good ovation when he steps up to the plate, usually because he's earned a round of cheers with a good catch from his centerfield position."[39]

Ernest Canada's time with the Wilson Tobs would prove to be the longest and most successful stay of any African American player with a North Carolina team yet. Overall, he batted a respectable .269 with 14 hits, including 2 doubles. According to Coastal Plain League historian Robert Gaunt, Canada was popular with both fans and teammates. He was released, however, with a couple weeks left in the season primarily because Boykin constantly shuffled players and wanted a power hitter as the team prepared for the playoffs. West had hinted at that shortcoming in Canada's skills, writing that he "doesn't appear to be a home run hitter; he is content with punching out singles." The roster move drew no mention in the *Wilson Daily Times*, though this was not uncommon. At the time in minor league baseball, official league stats were reported only for players who appeared in a minimum of 10 games for the season.

By appearing in 21 games, Canada became the first Black player noted in the permanent record for a North Carolina team.[40]

Unfortunately for Canada, service in the army during the Korean War interrupted his baseball ambitions. Upon returning from military duty, he briefly joined the Winston-Salem Twins of the Carolina League as a pitcher in 1954. He found more success in business, however, as owner of his own construction company. Canada was also later a member of the Greensboro Planning Board and a director of the Central YMCA in Greensboro. In 1970, he was one of eight founding members of the Black-owned Greensboro National Bank. Canada was inducted into the North Carolina A&T Sports Hall of Fame in 1982 for his accomplishments in baseball.[41]

Some of the challenges facing Black players in the Coastal Plain League in 1952 were of a logistical nature. As discovered by Danville's Percy Miller in 1951, Jim Crow laws mandated that Black players use separate facilities from their white teammates. This meant that team owners or managers had to arrange lodging, dining, and even changing facilities if they had Black players on their roster. To get around these unwanted complications, Rocky Mount owner Frank Walker did not take his Black players (England and Stallings) on any road games in 1952.[42]

Perhaps the most complicated Jim Crow situations arose at stadiums. The seating was still segregated, but no stadium would have had need for segregated locker rooms (previous use would have been by either all-white or all-Black teams). Robert Gaunt wrote that it "was a delicate subject, since many fans considered that they'd get used to blacks in baseball uniforms, but blacks sharing locker room facilities with whites was quite another matter."[43] The biggest example of this becoming an issue was in the league town of Edenton. As Black players began to appear in the league, it was reported that some Edenton fans had become concerned that visiting clubs might allow "Negro players to use the field house."[44] As the baseball facilities were city-owned, this put pressure on Edenton mayor Larry Prescott to enforce the rules of segregation if such a situation arose. The matter came to the attention of Ray Goodman, president of the Coastal Plain League. He informed the Edenton Colonials that, regardless of race, the rules of Organized Baseball stated that visiting teams be furnished field house facilities. If the Colonials denied the use of facilities to a Black player, the team would be subject to penalties for violating its obligations as a member of a professional league. The town government relented and agreed to lease the field house to the Colonials for a minimal amount. That way it was absolved of having to enforce any rules over how and by whom it was used.[45] (Ernest Canada did play at least once in Edenton, on July 20, 1952.)[46]

Among the rules that members of the National Association of Professional Baseball Leagues had to follow were those governing roster size and composition. By the early 1950s, the rule for Class D teams was that a team could carry only sixteen men on its roster any time. Of those, not more than three could be veterans, not more than five could be limited service (two years of experience), and not less than eight had to be rookies. These limitations meant that team owners had to be very careful when selecting veteran players. The rules also led to the frequent shuffling of rosters, especially with regard to rookies, if players did not contribute on the field.[47]

In addition to talent, African American players presented an attractive option in another way. Even if Black players had ten years of high-level experience in the Negro leagues, they were still considered rookies when they first joined a team in the National Association. This could essentially allow teams to get around some of the roster limitations. Of course, the best Black players would have had more options and likely signed for more money for bigger teams in the North. Based on experience, none of the four African American players who appeared in the Coastal Plain League in 1952 would realistically have been considered rookies, though that is what their contracts would have stated.[48]

The 1952 Coastal Plain League season had seen some small but significant inroads made into ending local segregation without any major issues. Fans undoubtedly were aware that decreased attendance left the clubs facing decisions that would have seemed unfathomable in the first few seasons after World War II. It would have been interesting to have seen how the 1953 season unfolded in the Coastal Plain League with regard to further integration, but as it approached, there was a struggle to find enough team owners willing to take the risk and invest. In the end, the league was forced to disband.[49]

Chapter 8
THE CUBAN CONNECTION

Beginning in the early twentieth century, one of the great sources of baseball talent was Cuba. Like the United States, Cuba is a country with a population of more than one race. Percentages of the population that is of African heritage vary greatly in reports, but it is most likely near 50 percent. The country has had racial struggles of its own, but despite that, the professional Cuban baseball league had been integrated since 1900. If its Black players sought to pursue a career outside the island, however, they were forced to face segregation.[1]

Players from Cuba, Venezuela, and other Latin American countries had always been allowed in Organized Baseball so long as they could be considered "white" by the standards of the day. An example of such a player is Cuban pitcher Dolf Luque, who won 194 games and two World Series titles in the major leagues between 1914 and 1935.[2] However, if talented players of obvious African descent wanted to pursue a career in the United States—such as Cuba's Martín Dihigo—they were limited to the Negro leagues. Dihigo began playing in the Negro leagues in 1923 and became one of Black baseball's biggest stars. In 1937, he was lured to Mexico by the offer of a big contract and became the first to integrate that country's professional league. Though he never played a game in Organized Baseball, Dihigo is still considered one of the sport's all-time greats and was enshrined in the National Baseball Hall of Fame in 1977.[3]

If one does not count Bobby Estalella, then the first Black Cuban to join Organized Baseball was Minnie Miñoso, who signed with the Cleveland Indians organization in 1948.[4] Others soon followed, and in 1952, two Cubans of African descent were members of the Danville Leafs in the Class B Carolina League. The Leafs had signed a working agreement with the Washington Senators, and the parent club had assigned several players to Danville. Among them was Cuban shortstop Juan Delis, who in late 1951 had been one of the first Black players signed by the Senators organization.[5]

The owner of the Washington Senators, Clark Griffith, was infamous for his refusal to embrace integration. Griffith was, in fact, resistant to many changes in baseball. Wrote baseball historian Ted Leavengood,

> Clark Griffith did not integrate his team for the same reasons that he refused night games, beer sales, and many other things that became standard fare at other stadiums. . . . Change was a risky business for an old man whose tiny stadium was in disrepair, and whose business was operating on a shoe string. Could the white southern fan base in DC have embraced Larry Doby [whom Griffith had been urged to sign] without any falloff in attendance? Perhaps so. But if an 80-year-old owner without deep pockets did not want to find out does that make him a racist?[6]

Griffith also profited from segregated baseball. For a decade he rented his stadium to the Homestead Grays. If the Negro leagues went away, which would be inevitable with integration, Griffith would lose a substantial amount of income.[7]

By the early 1950s, pressure was put on Griffith by local Black groups as well as by the media to make changes. "I will not sign a Negro for the Washington club merely for the sake of satisfying certain pressure groups," he stated in an interview with the *Sporting News*.[8] Griffith's solution was a "half-hearted concession"[9] that in one way was ahead of other major league teams: he signed talented Black (and non-Black) players from Cuba. The island had been a largely overlooked hotbed of talent for years, especially with regard to its players of African descent. In 1953, Shirley Povich, sports columnist for the *Washington Post*, wrote, "Mr. Griffith would give Washington fans dark players from other lands, but never an American Negro."[10]

On March 22, 1952, it was announced in the Senators' training camp in Winter Garden, Florida, that "two colored Cubans" had been assigned to the Danville infield. Ossie Bluege, a longtime big-league player who had spent five seasons as field manager of the Senators, was Washington's farm director and in charge of making all assignments. He called Luis Morales and Juan Delis "sensational" after watching them work out and made the decision to send the pair to the Carolina League. If he wanted to assign Delis and Morales to a Class B team, his options were limited, with Charlotte the only other team in the system at that level. The only higher option in the system was Chattanooga in the Southern Association, a league staunchly against integration. Perhaps he chose Danville because he knew of the team's experiment with integration the previous season.[11]

The manager of the Danville Leafs was former major leaguer Morrie "Smut" Aderholt, a native of eastern North Carolina and graduate of Wake Forest College. Aderholt had witnessed baseball's first integration in the International League in 1946, when his Toronto Maple Leafs had played against Jackie Robinson's Montreal Royals.[12] The *Danville Bee* reported he also was impressed by the Cuban duo, "according to the dispatches from the training camp."[13] The newspaper went on to reiterate that both players were natives of Cuba and stated, "Delis speaks no English, but Morales does and will serve as his teammate's interpreter."[14] Either way, the players—though of obvious African descent—were viewed differently than Percy Miller had been in 1951. "All the boys like 'em," said Aderholt. "They can hit, run, and field. And they want to play ball. They're helping us win games, too."[15] At least in terms of coverage by newspaper writers, there was a big difference between "colored Cubans" and "American Negroes." Cubans of African heritage were more of a curiosity on the baseball field, while having Americans of African heritage in the same situation bordered on scandal.

Playing primarily second base for Danville, Luis Morales hit .287 and appeared in 134 of the team's 139 games. He bounced around the baseball system for the next four seasons and played with several teams in the Washington system—including Charlotte for part of 1955—but never made the major leagues. Third baseman Juan Delis batted .298 for Danville but was limited to 66 games because of a fractured ankle. He spent the next two seasons with Havana, which was part of minor league baseball at the time. On April 16, 1955, he became the second Black player (after countryman Carlos Paula, who appeared in 9 games in late 1954) to play for the Washington Senators.[16] He made his major league debut as a pinch hitter against the visiting New York Yankees. Delis went on to spend the entire season with the team but saw action in only 54 games. With a batting average of just .189, however, his future with the Senators was not assured. Delis was released after the season and signed with the Havana Sugar Kings. He never made it back to the major leagues but spent several more years in the high minors with Seattle in the Pacific Coast League and Monterrey in the Mexican League.[17]

Chapter 9
TROUBLE IN THE TRI-STATE

One other brief yet important experiment with minor league integration took place in the region in 1952, and surprisingly it was in South Carolina. The Class B Tri-State League had been formed in 1946 with member clubs hailing from towns in South Carolina, North Carolina, and Tennessee. When it expanded from six teams to eight the following season, the town of Rock Hill (population around 25,000), in York County, South Carolina, decide to field an entry. The new team, named the Chiefs, was usually a contender in the league and made the postseason playoffs twice, winning in 1950. In 1950 and 1951, the Chiefs had a working agreement with the Chicago Cubs, but it was not renewed for 1952. That left Rock Hill as an independent club at a time when it was becoming more and more difficult to survive financially without major league support.

As an independent, the Rock Hill Chiefs were free to hire whatever players they chose (and could afford). One of the players they signed was among the biggest baseball stars in the Carolinas in the decade after the war: power-hitting first baseman Leo "Muscle" Shoals. The thirty-five-year-old veteran from West Virginia had previously played for Charlotte and Columbia, among other teams, in a career that had begun in 1937. With Rock Hill, Shoals had yet another outstanding season and batted .320. Fellow veteran Herb May, an outfielder, turned in a .316 average, but beyond those two players, the Rock Hill lineup was markedly unsuccessful. By August, the Chiefs were languishing in eighth place in the league. One manager had been fired, the team had lost key players due to injury, and attendance was down. They needed talent, so team president J. Earl Sherer, a sporting goods dealer, decided to take a chance and hire an accomplished Black player.[1]

Shoals recalled the events of that season with Rock Hill in his autobiography. "Nobody had the guts to put a black guy in their lineup because they knew what the reaction would be," he wrote. "It finally came about, but not before the season was almost over. I guess it happened that late because whatever heat was coming wouldn't last too long and

. . . breaking in a black player at that time would make it easier in 1953. Everybody knew it was inevitable, but a lot of people wanted to make it a white man's game in the Tri-State League for as long as they could."[2]

David "Pepsi Cola" Mobley was a twenty-eight-year-old native of nearby Lancaster, South Carolina. He had served in the war, during which time he played baseball for the 39th Signal Corps team while in France. After military service, Mobley returned home and played for the local Black team, the Lancaster Tigers. From there his baseball career took him to play for the Red Wings in Greensboro and eventually for the Indianapolis Clowns of the Negro American League. Mobley began the 1952 season with the Birmingham Black Barons but decided to go back to South Carolina to be near his ill mother. It is unknown how Mobley came to sign with the Rock Hill Chiefs, but somehow news of a player of his caliber returning to the area must have caught the team's attention.[3]

After the signing, Chiefs player-manager Leon Culberson, a former major leaguer who was a native of Georgia, announced that Mobley would be starting at left field. He then addressed his players, stating, "Look you guys, if you are going to play baseball for a living and if you expect to advance higher in minor league baseball, the chances are you will have to play with Negroes." Culberson took a vote and none of the players indicated they would not play with Mobley. The opposition team on Mobley's first night, August 26, 1952, was the Knoxville Smokies. When told of the Chiefs' intent to play Mobley, the Smokies' manager, Fred Gerken, made it known that neither he nor his players objected.[4]

The president of the Tri-State League was Bobby Hipps. A Furman University graduate who previously had a long minor league playing career, Hipps was an auto dealer in Asheville. His job for the Tri-State League was to make sure teams abided by rules and help resolve any disputes. While there was no official rule barring Black ballplayers, it was an unwritten tenet by which teams still abided. It had almost been tested at the beginning of the season when the Charlotte and Asheville clubs both gave tryouts to Black players, but none of the athletes involved made the rosters. When word reached Hipps that Rock Hill was about to sign Mobley, he asked the team not to do so. Whatever his personal opinions on the issue may have been, he knew that some teams would protest and the league could potentially collapse. He stated, "Due to the fact that objections have been raised, I asked Rock Hill if it would not use the player in question until all the league directors had time to discuss the problem and reach some conclusion on taking down the bars."[5]

At game time on August 26, Earl Sherer and the Rock Hill board of directors were in the midst of an emergency meeting to discuss Hipps's request. To the disappointment of some fans, Mobley was held out of the lineup while his future was discussed. The *Asheville Citizen-Times* reported that "many fans arriving for the game turned away from the gates after learning that Mobley would not play." Ultimately, the Chiefs' ownership group decided to ignore Hipps. Word was sent to Leon Culberson, and Mobley was inserted into the lineup in the fifth inning. He took over in left field in the sixth. In his first plate appearance, Mobley bunted and was thrown out in a close play at first. Leading off the eighth, he singled to center, which reportedly drew cheers from the fans. Unfortunately for the Chiefs, they lost the game, 5–4. More importantly, however, the color line had been broken in the state of South Carolina.[6]

The next day, Culberson had already penciled in Mobley to start the game, but it was not to be. According to Muscle Shoals, the Spartanburg club threatened to quit the league if Mobley continued to play. He also stated that players in Greenville took a vote and were in favor of Mobley playing, though the team owners were not. In Charlotte, team president Phil Howser had no problem. "If Greenville and Spartanburg don't approve of Negroes playing, they better get out of the league because we expect to have one next year in Charlotte," he said. "He's coming down from our Class C club in Drummondville, Quebec. I'm surprised there is any doubt in anyone's mind about my position on that. This is America and I see no reason why we can't play Negroes if they're good enough. Baseball is entertainment and we don't object to applauding other Negro entertainers, so why should baseball be any different."[7]

Despite the support, Mobley was released from the Rock Hill team. Under pressure by some league members who reportedly deluged his office with phone calls and facing the prospect of the league collapsing, Sherer reluctantly decided to release Mobley. He stated, "Our actions in taking Mobley's name off the roster is temporary and I feel that when the league meets in October, they [Negro players] will be voted in. It's the only way that some of the teams can continue to operate." The statement from league president Bobby Hipps read, "There is much to consider in playing a Negro in this league. The constitution of the league has nothing against it, and I have seen that the constitution is upheld. However, it is not as simple as that. Some towns favor it, others don't. It is of utmost importance that we have harmony for the betterment of the entire organization."[8]

The incident drew the attention of newspapers across the Carolinas and as far away as California's *Oakland Tribune*. The *Pittsburgh Courier*, one of the nation's top Black-owned newspapers, wrote, "Old man jim crow received a dramatic last-minute stay of execution when the Rock Hill (S.C.) Chiefs fielded a Negro player over the protest of the Tri-State League president, Bobby Hipps." Though the Spartanburg club was likely at the root of problem, the *Arizona Republic* of Phoenix firmly condemned Hipps, stating, "Tri-State President's Action Draws Ire of Fans, Members." Columnist Bob Quincy, of the *Asheville Citizen-Times*, wrote,

> Admittedly, the clumsy handling of the situation didn't help the league or race relations. . . . Rock Hill, if they thought a Negro would be beneficial to the club or to the box office, made the mistake of waiting too late in the season to make the move. It actually took the appearance of nothing more than a carnival stunt, although it may have been a sincere move to bolster the roster. But Rock Hill turned up the hole card in the long run. There has been a galloping rumor of long standing that South Carolina had blue laws which prevented the use of Negroes in white athletic contests. The Chiefs broke down that bruit with one hasty swing of their hatchet. But it left the Tri-State in something of a bloody mess.[9]

David Mobley went home to Lancaster but did make the newspapers again in September, when he played for the Lower State Colored All-Stars. He made another attempt at organized baseball the following season and signed with the Knoxville Smokies (which had left the Tri-State League and joined the Class D Mountain States League). Mobley played in 22 games before quitting the team. He returned to South Carolina, where he continued to play on semipro Black teams for several years.

Like the integration experiments in the Coastal Plain League during the 1952 season, the actions of the Rock Hill club were made purely for baseball reasons and done so at the local level. As more and more teams were forced to rely on major league support, roster decisions were often out of the hands of local team ownership. Even in the Tri-State League, this was becoming apparent. The Charlotte Hornets were an affiliate of the Washington Senators. The statement of Phil Howser in support of Mobley's appearance seemed to indicate that a Black prospect (Cuban catcher Douglas McBean) was advancing toward Charlotte in the Washington system. The Knoxville Smokies were an affiliate of the New York Giants. After Mobley's stint with the Smokies, that team's general manager, Jack Aragon, even received a letter signed "Ku Klux Klan" requesting that he not use Black players on his team. His reply, in the *Knoxville News-Sentinel*, stated, "I'll use any player that the New York Giants send me. There may be some Negro players among them in the future. If there are and they have the ability to make our club, we'll use them."[10]

The end of the 1952 season was essentially the end of an era for professional baseball in the Carolinas. In fact, the country's entire baseball system (below the major leagues) was struggling. This was especially true at lower levels such as Class D, where many of the early efforts at integration had been made. Before the 1953 season, the Coastal Plain League and the North Carolina State League, which was centered in the western Piedmont region of the state, ceased operations. Both had been founded in 1937. Fewer professional teams meant fewer opportunities for all players. In 1948 there were fifty-two professional baseball teams that called a town or city in the Carolinas home. In 1953, that number dropped to twenty-four.[11]

Chapter 10
BILL WHITE

Failure to integrate did not doom the many minor league clubs that ceased operation in the early 1950s, but a more concerted effort at hiring Black players might have prolonged their existence. Many Black fans stayed away from minor league games, perhaps out of protest but more likely because of lack of interest. When teams such as those in the Coastal Plain League in 1952 hired a Black player, attendance went up. Black fans suddenly had a stake in the games and someone to cheer for. A sustained increase in attendance by African American fans would definitely have helped the bottom line of many clubs, but in the long run, it would not have overcome the shift in American culture. Televisions and air conditioning began to keep people inside, and on those televisions, people were often able to watch Major League Baseball games featuring the very best players, both Black and white.

Despite the struggles of minor league baseball as a whole, the system did receive some praise relating to racial issues. As the 1953 season began, the Black-owned *Indianapolis Recorder* ran an article on the spread of baseball integration in the South, which noted, "Hey, what's this? Negro ballplayers are sprouting up on minor league teams of the Deep and Near-Deep South like mushrooms after a rain. With the present season, the Great Change that came over major league baseball with the signing of Jackie Robinson in 1946 has spread throughout almost the entire structure of the organized game. And Brother, that includes Dixie!" The article went on to list the more than twenty Black players who began the season with a minor league club in the South. Other newspapers, even in the Carolinas, were taking notice of growing baseball integration. On May 27, 1953, the *Burlington Daily Times-News* reported on the first signing of a Black player, Leonard Tucker, by the St. Louis Cardinals organization.[1]

The Class B Carolina League did survive the turmoil in the minor leagues after the 1952 season with no changes in league membership. Six of the eight members had major league working agreements, including

Danville, which switched from Washington to the New York Giants.[2] The Giants had been one of the first teams to sign Negro league players (six in 1949) and were committed to integration. While other early integration efforts—such as those of the Brooklyn Dodgers and the Cleveland Indians—had been led by forward-thinking team owners and executives, the person largely responsible for integration in the Giants organization was field manager Leo Durocher.

Durocher had been born in Massachusetts to French Canadian parents and made his debut in Major League Baseball in 1925. After a long and successful career as a player, he turned to managing. In 1948 Durocher managed Jackie Robinson and the Brooklyn Dodgers for part of the season before being hired by the New York Giants. In 1951, he started three African Americans in the 1951 World Series: Monte Irvin, Willie Mays, and Hank Thompson. Durocher demanded excellence from his players, and winning was much more important than race. Hank Thompson recalled the manager telling him, "I'm only going to say one thing about color: You can be green or be pink on this team. If you can play baseball and help this team you're welcome to play."[3]

In the summer of 1952, an African American college freshman named Bill White was invited to work out for Durocher. White had been born in poverty in 1934 in northern Florida, but his mother joined the Black migration northward when he was three years old. He grew up in northeastern Ohio and was a star student and athlete at a mostly white high school. An academic scholarship took White to Hiram College. After an outstanding performance in an amateur baseball tournament in Cincinnati following his freshman year, he had been spotted by a scout who worked for the Giants. That led to an invitation to try out for Durocher in Pittsburgh, where his Giants were playing a three-game series.[4] The Giants' manager was very impressed by White's performance and offer a $1,000 bonus. White stated he needed $2,500 to finish college, and Durocher agreed.[5]

The next spring, Durocher took White to the Giants' spring training camp in Arizona to essentially give him a taste of big-league baseball. His roommate for the stay was veteran outfielder Monte Irvin, a former star for Newark in the Negro National League. He had joined the Giants in 1949 and been a league all-star in 1952. When White was denied a seat in a Phoenix movie theater because it did not have a section for Blacks, Irvin told him to be patient. "Don't rock the boat," he said; "someday all this is going to change."[6]

The Black-owned *Pittsburgh Courier* commented on White's progress in a report from the Giants' training camp in Phoenix: "Perhaps the hardest working player in uniform is Bill White, rookie first baseman. Reason? White wants to go to a Class C league in the North rather than face discrimination if he goes into the Carolina League."[7] Wrote Hank Aaron in his autobiography, "The prospect of playing in even a suburb of the South was terrifying to most black players—especially those from the North, to whom the South was a land of horror stories."[8] After a stay in Arizona, however, the Giants did fly White south to Melbourne, Florida, where their Danville club from the Carolina League was in training. At the conclusion of camp, White and his new teammates took the bus to southern Virginia, a place White later admitted he knew nothing about. He soon found out, he wrote in his autobiography, that "Danville sure isn't going to be like Ohio."[9]

According to White, his time in Danville was lonely. He never interacted with teammates except on the field. Because of the laws of the time, he was kept from dining, lodging, and socializing with his fellow players. The team found White a boardinghouse in the Black Holbrook-Ross section of town, and he had to eat at Black restaurants. In the afternoons he would get on the segregated city bus, sit in the back, and ride to the ballpark. On road trips the team bus driver would drop the white players off at their hotel and then drive him to lodgings in the Black section of whichever town they were in.[10]

Despite the isolation, White's play on the field soon earned him respect with local sportswriters. After a preseason game at Raleigh's Devereaux Meadow, the *Danville Bee* wrote, "Hitting star of the game was Willie White, Leaf Negro first sacker, who smacked a tremendous 380-foot home run, a bases-loaded triple and a single."[11] By May, most newspaper reports had dropped the Negro reference and changed the diminutive Willie to his preferred Bill.

White also had his first real experiences with racism at the ballpark. In Danville it was not as bad as in other towns because white fans were generally respectful toward the Black players on their home teams. On the road in North Carolina, however, things were much different. Of all the towns White played in during his career, he called Winston-Salem in 1953 the worst of all. But no matter where he went, he faced harassment from the stands. "I had to put up with crap from the fans. I was called names I'd never heard," said White in a later interview. "I rebelled. I yelled back at the name callers. I was only 19 and immature."[12] In his autobiography,

Bill White's 1965 Topps baseball card. Collection of the author.

White wrote, "It seemed ridiculous to me. Here I was—smart, well-educated, a college student with top grades, and at $250 per month I was probably making more money than most people in the crowd. And yet these red-necked, stubbly-faced, gap-toothed, tobacco-stained crackers were looking down on me? I had to laugh—almost."[13]

Years later, White wrote, "The five months I spent in the Carolina League was probably the worst time of my life." He recalled that Willie Mays had told him that playing baseball in the South was a lot harder for

Black players from the North—who were not accustomed to Jim Crow segregation—than it was for those from the South. Said White, "Northern black players like me were treated even worse than most Southern black players, because unlike them, we had never had to learn how to hide our rage and frustration."[14]

Interestingly, White commented on the different responses of his teammates to the racial heckling. The southern players seemed embarrassed by it. He recalled that one of them, an outfielder from North Carolina named Charlie Allen, "told me in a soft Southern drawl, 'Don't let it get to ya, Bill.'"[15] The northern players showed no reaction, however. White couldn't determine if they could not believe it or just did not care. Even player-manager Andy Gilbert, a native of western Pennsylvania and the son of Czech immigrants, appeared to have no interest in the issue. He "never bothered to give me any support," said White.[16]

In one early-season game at Burlington-Graham, White was beset by a constant barrage of racial epithets. In the eighth inning he responded: as he ran off the field, he held up his middle finger to the fans along the first baseline. Coming from an African American, the obscene gesture was shocking when aimed at a white southern crowd.[17]

After the game, as White recalled, a large middle-aged woman walked up to him and poked her finger in his shoulder. "Boy, you got some nerve being disrespectful to all these people," she said. Bob Knight, a white outfielder from New Orleans, pushed the woman away and said, "Leave him alone. He's better than all of you." When the team was ready to board the bus after showering, they learned an angry crowd was outside waiting for them.[18]

White was not sure how his teammates would respond, but to his surprise, one of them suggested that they arm themselves with bats and exit as a group. White reported that they went out with "bats held high—for once as a true team—and headed for the bus." Seeing how serious the players were at protecting their own, the crowd fell silent and backed down.[19]

After that incident, White took out his frustrations on the field. "The more the fans gave it to me, the harder I hit the ball," he later said. "They eventually decided to leave me alone, which was a victory over bigotry."[20] White's outstanding performance soon made him a star. On June 20, his picture was in the *Danville Bee* with the headline "White Holds Lead as Top Leaf Batter." The terms used in describing the player referred only to his first-base position and not to his race.[21]

Though there was most definitely racial conflict at the fan level in Carolina League towns, there was not—at least officially—at the league level. No team ever threatened not to play because a rival fielded a Black player.[22] This was not true elsewhere in the South. The same papers that—for the most part—eventually ignored Bill White's race reported that in other southern leagues the issues were much greater. In the Class C Cotton States League, the Hot Springs, Arkansas, club attempted to use a Black pitcher named Jim Tugerson. He had been signed before the season, but after protests by other league members (most of which were in Mississippi), he was optioned to Knoxville in the Class D Mountain States League. Tugerson became that league's top pitcher, and Hot Springs, struggling in last place, wanted to recall him. It attempted to use him in a May game, but the league demanded Hot Springs forfeit for breaking league rules.[23] The league then attempted to remove the entire Hot Springs club. The commissioner of minor league baseball, George Trautman, stepped in and said the league had no right to do so. In his decision, Trautman stated from his Ohio office, "The employment of Negro players has never been, nor is now, prohibited by any provision of the Major-Minor League Agreement."[24] Despite the ruling, Hot Springs gave up and sent Tugerson back to Knoxville. There he was the league's top pitcher and won 29 games.[25]

Back in Danville, Bill White excelled for the entire season. In 134 games for the Leafs, he hit .298 with 20 home runs. He helped lead the team to a 79–59 record, second only to Raleigh in the league standings. White had to leave the team before the championship round due to the resumption of college classes, but the Leafs went on to win the Carolina League playoffs over Reidsville.[26]

"I took it out on the baseball," White said later. "I never had that much respect for Southern whites anyway. So I wasn't affected much by them. I just figured they were ignorant sons-of-bitches and they had nothing else to do. They went to work all day in the hosiery mills and they came out [to the ballpark] and they yelled and screamed. They weren't going anywhere. They were going to be there all their lives. I was just passing through. I had a chance to do something."[27]

In 1954, White received a welcome promotion to Class A Sioux City, Iowa. On May 7, 1956, at age twenty-two, he made his debut for the New York Giants in St. Louis. He went on to play thirteen seasons in the big leagues (eight of them with the St. Louis Cardinals), during which time he won seven Gold Gloves at first base and was a five-time all-star. After his playing career, White turned to broadcasting and became the first African American play-by-play announcer for a major league team when he was one of the voices of the New York Yankees from 1971 to 1988. White eventually became the highest-ranking Black executive in professional sports when he served as president of the National League from 1989 to 1994.[28]

Chapter 11
AMERICAN LEGION, EPISODE III

On May 17, 1954, in a unanimous decision, the US Supreme Court ruled in the case known as *Brown v. Board of Education* that "separate educational facilities are inherently unequal" and therefore violated the Equal Protection Clause of the Fourteenth Amendment of the US Constitution. Though there was a long, obstacle-filled road ahead, it was a landmark decision that established that racial segregation in public schools was unconstitutional, even if the segregated schools were otherwise equal in quality. It made headlines across the nation, particularly in the South. In Gastonia, North Carolina, things were no different as newspaper writers speculated on how the ruling would affect schools in the state.[1]

A few days after the *Brown* decision, a race-related article appeared on the sports page of the *Gastonia Gazette*. "In Junior Baseball Here Negroes Will Get a Fair Shake," the headline read. For the first time, Black high school students were trying out for the previously all-white American Legion baseball team. This was big news in Gastonia not only because of the racial aspect of the story but because anything relating to the American Legion program was newsworthy. The city of Gastonia already had a long and successful history in American Legion baseball. Over the previous two decades, teams from local Legion Post 23 had won several state and regional championships, as well as the national title in 1935. Local support for the Legion team was so great that a new ballpark was even donated to the post in 1950. Named Sims Legion Field, the facility was undoubtedly one of the nicest Legion ballfields in the country (most teams played on high school fields). The park even met professional standards and was later home to Gastonia's minor league team for over a decade. Despite the success of Gastonia's Legion team, it—like all other aspects of southern life—was segregated.[2]

In 1934, American Legion baseball and Gastonia made the news when Springfield, Massachusetts, sent a team with a Black member to town. That incident occurred when Gastonia was merely a host of the tournament. Twenty years later, however, Gastonia's own team was in the news for racial reasons. Gastonia Post 23 was coached by former major leaguer Lawrence "Crash" Davis in 1954. A Gastonia native, Davis had been a member of the 1935 Legion national championship team before going on to star at Duke University and play for the Philadelphia Athletics. After retiring from the Carolina League's Raleigh Capitals as a player in 1952, Davis returned home to coach the Gastonia High School baseball team (which he guided to back-to-back AAA state championships in 1953 and 1954). After the high school season ended, Davis switched to leading the American Legion program. It was so popular and had so many players trying out that the Legion decided to field two fifteen-player teams. Called the Blues and the Greens, they would both compete in North Carolina's Area IV, which also included Charlotte, Henrietta, Kings Mountain, Morganton, Hickory, Shelby, and Cherryville.[3]

Gastonia's American Legion teams were composed of players from several Gaston County high schools. Not included, however, were the two schools for Black students: Highland in Gastonia and Reid in Belmont. These two schools also produced outstanding baseball players. It is unknown whether a Legion official looking to strengthen the team approached players from these schools or whether the players took it upon themselves, but somehow four Black athletes from Highland High showed up at the first Legion practice on May 24. That day, *Gastonia Gazette* columnist Dwight Frady reported that "Coach Crash Davis is giving Robert Love, Edward McCoy, Robert Pharr and Haskell Clinton the look-see." He added, "It's nothing new for Negro boys to be playing on legion teams in the United States. It's just that here, the precedent has been set by the Highland boys being out for the first time. But right now, they have the same opportunity as anyone else to make the grade with the local entry." In another article, A. L. "Roy" Sudduth, athletic director of Legion Post 23, promised that "Negro boys, applying for positions on the city's junior Legion baseball team, would be given equal treatment with white applicants." After the first workout, Sudduth said that the forty white boys who were trying out "showed no resentment" and added that he "doesn't anticipate trouble." Sudduth also pointed out that "teams in other sections frequently have Negros on their rosters. But it is the first time to my knowledge the Negroes have tried to make teams in the South."[4]

After no issue arose during that first workout, a couple of other Black players joined the tryout, most notably Carl "Satch" Forney, a student at Reid High School in Belmont. According to the *Charlotte Observer*,

Forney "has had a tremendous strikeout total in pitching his team to the state championship in Negro baseball play." In three championship games, he struck out forty-eight batters in twenty-six innings. The *Gastonia Gazette* said, "The Negro pitcher has been slightly sensational over the past year, racking up nine victories. He's 17 years old."[5]

Newspapers around the region followed the story (referred to as a "precedent-shattering move" by the Associated Press) and reported on the progress of the Black players. Two, Pharr and Clinton, were cut early, along with eight white players. "The other Negro players will continue to practice with about 30 other white boys on the heretofore all-white team, usually one of the best in the state," noted the AP story that appeared in the *Index-Journal* from Greenwood, South Carolina. As the tryout period wrapped up, the *Gastonia Gazette* reported that "one of the Negro boys out for the team had to be dropped because it was found that he was not eligible. Edward McCoy, pitcher, could not make the age grade." The article added that "still officially out for spots are 'Satch' Forney, Arthur Anderson, William Davis, and Robert Love." The newspaper predicted that Forney and Davis were the most likely of the group to make the team.[6]

At the same time the Black youths were trying out for the Gastonia team, the local newspaper was filled with race-related articles. In addition to coverage of the *Brown v. Board of Education* ruling, other topics included how to deal with racial division in churches ("At Presbyterian Assembly, Church Preparing for Racial Fight") and election scandal ("Racial Issue Cloud Primary Picture"). On May 28, a special Democratic primary to fill an empty US Senate seat was held between interim appointee Alton Lennon, a judge from Wilmington, and former governor W. Kerr Scott. Just before the election, thousands of leaflets, which were a reprint of a newspaper advertisement, were widely distributed in the rural eastern part of the state. It was revealed that the advertisement was placed by the mayor of Winston-Salem in an attempt to harm Scott. The article "warmly praised Scott as a friend of the Negro." Scott and his supporters claimed the ad was a "falsehood," which was true because neither candidate was a supporter of school or any other kind of integration. Said Scott, "I have always . . . been opposed to Negro and white children going to school together."[7]

On Tuesday, June 1, sportswriter Dwight Frady reported the rosters had been set for both Gastonia teams. "Heading the Blues pitching staff will be Harold Stowe, Roger Sheppard, Carl 'Satch' Forney, and Allen

Jones," he wrote. He later added that in a practice game between the two squads, "Forney, the Reid High standout, hurled two innings and fanned four batters." In his rundown of the full teams, Frady said, "With the setting of the squad, four Negroes made the grade, two on each team. Forney and Davis are with the Blues, while Anderson and Love hold forth with the Greens. Love, outstanding Highland High athlete, has cinched the first base post with the Greens. Forney will probably see regular turns on the mound with Sheppard and Stowe on the Blues nine."[8]

After the article on June 1, news of the Black players disappeared from the *Gastonia Gazette* for over a week. The season opened on Thursday, June 3, and it appears that, of the four, only Forney remained on the team. He was apparently on the roster for the team's first 2 games (a loss to Shelby and a win over Hickory). The third game was against Charlotte, and the *Charlotte Observer* predicted beforehand that Forney, referred to as a "smoke-baller," would be the starter. Surprisingly, he, too, was cut from the roster before the contest.[9]

On June 9, an article appeared in the *Gastonia Gazette* that mentioned that Carl Forney and William Davis had been cut. It stated that American Legion programs were allowed to pull players from county high schools whose combined enrollment did not exceed 2,500. White boys on the teams came from five high schools: Gastonia, Belmont, Cramerton, Mount Holly, and Dallas. When the enrollments of Highland and Reid were added, the total number of students was well over 2,500. Said Dwight Frady of Forney and Davis in the *Gastonia Gazette*, "Both boys were held in high regard, but due to the enrollment block, Coach Crash Davis had no choice but to turn the boys down."[10] Interestingly, when Coach Davis was asked about the Black players later in the summer, the reason he gave for cutting them did not involve enrollment totals: "An infielder (William Davis) and a pitcher (Satch Forney) were pretty good ball players but I figured the colored boy who breaks into our Gastonia lineup will have to be terrific—another Robinson—to withstand the pressure."[11]

It is interesting that the enrollment total limit was not taken into consideration before the Black players tried out. The two largest high schools in the county were Gastonia High (around 1,250 students) and Belmont (around 600). Mount Holly had approximately 350 students in 1955, Cramerton's enrollment was 163, and Dallas was somewhere in between. At the two Black schools, Highland had an estimated enrollment of 425 in 1955, while Reid's was a little over 200.[12] As would be expected, the top players for Post 23 went to the larger schools: Jimmie Hall and Harold Stowe attended Belmont, Roger Sheppard and Reggie Heavener were stars for Gastonia High, and Max Sherrill was a standout at Mount Holly. Those three schools alone had a total enrollment of 2,200. When Cramerton and Dallas were added in, the total should have already exceeded 2,500.

Since Post 23 fielded two teams (the Greens and the Blues), it has to be wondered whether each could have technically had a separate group of schools to pull from. Even if it was on the Greens, the lesser of the two squads, replacing Belmont with Reid and Highland might have made the numbers work out. Of course, that would have meant that students at a white school would have been eliminated from consideration for a spot on one of the teams in favor of students from a Black school. That was not going to happen anywhere in the South in 1954.

That the Black high school players were given a chance to try out for the powerful Gastonia Post 23 program was a step in the right direction, but it seems there never actually was an avenue for them to find success. It is possible that someone innocently overlooked the enrollment limits or thought the two Black schools were already included. Or, perhaps the enrollment limits gave a convenient "out" to Legion officials if they decided not to actually go through with integration. It would have been easy enough to hide any discrimination and say the Black players were all released based upon some deficient skill, but no one did that (at least for the four players named to the roster). Coach Davis somewhat implied that none of the players had the character necessary to handle any discrimination they would have faced as racial groundbreakers. But these were high school amateurs and not professional athletes in the media spotlight. They were also local kids who grew up in a segregated society, which, doubtless, they knew how to navigate. It is perhaps even more likely that someone with clout made a complaint when it appeared that at least one of them (Forney) would actually play. The possibility of school desegregation was on everybody's mind in the summer of 1954. Professional sports was one thing, but mixing Black and white high school kids in American Legion baseball was way too close to the issue.

Racial issues aside, competition for a spot on the Gastonia Post 23 team would undoubtedly been tough. If Carl Forney, William Davis, or the others had made the team, they would have joined an extremely talented group of young ballplayers. Outfielder Jimmie Hall went on to spend eight seasons in the major leagues and was an all-star twice. The team's top pitcher was Harold Stowe. He would go on to star for Clemson University before signing a professional contract with the New York Yankees. Stowe pitched in the minors for several seasons and appeared in one big-league game in 1960. Other members of the Gastonia Post 23 team to play professional baseball—several seasons each—were outfielder Reggie Heavener, Max Sherrill, and pitcher Roger Sheppard.[13]

The Gastonia Post 23 team did have an extremely successful summer in 1954 and advanced all the way to the Junior World Series in Yakima, Washington. There, they fell to San Diego in the championship. "Harold Stowe has always said we would've won in 1954 if (black players) had been on the team," Carl Forney said of the Gastonia Post 23 team in an interview years later.[14]

In 1955, when Forney led Reid High School to another state championship, his talents caught the eye of former Negro league star Quincy Trouppe, who was scouting for the St. Louis Cardinals. Forney signed the professional contract offered to him by Trouppe and was sent to play for the Cardinals' farm club in Decatur, Illinois. It was not a successful stint in the Cardinals organization, however, and, plagued by bursitis in his arm, Forney was released during the spring of 1956. After attending unsuccessful tryouts with the Pittsburgh Pirates and the Brooklyn Dodgers organizations, Forney came home to play for the semipro Charlotte Black Hornets and later the Pepsi Cola Giants. In 1957, while playing for the Giants against the barnstorming Indianapolis Clowns, Forney was so impressive that the Clowns lured him to their team. Forney went on to spend several seasons playing for, and even managing, the Clowns in the waning days of Negro league baseball.[15]

At the same time that Black players were trying out for the Gastonia team, Martin K. Rosefield, state commander of the American Legion in South Carolina—in a rather surprise statement—said that "Negro youths would be given an equal opportunity with whites if they wished to try out for a Legion junior baseball team" in that state. There were no actual rules against integrated teams in the South Carolina Legion. The bylaws stated only that participants had to be between fourteen and seventeen years old and follow national regulations.[16]

Despite Rosefield's statement, Abe Fennell, South Carolina's commissioner for Legion baseball, was skeptical. Fennell stated he was "uncertain as to what action would be taken if Negro youths attempted to make all-white teams." He went on to point out that "most Negro members of the Legion have separate posts and last year, six Negro posts formed their own Legion baseball teams." It was the same argument that was so often made for continued segregation in schools and other situations: let them do their own thing and we'll do ours. Everything is fine, no need to mix things up and change the system.[17]

Chapter 12
BLACK PIRATES AND LUCKIES (ALMOST)

Before spring training began in 1954, Wendell Smith, the nation's most prominent African American sportswriter, wrote in the *Pittsburgh Courier*, "The excitement over Negro players in organized baseball is apparently dying down. People are accepting their presence as matter of fact." While that may have been somewhat true in towns of the North, the statement was premature. The integration of the Class A South Atlantic League in 1953 had certainly been a positive sign, but there was a long way to go in the Carolinas and the South. Even in the major leagues, eight clubs had still not fielded a Black player (three of those would do so at the beginning of the 1954 season). In the same article, Smith also predicted a resurgence of the struggling Negro leagues, something that would not happen.[1]

On April 17, 1954, an editorial titled "What Price Prejudice" was printed in the *Carolina Times*. It addressed what it referred to as "the terrible plight of organized minor league baseball, especially in North Carolina." The article pointed out that the number of professional teams in the state had dropped from forty-seven in 1948 to only thirteen in 1954 and proposed a solution: faster integration. "We think the management of organized baseball in this state is paying an awful price to keep the league generally speaking 'for whites only,'" opined an editorial in the newspaper, "when this state, which has the largest Negro population in America, one million to be exact, could furnish enough fans to heal what ails the game if they would only include Negro players on all teams. Not only would this increase the interest of Negro fans to the extent that it would start the turnstiles clicking with Negro fans but we believe it would increase the interest among white fans." Though a case could be made for the financial importance of support from Black fans, especially in the southern states, the author of the *Carolina Times*' editorial was naive in their belief that the solution to the struggles of minor league baseball was so simple.[2]

The problems facing the minor leagues were nationwide, not only in the Carolinas. In states where the percentage of Black residents was high, African Americans might have made some difference at the turnstiles, but in many other states, such an outcome was doubtful. In 1950, the population of North Carolina was 4,060,000, with 25.8 percent of the residents listed as Black. The state ranked tenth in the country in total population. Just behind it was Indiana, with a total population of 3,952,000. Only 4.4 percent of that state's population was listed as Black, however. Iowa had a population of over 2.6 million, but only .08 percent were Black. Like North Carolina, these states were facing the same struggles with their minor league teams; the Class D Ohio-Indiana League shut down after the 1951 season, while the Class D Mississippi–Ohio Valley League would struggle through the 1955 season before calling it quits. In these and many other states, the small percentages of Black residents who would have been potential fans were not high enough to make much difference to teams financially.[3]

On the field, the integration of minor league teams in the Carolinas continued at a slow pace. In the Carolina League, the first steps toward integration had happened at Danville, followed by Fayetteville, but in 1954 Burlington-Graham joined the very short list. That season, fans who had so ruthlessly heckled Danville's Bill White in 1953 had to deal with Black members of their own team. The Burlington-Graham Pirates were a Pittsburgh farm club, and among the players assigned to the team were two African Americans: R. C. Stevens, a 6′5″ nineteen-year-old first baseman from Moultrie, Georgia, and Herb Bush, a twenty-six-year-old outfielder from Mobile, Alabama. Bush was an air force veteran who had attended Xavier University of Louisiana.[4]

The parent Pittsburgh club itself would also have its first Black player that same season. It had not integrated before 1954, but running the club was Branch Rickey, the man who had brought Jackie Robinson to the Dodgers. With Pittsburgh, he continued to seek top players for the organization regardless of race. An infielder named Curt Roberts was the first African American to play for Pittsburgh in the spring of 1954. He never became a regular player in the major leagues, but he opened the door for another Black player who debuted for the Pirates in 1955 and became one of the biggest stars in game history: Roberto Clemente.[5]

As the 1954 season approached, Burlington's *Daily Times-News* reported on the progress of baseball prospects from the Pittsburgh Pirates' minor league training camp in Brunswick, Georgia. There, in

R. C. Stevens. Collection of the author.

early March, 250 baseball players showed up—some under Pittsburgh contract, some just trying out—in an attempt to win a spot on one of the minor league clubs in the system. The newspaper speculated on which players might be assigned to Burlington-Graham but admitted that would not be known until higher-level clubs made cuts. Finally, on April 12, some of the roster was announced. That day, the headline on the *Daily Times-News* sports page read, "Bur-Gra Pirates Get 19-Year-Old Negro

First Baseman." The article, by sportswriter Bill Hunter, introduced R. C. Stevens, mentioned that he had two years of experience in the Pirates' organization, and noted that he would be "the first Negro ever to play on a professional baseball team in Alamance County." Hunter downplayed the significance of the assignment, stating, "Another Carolina League team, Danville, has had Negro players for the past two seasons, so the introduction of Stevens is nothing new to the league." He added that Winston-Salem had five Black players in its camp and High Point–Thomasville had one. The Danville team, he assessed, "will almost definitely use a Negro player this season."[6]

L. C. "Red" Fowler, president of the Burlington-Graham club, had no problem with the assignment of Stevens. He stated, "I believe that Bur-Gra should use Negro players when necessary if they have the qualifications to play ball. Stevens has those qualifications. The thing I most desire is a pennant for the Bur-Gra team. With Stevens at first base, I think we will have a contender this season." Fowler added, "I am against holding up the advance of any ball player. If Stevens needs a year of Class B baseball on his way upward, and if he gives me a much stronger ball club, then I am for using him." At least for team ownership, success on the field was more important than race.[7]

The following day, Hunter dedicated half of his weekly column to Stevens's signing. "Only time will tell how Bur-Gra Pirates fans will accept R. C. Stevens on the Alamance County team," he wrote. "The great majority of fans, naturally, will only care whether or not he is a good ball player. There is always that small minority which will complain in any situation like this, and this case will probably be no exception." He went on to add that there were more than a dozen Black players in the Pirates' Georgia training camp and that he had seen no dissension at all in his visit. Hunter stated that "the boys from the deep South have no trouble at all with the Negroes on the field or off." No matter how he felt personally, it is doubtful that any young job-seeking player would have complained if he wanted to remain in the good graces of the Pittsburgh Pirates. Hunter also speculated that the Burlington team might receive another Black player before the roster was finalized. He wrote, "Pittsburgh officials, who have handled matters of this type for several years now, think it is better to send two Negro players to a team. It gives added companionship to each other and it helps the situation all around." His prediction proved true, and the assignment of outfielder Herb Bush was announced the next day.[8]

Stevens and Bush were two of the earliest Black players signed by the Pirates organization. The Pirates had sent Stevens to Batavia, New York, in 1952 while Bush played for the team's Class C affiliate in Saint-Jean-sur-Richelieu, Quebec. Both played for the Saint-Jean Canadiens in 1953, where Stevens had a .313 batting average and Bush batted .342.[9] Assessed author Alan Cohen, "The next stop on the Pirates' minor-league ladder was less hospitable: the Burlington-Graham Pirates."[10] But it was a step toward the major leagues as well as an increase in pay; with the Saint-Jean Canadiens, both players were paid $200 per month, but at Burlington they both made $250 for thirty days and $275 per month afterward. These salaries were in line with those of white players with the same amount of experience.[11]

In early May, after only a few games, Bush was injured during a game at Greensboro. Attempting to slide back into first base on a pickoff play, he fractured his left ankle.[12] He eventually returned in late July, but during his prolonged absence, Stevens was left as the only Black player on the team. In one game, "an opposing fan brought a black cat to the game and taunted Stevens with racial epithets."[13] And like other Black players who had come before, he faced the same segregation with regard to accommodations and dining.[14] Despite the challenges, he turned his focus to the field, just as Bill White had the previous season. The result was a .293 batting average with 100 walks, 31 doubles, 25 home runs, and 115 RBIs. The July 28 game against Reidsville was a highlight as he hit a grand slam and a 2-run home run.[15] Stevens's bat helped power the Pirates to a second-place finish in the Carolina League. They advanced to the championship round of the playoffs but fell to Fayetteville. In ten playoff games, Stevens hit 3 home runs.[16]

Due to his injury, Herb Bush appeared in only 30 games. He did hit .343, which boded well for his future, and contributed a grand slam home run in the playoffs. Bush came back to Burlington in 1955, but after a slow start (.194 in 19 games) he was demoted to Class D Dublin in the Georgia State League. After 30 games there he was released, ending his professional career. Bush then returned to the Burlington area, which he made his permanent home. He served as a member of the Burlington Recreation and Parks Commission, and a softball tournament was later named in his honor.[17]

R. C. Stevens was highly regarded in the Pirates organization. Wrote Branch Rickey in a scouting report, "This big, agile, right hand hitting negro is a 'hitter-upper.' He can scratch more clouds than most anybody.

He has power enough to drop the ball out of the park on occasion. He is a young fellow and his ownership should be protected."[18] Stevens was promoted to Hollywood in the Pacific Coast League in 1955 and eventually made his Pittsburgh debut in 1958. Though he had power, Stevens was never quite able to consistently hit major league pitching; in 104 games over parts of four seasons, he batted only .210. Stevens was more successful at the AAA level; he played for parts of three seasons for both Salt Lake City and Toronto. He retired from baseball in 1963 after finishing the season with Quad Cities (Davenport, Iowa). Stevens settled permanently in Davenport and went to work for International Harvester. He retired as a department manager.[19]

Other than at Burlington-Graham, integration continued in the Carolina League at Danville with Marshall Bridges, a pitcher from Mississippi, and Willie Kirkland, an outfielder from Alabama. Both went on to have average big-league careers. Another player of African descent on the Leafs' roster was infielder Ozzie Virgil. Not only would he make the major leagues, but he was the first native of the Dominican Republic to do so. After spending parts of two seasons with the Giants, Virgil was acquired by the Detroit Tigers. On June 6, 1958, he became the first Black player to appear for that team.[20]

Interestingly, Virgil was never seen as a "true representative" by African Americans, according to author Ron Briley. This was despite the fact he had graduated high school in the Bronx, New York, and served in the US Marine Corps. Said Virgil in an interview with Briley, "The only thing I didn't like was that the black people in Detroit didn't accept me. They thought of me more as a Dominican Republic player instead of a Negro. If they called me black, fine. If they called me white, fine. If they called me Latino, fine. I didn't care what they called me, I just wanted to play." Virgil, who had been hitting .293 at AAA Charleston at the time of his promotion, felt he had been called up to Detroit solely because of his outstanding play.[21]

Burlington-Graham and Danville were among the five teams in the Carolina League that had major league agreements in 1954. Of the three independent clubs, the only efforts at integration took place in Reidsville. This is perhaps more important because the players whom these teams hired were of their own choosing. In Reidsville, as opposed to Burlington-Graham and Danville, player assignments were not dictated by a baseball executive far away in the North.

Since they were not stocked with as many young prospects, independent teams often had an average age greater than that of farm teams.

The 1954 Reidsville Luckies comprised many veterans, including two—Jack Sanford and Garland Lawing—who had spent short stints in the major leagues. The rest of the team consisted of players who earned a roster spot with outstanding play in the preseason. Among those given a tryout by the Luckies and manager Fred Harrington were two African Americans.[22]

On April 4, in the first official exhibition game of spring training, two Black players took the field for the Luckies against a semipro team from Oak Ridge in neighboring Guilford County. Though Reidsville, in its seventh season as a member of the Carolina League, had never had a Black player on its team, the event drew only casual mention in the local newspaper. In the *Reidsville Review*, the fourth paragraph of the report of the game read, "Roosevelt Robinson, one of the two Negroes in the starting lineup, pitched the first three innings. He got by the first inning without trouble, but control trouble and spotty support by his mates figured in one run scored by the visitors in the second and five more in the third." Later, the article added, "Robinson and center fielder Bill Harrison became the first Negroes to play on a Reidsville team Friday afternoon."[23] Ten days later, both players were still among the candidates to make the team. On April 15, a preview of the exhibition game against a team from Fort Bragg read, "Reidsville's young Negro hurler will see action on the mound for the Luckies." The article went on to state that thirteen pitchers were still in consideration for one of eight roster spots. Bill Harrison was also listed as a candidate for the outfield.[24] Robinson performed well against Fort Bragg. He "pitched scoreless ball during his three-inning stint and except for a spell of wildness, looked good."[25]

Though Harrison did not make the final cut, Robinson did and went on to appear in 5 games with no wins and one loss. On May 5, he was given his release by the team. This appears to be nothing more than a baseball decision as the Luckies sought to build a strong pitching staff while reducing the roster to the required seventeen by the mid-May deadline. The *Reidsville Review* made only minor mention of the roster moves: "Over the weekend, Joe Ares was returned to Richmond while Joe Scalise, Bill Bustle and Roosevelt Robinson were released. Scalise is an outfielder, the other three are pitchers."[26]

Though the appearance of the first Black players for clubs did not seem to be big news in the mainstream newspapers, it did draw attention in the Black press. In the *Carolina Times*, based in Durham, an editorial in the April 24 edition called for Black fans to boycott the Durham Bulls. That team had not yet fielded any Black members. The editorial also called on the team to give talented Black players a chance: "There are several Negro players in Durham that are by far better than the average ones seen in action on the Bulls team last year and we see no reason why they cannot be given a chance to play with the club the same as is being done in Burlington and Reidsville."[27] Though this argument seemed logical on the surface, it was most likely unrealistic. The Durham Bulls were a farm club of the Detroit Tigers. Players were selected and paid by the Tigers and assigned by that organization to Durham from all over the country. In 1954, there were not even any local white members of the team. The fact that the Bulls had an all-white roster was essentially a reflection of the attitude the Tigers and owner Walter Briggs had toward integration. Briggs, who had been opposed to integration, died in 1952, but his family still owned the team and his policies lingered. As of 1954, there were no Black players in the entire Tigers organization.[28]

The same *Carolina Times* editorial praised the Burlington and Reidsville clubs for their efforts at integration, stating that it "congratulates the managements of the Reidsville and Burlington Clubs that they had the foresight and the courage to take the forward step and give Negro players in their respective cities a chance. We urge Negro fans in those two cities to support the teams morally and financially in order that America's greatest pastime may continue to furnish pleasure and amusement for the people of this country." In Burlington it was merely coincidence that Black players had been assigned to the team by the Pittsburgh Pirates. In Reidsville, however, team ownership and management did deserve praise for making small but positive steps toward integration on their own.[29]

Chapter 13
FRANK ROBINSON

The Class A South Atlantic League, frequently called the Sally League, had been founded in 1904. For half a century, it had operated as one of the top leagues in the Southeast, second in prestige only to the Southern Association. Member cities changed over the years, but Columbia, Charleston, Charlotte, Spartanburg, Greenville, and Asheville were frequent participants. Others in the league included such cities as Savannah and Macon in Georgia and Knoxville, Tennessee. Of course, like all southern leagues, the Sally was for white players only. That all changed in 1953, however, when the Milwaukee Braves assigned Hank Aaron, Horace Garner, and Felix Mantilla to their Jacksonville affiliate, and the Philadelphia Athletics sent Al Isreal and Fleming Reedy to Savannah.

Before the 1953 season, Arthur Ehlers, general manager of the Philadelphia Athletics, was interviewed by W. Rollo Wilson, veteran sportswriter for the Black-owned *Pittsburgh Courier*. He discussed integrating the Sally League: "As you know, we have assigned Reedy to the Savannah team for 1953. He played one game with Savannah against the A's during spring training in 1952 although he was a member of the Lincoln [Nebraska] club. We tried it for an experiment to see how the people down there would react to a Negro on the home team and the result was favorable. He played a fine game that night, was applauded by the home fans and I was greatly encouraged." He continued, "Perhaps you remember that I told you about three years ago I just wished I had enough nerve to assign a colored player to our team in Savannah because his presence would get us support of the Negro fans? After that I saw how warmly the Brooklyn players were greeted when they played there. Then I used Reedy that night. Now I have the nerve."[1]

Reedy, Aaron, and the others officially broke the color line in South Carolina on April 21, 1953. On that day, Savannah traveled to Charleston and Jacksonville visited Columbia for games. Both away teams were victorious. Having a Black player on a visiting team was certainly not the same as having one on the home team, but it helped set the stage for future seasons in the Sally League.[2]

In 1954, the list of integrated teams in the South Atlantic League grew to include Charlotte, Columbia, and Montgomery. One of the major league teams that helped expand that integration was the Cincinnati Reds. In the late 1940s, the Reds had been notorious for their harassment of Jackie Robinson and other Black players. After the 1951 season, Gabe Paul was promoted from within the organization to take over as general manager. Paul, who was Jewish and had certainly had his own experiences with prejudice, was determined to work toward integration of the Reds. Not long after taking office he hired two Black scouts, and before the 1952 season they had signed five Black players. It was not an easy road to Cincinnati for these athletes. Author Rick Swaine wrote, "Another obstacle to Paul's integration efforts was that the Reds' top farm clubs were located in Tulsa, Oklahoma, and Columbia, South Carolina, not exactly ideal spots for vulnerable, impressionable young black players." Nevertheless, Chuck Harmon from Indiana and Nino Escalera from Puerto Rico did advance through the system, played for Tulsa in 1953, and on April 17, 1954, became the first Black players to take the field for the Cincinnati Reds.[3]

As the 1954 Sally League season approached, sportswriters began to speculate that the Cincinnati Reds would likely send Black players to their Columbia farm club. On March 30, the headline of the sports section of the *Columbia Record* announced, "Reds Sign Negro Shortstop." Sportswriter Van Newman went on to say that Lazaro "Chico" Terry, a native of Cuba, "will become the first Negro player to perform in a Columbia uniform in Capital City Park." After a standout season with Class C Ogden, Utah, in 1953, during which he batted .327, the twenty-one-year-old Terry was promoted within the Cincinnati system. Newman noted that "Terry is expected to be joined on the Columbia roster by at least one more Negro player before opening day." The two most likely candidates were infielder-outfielder Frank Robinson, who had also had an outstanding season at Ogden in 1953, and pitcher John Jackson.[4] *The State*, Columbia's other newspaper, also hailed the arrival of Terry. "A strong pitching staff and a solid defense, built around Negro shortstop Chico Terry, will probably be Columbia's strongest assets this season in the Sally League pennant race."[5]

As predicted, another Black player was assigned to Columbia during the preseason: pitcher John "Stony" Jackson, a twenty-seven-year-old

The 1955 Columbia Reds, with Frank Robinson (*back row, second from left*), Marvin Williams (*second row, far right*), and manager Ernie White (*front row, center*). Courtesy of *The State* Newspaper Photograph Archive, Richland Library, Columbia, SC.

right-hander from Mississippi. After playing baseball for Southern University in Baton Rouge, Jackson had joined the Kansas City Monarchs in 1951. Jackson pitched in both the 1952 and 1953 East-West Games in the Negro leagues. He signed with the Cincinnati Reds organization before the 1954 season.

On April 13, opening day, Terry made his Columbia debut against visiting Charlotte in front of 3,500 spectators. He was 2-for-4 at the plate with a triple and two runs batted in as the Reds defeated the Hornets, 6–1 (the game also featured Charlotte's first Black player, Terry's countryman Carlos Paula). The following day, newspapers were cautiously accepting. An article in the *Columbia Record* was titled "First Negro Red

Apparently Will Be Welcomed Here If He Can Produce." It went on to state that Terry was given "a hearty round of applause the next time up after his triple" and that "when the plate umpire made a questionable call on a third strike the white spectators were the first to voice disapproval." Included also was a quote from a spectator: "It don't make no difference what color he is, as long as he can hit that ball." Another article on the same page announced "Reds Use First Negro Pitcher." Stony Jackson was scheduled to start the second game of the season.[6]

A few games into the season, the Cincinnati Reds transferred eighteen-year-old Frank Robinson from Tulsa to their farm club in Columbia. Robinson was a highly regarded prospect from Oakland, California, who had won the 1950 American Legion national championship with Bill Erwin Post 337. After graduating from McClymonds High School in 1953, he was signed to a $3,500 contract by the Cincinnati Reds. In his first season of professional baseball, Robinson batted .348 for Class C Ogden. He was promoted to Tulsa in 1954, but when he didn't win a starting job, the Reds moved him to Columbia, where he would have more playing time. Robinson, who was a versatile fielder as well as a powerful hitter, made his Columbia debut on the road at Savannah. In 2 games there, he hit 4 home runs and drew instant praise from the Columbia press. After Robinson's early home runs and a complete game victory by Stony Jackson in which he also hit a home run, Associated Press sportswriter Vernon Butler wrote, "Columbia's investment in Negro baseball players has already paid a sizeable dividend."[7]

While the Black members of the Columbia Reds may have been finding success and acceptance by the white community while on the field in 1954, the same was not true for African American members of the local population. On June 22, Sarah Mae Flemming, a Black maid, took a front seat on a segregated Columbia city bus. The driver accused Flemming of sitting in the part of the bus reserved for white people, struck her, and ejected her from the rear door. The incident occurred seventeen months before Rosa Parks took her stand against segregation on city buses in Montgomery, Alabama, on December 1, 1955.[8]

Modjeska Monteith Simkins, a Columbia native who was state secretary for the South Carolina NAACP, heard about Flemming's incident and convinced local white attorney Phillip Wittenberg to represent her. He filed a suit against South Carolina Electric and Gas Company, the operator of the bus, in federal court claiming Flemming's Fourteenth Amendment rights had been violated and asked for $25,000 in damages.

Interestingly, the first news reports of Flemming's suit mentioned nothing about race. The story, on page 3 of *The State*, merely noted that "a $25,000 suit had been filed against the South Carolina Electric and Gas Company by a Columbia woman who alleges that one of the company's bus drivers struck her 'a severe blow in the abdominal region.'"[9]

On August 11, *The State* finally printed a more detailed account of the incident. It reported that Flemming had been removed from a seat on the bus due to a "violation of the 14th amendment of the U.S. Constitution and article 4, section 2 of the United States Constitution." The article also claimed that the bus driver had acted "in accordance with customs and useages [*sic*] prevailing in Columbia and because she was a Negro ordered her from the seat." Flemming stated she had been standing on the full bus when a seat became open. As no white passengers were standing, she sat. There were white passengers seated behind her, however, so the driver pulled over, ordered her out the back, and struck her in the stomach as she exited.[10]

A district court judge in Columbia dismissed the case in early 1955 on the grounds that South Carolina statutes were valid based on the *Plessy v. Ferguson* decision. On appeal, the decision was reversed by the US Court of Appeals for the Fourth Circuit in Richmond. The bus company, joined by the State of South Carolina as well as the City of Columbia, appealed, but on April 1956, the US Supreme Court refused to review the Fourth Circuit decision. Technically, the ruling in the *Flemming* case—though widely ignored—struck down segregation on city buses. It was cited, however, in the decision from the far-better publicized *Browder v. Gayle* case from Montgomery, Alabama, which did lead to the end of segregated buses.[11]

Though he may not have been allowed to sit at the front of the bus, Frank Robinson was praised by Columbia baseball fans in 1954. On the day Flemming's suit was announced in *The State*, the sports page applauded Robinson's 19th home run of the season. It helped lead Columbia to victory over the visiting Jacksonville Braves. The article also stated that the league's top pitcher, Humberto Robinson, was scheduled to take the mound for Jacksonville at Capital City Park that night. Humberto Robinson, who was also Black, would become in 1955 the first native of Panama to appear in the major leagues.[12]

While they may have been finding success on the field, being the first Black players to represent a South Carolina team in Organized Baseball took its toll. A decade later, Robinson wrote,

> I was eighteen, I'd had no real experience with segregation or that sort of thing. South Carolina was like enemy country. I had to ride in the back of buses, I could never find a Negro cab after games. We had three Negroes on the team. We shared one small room in a boardinghouse with no shower. We had to line up to get into the tub. I stayed in my room evenings because I couldn't go to the movie theaters in town. I just wouldn't sit up in the last row in the balcony—and I like movies. I like good clothes, too—the stores that sold 'em in Columbia wouldn't let me in. And worse, I couldn't figure out why I could do as I pleased in California and Utah, but not in South Carolina. I didn't know how to take it. I was blue, homesick, ready to quit.[13]

In his 1968 autobiography, Robinson wrote that he would always remember one event that took place in Columbia in 1954. The team was playing Savannah, and before the game, manager Ernie White, a South Carolina native and former big-league pitcher, was going over the opponent's roster with his team. Robinson recalled that when White reached the name of one large power-hitting player, he said, "How are we going to pitch to this big black n——?" Wrote Robinson, "A deathly quiet fell over the clubhouse—I was one of two Negroes on our team—but White, who is a Southerner, didn't realize what was going on. That was just his way and he didn't mean anything by it."[14] Despite Ernie White's insensitive language, the manager was very supportive of Frank Robinson and helped his career develop.

Even though he was heckled by fans and insulted by players on opposing teams, Frank Robinson excelled on the ball field. "There was one way to get out of the South—by playing the best ball I knew how," he said. Robinson was the Columbia Reds' best player in 1954 and led the team with a .336 batting average and 25 home runs. His 112 runs scored were the most in the league, and he was named to the post-season all-star team.[15]

Neither of Frank Robinson's Black teammates at Columbia in 1954 went on to baseball fame. Stony Jackson posted a 7–12 record for Columbia in 1954. In August, he was demoted to Class D Douglas, Georgia. He finished the season there with a perfect 6–0 record. The following season, Jackson pitched for three teams in the Reds system, including Columbia (he was 1-for-4 in 9 games). It was his final season in professional baseball. Chico Terry appeared in 40 games for Columbia but batted only

.183. Perhaps the stress of the racial situation combined with a language barrier affected him, or perhaps his skills were not at the level of competition in the South Atlantic League (he had jumped from Class C to Class A). Either way, he was returned to Ogden in June. There, he found his swing and led the team with a .333 batting average. Terry went on to have several successful seasons in the minor leagues and advanced as high as AAA Indianapolis but never made the major leagues. He did, however, play a role in integrating the teams of two other cities. In 1957, Terry played a few games for the Durham Bulls in the Carolina League during their first integrated season. Two years later he was back in South Carolina and spent almost all of the 1959 season as one of the first Black players to represent Charleston in the Sally League.[16]

With Frank Robinson's success at Columbia in 1954, it would have appeared he had achieved his goal and "played" his way out of the South. It was not to be, however. Late in the 1954 season, Robinson had begun to experience pain in his throwing arm. He thought it would recover after rest, but the Reds sent him to Puerto Rico to play winter ball. There, he stated in his autobiography, he felt pain in his arm "like the stab of a knife," followed by swelling and numbness. He was sent to specialists for treatment; they prescribed more rest.[17]

Robinson was invited to spring training with the Cincinnati club in 1955, but the pain in his arm still prevented hard throws. Rather than given a shot at the major league roster, Robinson was told he was being sent back to the minor leagues to give his arm a chance to recover. He asked to be sent to Columbia instead of Tulsa. "Ernie White was glad to have me," wrote Robinson. "White was a fiery type leader who hated to lose, but he was very patient with me. He played me at first base so I wouldn't have to make long throws."[18]

In Columbia, Robinson was joined on the team by one other African American. Marvin Williams, a thirty-five-year-old native of Texas, was a veteran of the Negro National League as well as the Mexican League. When desegregation finally presented an opportunity, he signed with Sacramento of the Pacific Coast League. Williams spent the 1954 season with the independent Vancouver Capilanos in the Western International League before signing with the Cincinnati Reds organization.[19]

Because of his arm trouble, Robinson struggled early in the 1955 season. "My hitting had fallen off next to nothing. At one time, my batting average was .190, and the fans, even the home fans, began to get on me." Robinson wrote of one game in Columbia at which three drunk white fans heckled him incessantly. The racial taunts became too much to take, and when the game ended, Robinson grabbed a bat that was lying on the base path and headed toward the stands to confront them. His teammate Marv William rushed to restrain him. Robinson recalled that Williams told him, "It isn't worth it." Said Robinson later, "And really, he was right, but it didn't seem right at the time." Manager Ernie White ran over and asked what was wrong. Robinson wrote in his autobiography, "I told him and he said, 'Tell me who they are, I'll get them for you.'" White did find out the name of the owner of the car in which the fans fled. He wrote a letter to the person and said that if the courage of Frank Robinson was doubted, he would arrange a personal meeting. It was not answered, but Robinson was not bothered by them again. Robinson told a slightly different version of this story in the essay he wrote for Jackie Robinson's 1964 book, *Baseball Has Done It*. In it, he wrote, "Ernie White tried to calm down the fans who were ganging up on me. White told the one who had done the worst name-calling that he knew them and would have them barred from the park."[20]

The combination of injury and Jim Crow restrictions caused Frank Robinson to reconsider his career choice. "I had plenty of time to think, you know, living in Columbia and not being able to go where I wanted. I always liked to be around people and this was like a prison. I just couldn't sit and stare at the four walls of my room. I was very lonely, and bitter. I felt I was giving everything I had to give even though I was not in good physical shape, and I was not earning any respect in return. I was at a point where I couldn't take it anymore."[21]

Before one late July road trip to Charlotte for a three-game series, Robinson considered leaving the team. "I told my roomie, Marv Williams, who was the only other Negro on the club, 'I might as well go home.'" Williams said if Robinson wasn't going to Charlotte, then he was not either. The team left on the ninety-mile trip, and two players stayed behind. Fortunately, the game was rained out. Wrote Robinson, "That gave me time to think about what I had done. And it began to dawn on me that I was throwing away any chance I had to become a major-leaguer, that I was throwing away my whole life. . . . I told Marv, 'I've changed my mind. Let's go back.' He said okay and a friend of ours drove us to Charlotte and we didn't miss the game. We played a doubleheader that night and I started to hit better."[22]

Robinson's throwing arm was still a problem, but after he took himself out of the lineup for two weeks—during which time he did not touch a baseball—he began to recover. He played a total of 80 games in 1955 and batted .263 with 12 home runs. It was not the stellar season he had had in 1954, but it was a respectable performance. Marv Williams batted .328 in 97 games for Columbia in 1955. The Reds assigned him to Tulsa in 1956, and he played several more seasons in the Texas League before retiring at age forty-one.[23]

Frank Robinson made the Cincinnati ball club in spring training in 1956 and never looked back. He was the 1956 National League Rookie of the Year and appeared in the first of 12 all-star games. In 1966, the year he won the American League Triple Crown, Robinson was named the MVP of the World Series as he led the Baltimore Orioles to the title. In total, his major league playing career spanned twenty-one seasons with five clubs, and he retired with 2,943 hits, 586 home runs, and a .294 batting average.[24]

In 1975, Frank Robinson became the first Black manager in major league history when he was hired by the Cleveland Indians. He eventually spent sixteen seasons as a big-league skipper with Cleveland, San Francisco, Baltimore, and Montreal/Washington. Robinson was inducted into the Baseball Hall of Fame in 1982 and awarded the Presidential Medal of Freedom in 2005. Over fifty years after the seasons in Columbia that helped shape him as a player and a person, he retired from baseball completely in 2006.[25]

Chapter 14
THE CUBAN CONNECTION, CONTINUED

One of the Black Cuban players signed by Clark Griffith's Washington Senators as a partial concession to integration was powerful 6′3″ outfielder Carlos Paula. After spending the 1953 season with the Class B team in Paris, Texas, the Senators assigned Paula to one of their top affiliates, the Charlotte Hornets of the Class A South Atlantic League. There, in 1954, he joined fellow Cubans Cholly Naranjo, Jose Aguiar, Enrique Gonzalez, and Jose Nakamura (none of whom were considered Black).[1]

After the 1953 season, Phil Howser, Charlotte's team president, had pulled his team out of the Class B Tri-State League and applied for entry into the Class A South Atlantic League. One reason he gave was that the South Atlantic League, an eight-team circuit that included the Columbia Reds, had allowed Black players in 1953 while the Tri-State continued to ban them. He stated that he would likely use three from the Washington organization in 1954. "This is no promotional stunt," he said. "We're going to put the best club we possibly can in Charlotte next summer, and we believe we have some Negro players who can make the grade."[2]

Charlotte's manager in 1954, for the second season, was former big-league pitcher Pete Appleton. Born to Polish immigrants in Connecticut, he was an example of a player who anglicized his birth name in order to be more acceptable to fans, a fairly common practice at the time. Perhaps to make his name more easily pronounceable or perhaps to avoid any discrimination—no one is exactly sure why—he legally changed his name to Appleton from Jablonowski. Sportswriter Shirley Povich postulated it was because the pitcher believed his ethnic surname "was no fit name for the national pastime." Regardless, it is likely that Appleton somewhat understood the struggles of perceived outsiders trying to fit into the game.[3]

As the Hornets prepared for the season at Daytona Beach, all eyes were on Carlos Paula. After a spring training game against the club from Reading, Pennsylvania, in which Paula had 4 consecutive hits including 2 triples, stole a base, drove in 2 runs, and scored another, the

Carlos Paula. Photo by Osvaldo Salas. Courtesy of National Baseball Hall of Fame and Museum, Cooperstown, New York.

sportswriter for the *Charlotte News* wrote, "Paula had everyone passing out raves, including General Manager Hank Greenberg of the Cleveland organization." The *Charlotte Observer* also praised the performance of "the dusky, 195-pound Cuban." The article further mentioned that manager Appleton had specifically requested that Paula join his team. After the game, Paula was named as the starting left fielder in the upcoming exhibition game against the New York Yankees in Charlotte.[4]

In 132 games for the Hornets that season, Paula did not disappoint: he hit an impressive .309 with 24 doubles, 13 triples, and 14 home runs. He was called up to Washington in September and became the first Black player to take the field for the Senators, making his debut at Griffith Stadium on September 6, 1954.[5] In 1955, Paula made the Senators' roster out of spring training. He played in 115 games that season and hit a very respectable .299. He spent most of the 1956 season with Denver and Louisville in AAA but did make it into 33 big-league games. In 1957, Paula was again assigned to an AAA club. The Senators finally decided to give up on him as a prospect in the spring of 1958 and traded Paula to

Sacramento in the Pacific Coast League. He played a few more seasons in the minor leagues but never made it back to the majors. According to historian Larry Brunt of the National Baseball Hall of Fame, no one ever denied Carlos Paula's strength, speed, and overall raw talent. Instead, it was his fielding, base running, and somewhat lackadaisical work ethic that led the Senators to trade him. Twenty years after his career, jokes were still being made, and a poor fielder was referred to as "a reborn Carlos Paula."[6]

One of Paula's teammates at Charlotte in 1954 also played a role in the integration of professional baseball in the South, though in a different way. Though the integration of previously all-white minor league baseball that took place during the 1940s and '50s primarily involved players of African descent, there was also a notable example of one with Asian heritage: Jose Nakamura.

In the United States, many immigrant groups—such as Italians and Poles—readily accepted baseball as their sport of choice. Baseball was also popular among Americans of Japanese descent, particularly on the West Coast, during the first half of the twentieth century. They were never officially kept from Organized Baseball, but very few ventured beyond segregated teams. Also, after World War II, there was undoubtedly some negative sentiment toward anyone with a Japanese name.

The first player of Japanese descent to play in the Carolinas also happened to be Cuban. Born in Cuba to Japanese immigrants in 1928, left-handed pitcher Jose Nakamura signed with the Havana Cubans at age eighteen. There he was discovered by scout Joe Cambria and sent to the Abilene, Texas, club in the Class C West Texas–New Mexico League. Nakamura's appearance in Abilene in 1949 most likely made him the first member of the Japanese diaspora to appear in Organized Baseball in the postwar years. "There was just one," said Nakamura in a 2005 interview. "*Yo era el unico*, the only one, a Japanese Cuban."[7] (California's Stockton Ports did sign a pair of Japanese Americans who played briefly later the same season.)[8]

In 1951, Nakamura—whose first name was often anglicized to Joe in the newspapers—signed with the Shelby Farmers of the Class D Western Carolina League. In three seasons with Shelby, Nakamura essentially dominated the league. He posted records of 17–6, 3.28 ERA in 1951; 13–5, 2.49 ERA in 1952; and 19–11 with a league-leading 2.40 ERA in 1953. After the 1953 season, Nakamura's contract was purchased by the Washington Senators, and he was assigned to the Charlotte Hornets.[9]

At Charlotte in 1954, Nakamura joined Carlos Paula and several other Cubans. Despite playing for a losing team, he pitched well, primarily in a relief role, for two seasons. In 1956, Nakamura earned a brief promotion to Louisville—one step from the major leagues—before deciding to sign with a team in Mexico. He retired from playing after the 1958 season and eventually managed a sugar-processing facility in Cuba.

Despite having a Black star of their own—Carlos Paula—in 1954, Charlotte fans taunted players on other teams. A Black player who later related his experiences in the South Atlantic League was Elbert "Al" Isreal, a third baseman from Rockville, Maryland. Isreal was a veteran of the Homestead Grays and the Philadelphia Stars in the Negro leagues and in 1952 was signed by the Philadelphia Athletics organization. Said Isreal years later,

> I had trouble in Charlotte. I said something to one fan who was yelling at me. "You know, you're paying to see me play, and I love to play ball. You're telling me I can't play, but still you come and pay to see me." That night, when I come out of the ballpark, I had to be escorted out by the police because a whole bunch of white guys was waiting for me with sticks and bottles. I didn't pay attention to that. I didn't pay it no mind. We were there to play ball.

Isreal would later spend part of the 1956 season and all of 1957 with Columbia in the same league before retiring from the game at age thirty.[10]

Interestingly, in 1954 editions of the *Charlotte Observer*, the issue of race in sports is ignored. In fact, the issue of race in any context—or even the existence of non-white Americans—is generally ignored. With the exception of the occasional photo of Carlos Paula or sometimes top boxers of the day, a reader unfamiliar with the city might have assumed every resident was white. Some mainstream newspapers in the state gave at least a partial page to a section often called "News for Negroes," but not in Charlotte. One notable exception was a three-photo feature in the sports section on a longtime Black veteran of semipro baseball in Mecklenburg County. Herman Helms, a young sportswriter who would go on to have a very distinguished career, published a long interview with an African American player named Pete Hogan.[11] Much like Satchel Paige, Hogan was considered ageless and claimed to have been playing for Black teams in the area for thirty-six years. Helms did address the issue of race. He wrote, "Back in his younger days, Hogan says managers of white teams told him, 'If we could paint your face white, we'd sure like to have you on our team, Pete.' There is no bitterness to the fact that the doors to professional baseball were once closed to members of his race, but he's glad things have changed, and Negroes can now play in the pro loops and the majors."[12]

Chapter 15
TROUBLE IN THE TRI-STATE, AGAIN

In the Tri-State League the conflict over using Black players that had arisen in 1952 resurfaced in 1954. The season began with six members, down from the eight it had in 1952: Greenville, Anderson, Rock Hill, Spartanburg, Asheville, and Knoxville. Despite the fact that Black players were playing for Columbia and Charlotte in the neighboring Sally League, some members of the Tri-State League still resisted. Those teams did not necessarily oppose integration but were reluctant to challenge the status quo and upset a league financial situation that became more tenuous each season.

Leo "Muscle" Shoals, who had been a teammate of David Mobley during his brief trial with Rock Hill in 1952, began the 1954 season with Kingsport in the Class C Mountain States League. When teams dropped out due to financial difficulty, the entire league disbanded on July 20. Players who were part of a major league farm system were reassigned; those who were not were given an official release, allowing them to seek a new job wherever they could. The Knoxville Smokies purchased the contract of veteran star Shoals as well as young—and Black—Cuban prospect Aldo Salvent. Shoals had finished second in batting in the Mountain States League with a .351 average while Salvent was third, one point behind at .350.[1]

Recalled Shoals, "Aldo . . . wasn't going to go at first because of the fact that he would be the only black on the team. I told him to at least give it a try. I told him to look at Jackie Robinson, he was the only black in major league baseball in 1947 and he made it." Salvent decided to join Knoxville, and the pair drove there together. They were inserted into the lineup for the Smokies' game against the Greenville Spinners on July 23. Salvent was the star of the game with 2 hits, an RBI, and a stolen base as he led his new team to a 3–1 victory.[2]

The hiring of twenty-five-year-old Salvent seemed to be an astute move for the Knoxville team. It was also definitely bold, considering the failure of the Mobley experiment just two seasons previous. According to Shoals, "There were a couple towns in the league which had an ordinance against blacks and whites mixing on the baseball field." Those two were Anderson and Spartanburg, and problems soon began to arise. On July 26, the Smokies traveled to South Carolina to take on the Anderson Rebels. The *Greenville News* reported, "Aldo Salvent, the Negro signed last week by Knoxville, is sitting out the three-game series here at the request of the directors of the Anderson Baseball Association." The Smokies then traveled to Asheville. The Tourists did not make a request that Salvent stay on the bench, and he appeared in all 4 games of the series at McCormick Field. Next up, however, was Spartanburg.[3]

The owners of the Spartanburg Peaches were R. E. Littlejohn and Leo Hughes. Littlejohn, who had played baseball at Furman University in the early 1930s, built a very successful trucking and oil distribution business. When the Tri-State League formed in 1946, he purchased a franchise. As an original owner and prominent businessman, he doubtless had considerable clout in league issues—something that had already been seen in the Mobley affair of 1952.

Littlejohn reportedly pressured the ownership group of the Knoxville Smokies to not use Salvent in the three-game series between the teams at Knoxville that began on August 1. In the first game, however, Salvent did play. Afterward, Spartanburg manager Jimmy Bloodworth told Knoxville general manager Ira McCollister that he had orders to take his team back to South Carolina if Salvent played. McCollister called Littlejohn, pleaded with him to keep his team in town, and said that Salvent would be held out for the rest of the series. But the owners of the Knoxville team, Jim Burke and Dr. Edgar Grubb, disagreed and told field manager Ken Polivka to start Salvent. Bloodworth then did as instructed and returned his team to Spartanburg before the second game was played. Not only did the Peaches forfeit the game, but Littlejohn told league president Bobby Hipps that he was completely withdrawing from the league.[4]

Littlejohn issued a statement on the matter. "I promised the Spartanburg City Parks Board that I would not allow my team to play against teams using Negro players," he said. "I stuck to my word by bringing the team home and I intend to remain firm in my convictions." As in Anderson, local rules in Spartanburg did not allow racial mixing on the baseball field. Based upon that policy, not allowing Salvent to play when Knoxville was in Spartanburg is understandable, but why the Spartanburg City Parks Board would have any say in what took place in Tennessee is not. Despite the weak excuse given by Littlejohn, his withdrawal from the league caused considerable alarm among other members. If the league folded, everyone from team owners to concession vendors to players would be out considerable amounts of money. Columnist Mal Malette, in the *Asheville Citizen-Times,* stated league failure would affect "six umpires, 110 ballplayers, thousands of fans and five big league farm chains."[5]

Since 1947, the Spartanburg Peaches had been a farm club of the Cleveland Indians. In 1954, they were one of seven minor league affiliates—in locations stretching from northern Florida to Quebec, Canada—to which Cleveland assigned players. The Indians did not actually own any of these franchises, only the contracts of the players.

The person in charge of all Cleveland Indians business was general manager Hank Greenberg. As the Jewish son of Eastern European immigrants, he was certainly no stranger to discrimination. Undeterred, he had a playing career that would lead to enshrinement in the Hall of Fame. Upon retirement Greenberg joined the front office of the Indians. The Indians were the first team in the American League to integrate, and Greenberg continued to push for equality. When star player Larry Doby told him how demeaning it was not to be able to stay with teammates during spring training, Greenberg responded by having the traveling secretary of the Indians inform hotels that all members of the team stayed together, or they stayed elsewhere.[6]

In the early 1950s, the Indians had several Black players in their minor league system. Greenberg and his staff faced the tricky job of helping these players develop in atmospheres that would not distract their focus from the baseball field. That meant keeping them away from the South, though that was not always possible. During spring training in 1953, a team of Indians minor leaguers was scheduled to play in Winter Garden, Florida. Two Black members of that team, Billy Harrell and Brooks Lawrence, were barred from playing by a city ordinance that did not allow Black and white players to share the field. Greenberg was outraged by the incident and stated, "In the future if our Negro boys are not accepted, there will be no game." Harrell and Lawrence both made the major leagues but did so by following a northerly path. Their developments saw them play in places such as Reading, Cedar Rapids, and Dayton. Cleveland's most promising Black player in 1954 was pitcher Jim "Mudcat" Grant, a native of Florida. The future big-league all-star was assigned to Fargo, North Dakota, that season and Keokuk, Iowa, in 1955.[7]

Though the Indians could control their players, they had less influence over the actions of the teams in their farm system. When informed of the Aldo Salvent incident, Greenberg stated, "We have no jurisdiction over Spartanburg. We're disappointed in their action but, having no financial interest in the team, all we can do is protect our own players." If a solution was not reached, the Indians would either have to reassign their prospects elsewhere or send them home early. Asheville columnist Mal Malette speculated the incident might cost Spartanburg any relationship with Cleveland going forward.[8]

In Kingsport, Tennessee, an attempt was even made to raise money to move the Spartanburg franchise and its Cleveland-owned roster to Kingsport for the remaining weeks of the season. It was considered when league directors assembled for an emergency meeting at Asheville's Battery Park Hotel on August 3. After three and a half hours of discussion, however, another solution was reached—Salvent was sold to Hagerstown, Maryland, of the Class B Piedmont League. Littlejohn, who had the support of team owners from Anderson and Rock Hill, had offered to return to the league if Knoxville got rid of Salvent and promised that such an incident would not reoccur. Ira McCollister and the Smokies had no other option but to agree.[9]

In his column on August 5, Mal Malette of Asheville wrote, "I'm told that Tri-State officials had a gentleman's agreement not to use Negro players this year. Most of them recognize that the ban will have to be dropped soon but wanted to hold off a while because of park lease restrictions in Anderson and Spartanburg." Malette also printed a letter from a reader who identified only as R. V. S.; it read, "Knoxville should be congratulated for their sincere effort in trying to follow the ideals this great country was founded on. These ideals being that every man, woman or child is created equal, regardless of race, color or creed. It seems to me that these rights and guarantees were waived in this case involving Knoxville's excellent Negro third baseman." The reader went on to say, "I am personally very sorry to hear of the sudden departure of Salvent and only hope that wherever he goes, he will be accepted as an individual and also for his baseball skills and spirit."[10]

The next day, sports columnist Bob Terrell, also writing in the *Asheville Citizen-Times*, wrote, "Apparently Aldo Salvent was a victim of circumstances. From outward appearances he was the tool the Knoxville Smokies chose to use to force an issue of five other Tri-State League cities. Perhaps the Smokies did not realize how bomb-like the signing of the Negro third baseman would be. At any rate, the move almost cost us a baseball league." Terrell went on to ask, "Was it worth it? Is Salvent that good of a third baseman?" He listed three players he felt were better: Mel Kerestes of Rock Hill, Tom Marino of Greenville, and Jack Whitehead of Asheville. Marino, named to the league's postseason all-star team, was an excellent hitter and batted .332 with 8 home runs in 92 games. Kerestes was also solid at the plate and turned in a .303 average but lacked power (0 home runs). Whitehead hit only .221 and led the league with 31 errors. After his move to Hagerstown, Aldo Salvent appeared in 32 games and batted .354 with 8 home runs.[11]

Despite being forced to give up a talented player, the Knoxville Smokies finished second in the 1954 Tri-State League standings and then went on to win the postseason playoffs. Spartanburg finished a distant fourth and was last in the league in attendance.[12] When the season ended, Littlejohn stated the Spartanburg team had lost money for the second year in a row and that he planned to dissolve it. A meeting led by Mayor Neville Holcombe was held to discuss options for keeping a Spartanburg team on the field in 1955. A reported thirty people attended, including six who were African American. On the agenda were items such as season tickets and creating a nonprofit organization to run the team. Reportedly, the Black attendees "requested that the committee consider hiring Negro players, capable of playing Class B ball, next year." The mayor's response was that "the committee was concerned only with keeping professional ball here and that it would be up to the new organization to act on the matter." During the off-season, Littlejohn and Hughes decided to keep the team for another season. The Tri-State League managed to limp through the 1955 season with only four members (Asheville, Spartanburg, Greenville, Rock Hill) before throwing in the towel.[13]

As for Aldo Salvent, he played a full season for Hagerstown in 1955 and batted .280 with 23 home runs. He then moved to the Mexican League, where he had several successful seasons and won the batting title with a .359 average for Veracruz in 1957. He retired in 1962 at age thirty-two.[14]

Chapter 16
THE SAD TALE OF TOM ALSTON

In addition to the Senators' Carlos Paula, another of the first Black players to integrate a major league team had a Carolina connection. In the early 1950s, the St. Louis Cardinals were essentially the major league team of the South. As such, they were in no hurry to integrate. That changed in 1953, when brewing company Anheuser-Busch bought the franchise. Company chairman August A. Busch Jr. soon realized that no Black players on the field meant very few Black faces in the crowd. To remedy the situation, he hired former Negro league player Quincy Trouppe to scout players who could possibly integrate the team. Baseball historian Warren Corbett stated that Busch was "no civil rights crusader." Instead, his intentions were primarily capitalistic, and he wanted to sell beer to everyone regardless of race. More Black fans would mean more sales.[1]

One of the more than a dozen players Trouppe signed was a 6′5″ first baseman from North Carolina named Thomas Edison Alston. Alston had grown up in Greensboro and began playing baseball in the navy in 1944. After the war he enrolled at North Carolina A&T (where he was a baseball teammate of Ernest Canada) and graduated with a degree in physical education.[2] While in school, Tom Alston also played for the Goshen Red Wings, a traveling Black team based in Greensboro. That led to an offer to play with the barnstorming Jacksonville Eagles after graduation. From there, Alston's promising baseball career took him to an independent team in Saskatchewan, Canada, and eventually to Organized Baseball in California in 1952. When Trouppe signed Alston, he was playing for San Diego in the Pacific Coast League. In his second season with the Padres, Alston hit .297 with 207 hits, 101 RBIs, and 23 home runs. He appeared primed for major league stardom. The Cardinals apparently had the same assessment of his potential and paid $100,000 and gave four players for his contract.[3]

After time in Canada and California, returning to the Jim Crow South would have been a big change. "When we played exhibition games down south, the Negro players had to stay in shabby hotels while their white

Tom Alston. Collection of the author.

teammates stayed in the good hotels," said Alston in an interview years later. "Segregation was an accepted way of life back then. The Cardinals had the rap of being bigoted. I didn't experience anything real bad. None of the players were friendly to me, but they weren't rude."[4] Despite the challenges facing him, Alston played well in spring training and made his debut in St. Louis on opening day in 1954.

Overall, his first season with the Cardinals was moderately successful, and he hit .246 with 34 RBIs in 66 games. He soon began to struggle, however, and spent most of the next two seasons in the minor leagues with only short stints in St. Louis. Alston also lost weight, leading one sportswriter to refer to him as a "stringbean first baseman" with a "$100,000 price tag."[5] Alston's behavior also became increasingly erratic (he reportedly heard voices), and the club sent him to a psychiatrist a few weeks into the 1957 season. He was diagnosed with neurasthenia, a mental disorder with physical symptoms such as fatigue and anxiety. The Cardinals wanted him to stay in St. Louis for treatment. Of a psychiatrist visit, recalled Alston years later, "The doctor didn't say a word to me. Just came in and gave me electro-shock treatment." He eventually decided to leave the Cardinals and go home to North Carolina.[6]

Unfortunately, Alston never returned to baseball. His illness ended his career, and he never reached the potential many believed he had. Some blamed his illness on the expectations put on him as a bonus player who had cost so much. Said former teammate Wally Moon, also a rookie in 1954, "I think Tom—and this is my personal opinion—felt a great deal of pressure. I know he did. I talked to him." Red Schoendienst, another teammate, remembered Alston as "a little nervous." Perhaps both the pressure to perform and being a racial pioneer (and the scrutiny and isolation that went with that) were too much for him. Perhaps the pressure exacerbated underlying conditions that psychiatric medicine in the 1950s was not adept at treating (and for a Black man at the time, proper treatment was doubtless even less available).[7]

Back in Greensboro, Alston's struggles continued. For unknown reasons he burned down the New Goshen Methodist Church. He was arrested but determined to be mentally incompetent to stand trial. That led to him being sent to Goldsboro's Cherry Hospital, a state mental institution. Alston remained there nearly eight years before being released in 1967. He wasn't free for long before he set his apartment on fire. Diagnosed as schizophrenic, he was taken to John Umstead Psychiatric Hospital in Butner, North Carolina, where he stayed two years. After his release, Alston was unable to find a steady job due to his mental and physical problems. Living in a small apartment in Greensboro, he struggled by on disability and Social Security.[8]

Former St. Louis Cardinal turned television personality Joe Garagiola discovered Alston's plight in 1990. He arranged for an organization that offered assistance to former baseball players to provide Alston with financial help. Because of Garagiola, the Cardinals also invited Alston to throw out the first pitch at a game in St. Louis in June 1990, at which his place in team history was acknowledged. Tom Alston died at a care facility in Winston-Salem in 1993 at age sixty-seven. He is buried at New Goshen Methodist Church in Greensboro, not far from the baseball field on which he once played.[9]

On a side note, the St. Louis Cardinals' first Black pitcher also had a Carolina connection. Bill Greason, a native of Atlanta, began the 1948 season in the Negro Southern League with the Asheville Blues, though his contract was soon sold to the Birmingham Black Barons. He eventually made his way to Organized Baseball and signed with Oklahoma City (where he was the first Black player in the state) in the Texas League, which sold him to the Cardinals organization. In 1954, two months after Tom Alston made his debut, Greason took the mound for St. Louis. Unfortunately, he appeared in only 3 games before being sent back to the minor leagues. After several seasons in AAA, he retired in 1959. Greason then embarked on a new career; as a church minister in Birmingham, he became very active in the civil rights movement of the 1960s.[10]

Chapter 17
MVP

In the Carolina League, Black players were becoming slightly more common in 1955. Herb Bush (briefly) returned to Pittsburgh's Burlington-Graham farm club for a second season and was joined by Frank Washington and pitcher Cleo Lewright (in 1949, Lewright, a native of Missouri who had attended Lincoln University, had been the first to integrate the California League with Bakersfield, a Cleveland Indians farm club).[1] For the Winston-Salem Twins, thirty-year-old infielder George Handy appeared in 9 games. A native of Wilson, North Carolina, Handy began his career in 1947 with Memphis in the Negro American League and spent most of the 1955 season with Norfolk in the Piedmont League.[2]

While Bill White and R. C. Stevens had turned in outstanding performances the previous two seasons, the Carolina League featured the state's first Black superstar in 1955. Danny Morejon was a twenty-four-year-old Cuban who had joined the Cincinnati Reds organization in 1954. His rookie season had been divided between three teams in the farm system: Havana, Portsmouth, and Miami Beach.

During spring training in 1955, the Reds assigned Morejon to their affiliate in High Point–Thomasville. In his preseason assessment of the Hi-Toms, *High Point Enterprise* sports editor Bill Hodges mentioned the arrival of the team's first Black player. It did not appear to be big news, however, as it wasn't until the eighth paragraph of his column that he noted it. "Tomorrow night will be a sort of milestone in Hi-Tom history," he wrote. "It will be the first time in history that a player of the Negro race has performed for the Hi-Toms in a regular season game. The locals have two—center fielder Dan Morejon and pitcher Jesus (Bron) Ayon—and if their play so far is any indication, they'll be a valuable addition to the club."[3] On April 22, the *Enterprise* featured a photo of Morejon and Ayon with manager Jimmy Brown. The caption, "A Problem in Comparative Linguistics," pointed out the fact that that the manager didn't speak Spanish and the two Cuban players didn't speak English. It also mentioned that the players "represent something new on the local baseball

Left to right: **Manager Jimmy Brown with pitcher Bron Ayon and star outfielder Dan Morejon. Collection of the author.**

scene since they are the first players of the Negro race to ever perform for the Hi-Tom club."[4] In his preview of the game, Hodges reiterated his previous statement, writing, "Brown's selection of Ayon as the starting hurler and Morejon as the center fielder is a milestone in Hi-Tom history."[5] Interestingly, no mention of either player's race was found in the *Enterprise* afterward. The only words that ever preceded their names were their positions on the field or superlatives relating to skill.[6]

The opening game of the 1955 season proved to be Ayon's only start for the Hi-Toms before he was switched to a relief role. The twenty-year-old appeared in 18 games, with 2 wins and 1 loss, before being transferred to Duluth in the Class C Northern League. Left as the only Black player on the team in a place where he did not speak the language, Morejon overcame the incredible isolation he must have felt to become the team's—and the league's—biggest star.[7]

In the Carolina League, the midseason all-star game was a matchup between the first-place team, which hosted, and a team of voted-upon stars from the other members. Morejon was the first Black player in the league to be chosen as an all-star for the July 11 contest (R. C. Stevens had played in the game the previous year, but it had been as a member of the host Burlington-Graham Pirates). He hit a double as the All-Stars defeated the Fayetteville Highlanders, 5–1.[8]

Morejon went on to lead the Hi-Toms to a first-place finish in the league standings, and he won the batting title with a .324 average, hitting 30 doubles, 10 triples, and 13 home runs. His 254 total bases were 1 short of the league lead.[9] The performance earned him the league's Most Valuable Player award, for which he was given a plaque and a $100 war bond. Morejon also finished in a tie for "Most Popular Hi-Tom," an award voted on by fans. He and shortstop Fred Harrington each received a watch courtesy of a Thomasville jewelry store.[10]

Promoted to Savannah the next season, Morejon eventually made his debut for Cincinnati on July 11, 1958. It was a short stay in the major leagues, however, and Morejon was sent back to the Reds' Havana affiliate after 12 games. With Havana the entire 1959 season, he helped lead the Sugar Kings to the Little World Series (the AAA championship) against Minneapolis. Morejon hit .407 for the series against the Millers and drove in the winning runs in both Game 6 and Game 7.[11] He never made it back to the big leagues and eventually moved to the Mexican League, where he played for four teams over nine seasons. Morejon was elected to the Cuban Baseball Hall of Fame in 2007.[12]

Though Morejon's career did not turn out as he would have hoped, he remained close to the game for the rest of his life. He settled in Miami after his playing days and in 1979 began working at Tropical Park, where he managed and maintained the baseball fields. He held that position for thirty years. After his death in 2009, the Miami-Dade Board of Commissioners honored him by renaming Field No. 4 at Tropical Park as "The Daniel Morejon Field." Perhaps his greatest contribution to the game, however, was that he showed white fans that a Black man could be a superstar in the South, something that was acknowledged when he was voted the Carolina League's best player in 1955.[13]

Chapter 18
SATCHEL

As the end of the 1955 Carolina League season drew close, the Greensboro Patriots had still not fielded a Black player. This was likely due to their affiliation with the Boston Red Sox, the major league team most staunchly against integration. On August 14, however, Greensboro team owner Rufus Blanchard signed a contract with legendary pitcher Satchel Paige. After a long career in the Negro leagues, Paige had been recruited by the major leagues and played several seasons for the Cleveland Indians and the St. Louis Browns. At least in his late forties by 1955 (his age is disputed), Paige was still a big draw at the gate. Fans both Black and white wanted to see the man regarded as one of the best pitchers ever. Greensboro attendance was averaging 845 fans per game in 1955, down from nearly 1,200 the previous season, so a big crowd would be a financial boon to the team. That led Blanchard to sign Paige and promote him in the media as the starting pitcher against the Reidsville Phillies on August 17.[1]

According to author, historian, and former minor league baseball executive Marshall Adesman, prior to the restructuring of the minor leagues in 1963, a big-league team could send any number of players to their farm clubs:

> They could stock the entire team if they wished (and had enough players), or just a few. And conversely, the minor league team had the right to sign their own talent if the parent club couldn't help. Greensboro, for instance, might have a need for a starter, so they call Boston and ask if they've got anyone available. "No? Well, mind if we sign a local kid? OK, thanks." And they bring a youngster right out of high school, or a former player who thinks he may be ready to make a comeback, something like that. Except in this case, it wasn't a teenager or rehabbing vet, it was Satchel Paige.[2]

When news of the plan reached the Philadelphia Phillies, Reidsville's parent club, farm director Eddie Collins Jr. protested to George

Trautman, the commissioner of minor league baseball, and asked him to invalidate the contract of Paige, whom he considered a circus sideshow. Collins called the Paige appearance "a travesty of the game" and "a farce." Trautman ruled that Greensboro could use Paige only in exhibition games. That meant he could not pitch in the sold-out game against Reidsville, a take of perhaps $4,000 at the gate according to the *Greensboro Daily News*.[3] Blanchard protested and wrote to Trautman, arguing that to change the game to an exhibition would "defraud the public." He added, "If you want to have a farce, that would be it." The issue turned out to be moot because Hurricane Diane hit North Carolina on game day and washed the contest out. Greensboro decided not to argue its case any further, and Paige was released from his contract before he ever took the mound.[4]

The incident is interesting primarily because it shows the influence and power that major league clubs had over the minor leagues. The episode with Satchel Paige may or may not have been related to racism. The Philadelphia Phillies were notoriously racist as an organization and had taunted Jackie Robinson with the encouragement of manager Ben Chapman. General manager Herb Pennock was also openly against integration. He died in 1948, but Eddie Collins Jr. had been his assistant and was married to Pennock's daughter. There are no reports, however, of Collins himself being prejudiced against Black players.[5]

Why the Phillies would have cared about an opponent of a farm club fielding a Black player when there were already other Black players in the league is unknown. Perhaps Collins was just strictly following the rules of baseball. At the time that Greensboro signed Paige, Collins was actually in Reidsville on his way to a meeting in South Carolina.[6] It is plausible that somebody with the Reidsville team complained and Collins took on the case in an effort to show that the Phillies cared about keeping their farm club happy. Therefore, he called Trautman. Stated Marshall Adesman, "Why Trautman put his foot down, though, is rather puzzling. Minor league teams didn't promote back then the way they do now, but there were some exceptions. Joe Engel [the team owner] had been rolling out innovative promotions in Chattanooga for decades. No doubt there were others, and Trautman ought to have seen this as just one more. But he didn't, based on a phone call from Eddie Collins. Maybe Trautman just didn't want to anger a major league executive."[7]

The following season, Satchell Paige was signed to a contract by the AAA Miami Marlins of the International League. He pitched three seasons for the team and had a combined record of 31–22. After Miami, Paige continued to play and make appearances, including one inning for the Kansas City Athletics in 1965 (which no one denied was a publicity stunt). He pitched his final official professional game at age fifty-nine on June 21, 1966, in Hampton, Virginia, for the Peninsula Grays of the Carolina League. Paige pitched two innings and gave up 2 runs to an opponent that was none other than the Greensboro Patriots.[8]

Chapter 19
THE UNDEFEATED

With both ups and downs, 1955 was a watershed year for civil rights in the United States. In late August, fourteen-year-old Emmett Till was murdered in Mississippi for supposedly flirting with a white woman. The civil rights movement was already growing, but the horrific nature of Till's death truly ignited it. Several months later, in one of the most famous examples of nonviolent protest in the nation's history, Rosa Parks was arrested for not giving up her seat to a white passenger on a Montgomery, Alabama, bus. In the Carolinas, incidents also took place. Six African American men, led by dentist Dr. George Simkins, were arrested in Greensboro for attempting to play on a city-owned golf course. That led to two cases, *Simkins v. City of Greensboro* and *Wolfe v. North Carolina*, the latter of which eventually went all the way to the US Supreme Court.[1]

In the world of baseball, outcomes were somewhat more positive with regard to race. Early October saw the Brooklyn Dodgers, with five Black members—Jackie Robinson, Jim Gilliam, Sandy Amoros, Roy Campanella, and Don Newcombe—defeat the all-white New York Yankees, 4 games to 3, to win the World Series. Campanella was voted the National League's MVP (three of the top four vote-getters were Black). In the Carolinas, Danny Morejon was the Carolina League MVP, while Marvin Williams of Columbia was the top hitter in the South Atlantic League with a .328 average. He missed out on the batting title, however, after being just short in plate appearances. Instead, the title went to fellow African American Wes Covington; the North Carolina native hit .326 for Jacksonville. Still, while the world of professional sports may have been somewhat insulated from everyday struggles, Black players certainly faced discrimination. In 1955, the most important example of this—perhaps in the country—took place in South Carolina, but the discrimination was not targeted at adult or even high school–age players. Instead, the victims were ten- to twelve-year-old boys.[2]

Little League Baseball Inc. was founded in 1937 in Williamsport, Pennsylvania, as a program for boys aged nine to twelve. It began with just a few local teams but rapidly expanded to other areas around the state. In 1947, the first Little League programs outside Pennsylvania were established. That same year, the first Little League Baseball World Series was played in Williamsport. By 1951, leagues had been established in Canada and the Panama Canal Zone. The rapid expansion was due to the fact that there had been a need for an organized youth baseball system. Before, grassroots baseball had been limited to scattered individual local recreation programs, only some of which were well-funded and organized. More often than not, the only option for young baseball players, especially in rural areas, was informal sandlot play until they reached high school. Little League Inc. promoted sportsmanship, followed uniform rules, and offered a structured system of tournament play. Most importantly, Little League Inc. had a firm nondiscrimination policy.[3]

In 1953, Robert F. Morrison, a Black businessman who owned an Esso station and was a member of the NAACP, filed a charter with Little League's national office to form a new league based at the Cannon Street YMCA in Charleston, South Carolina. Originally named the Charleston Negro YMCA, the organization had been created to serve the needs of former slaves in 1866. It first operated out of churches and meeting halls, but a permanent facility was finally constructed in 1950 at 61 Cannon Street. African American youth of the area were greatly underserved, so the Cannon Street Y began to offer youth recreational programs.[4]

Little League Inc. welcomed Morrison's league, but as youth baseball was segregated in South Carolina, there were many complications. The main one was the lack of competition. White teams from different leagues played each other in tournaments all over the state, but teams of Black kids could play only among themselves. Fortunately for Morrison, the interest for his program was so great that he had enough participation to create several separate teams. In 1954, the first year of play, the Cannon Street YMCA Little League consisted of four teams, each sponsored by a prominent local Black business or organization: Fielding Funeral Home, Police Athletic League, Pan Hellenic Council, and Harleston Funeral Home. Each team was allowed 15 players, but reportedly over 100 boys tried out for one of the 60 spots in the league.[5]

After a year of only interleague play, Morrison decided to enter a team to compete for the city championship. To do so, he and the coaches of his teams—Rufus Dilligard, Ben Singleton, Archie Graham, Walter Burke, and Lee Bennett—got together to decide on an all-star team to represent the league. The roster they assembled consisted of the best players from each team. Chosen were John Mack, Arthur Peoples, John Bailey, Vermont Brown, Norman Robinson, Allen Jackson, Charles Bradley, Leroy Major, John Rivers, Carl Johnson, Maurice Singleton, Buck Godfrey, David Middleton, Vernon Gray, and alternates Leroy Carter and George Gregory.

When word got out that Morrison was entering the Cannon Street All-Stars into the city tournament, white leagues reacted quickly. Led by Danny Jones of North Charleston, who was also the state commissioner for Little League, they drafted a resolution requesting a white people-only tournament. The national office of Little League Inc. responded immediately, informing the other leagues that racism would not be tolerated and that they would have to play or forfeit. That is exactly what happened: the other teams in the city forfeited, leaving the Cannon Street All-Stars to be declared South Carolina District 7 Champion without playing a game. That entitled them to a place in the state tournament. Said Peter J. McGovern, president of Little League Inc., "Our rules, based on fair play, do not recognize barriers of race, creed, or color. The program will withstand such storms as long as we adhere firmly to the democratic principle which made its phenomenal growth possible."[6]

There is speculation that the other teams in Charleston did not want to play because they did not want to risk the humiliation of losing to a team of Black kids. It was only a year after the *Brown v. Board of Education* decision, and if white teams lost, it would only have been ammunition for those promoting equality among the races. "I heard rumors, but I never saw Danny Jones at Harmon Field," said Coach Rufus Dilligard years later. "Other whites came and they could have scouted us, but I didn't care. They knew we were good. Somebody must have seen us. I know the worst thing that could have happened was for them to play us and get whipped. They probably did not want to risk that. White fellas used to be at practices and games and that All Star team was a bunch no one could take lightly. So it wouldn't surprise me that word got back to top level whites that we were good, too good." Jim Crow laws provided a convenient excuse for not facing tough competition.[7]

The state Little League tournament had been scheduled for Parris Island, but Danny Jones announced it was called off when forty-five of the fifty-five white teams withdrew from competition following the entry of the Cannon Street All-Stars. The Greenville Junior Chamber of Commerce stepped in and offered to host instead, and dates were set for August 8–11. B. B. Owings, vice president of the Greenville Jaycees, stated that the tournament would have "the official sanction of State Little League Commissioner Danny Jones of North Charleston." He also made it clear that invitations were extended to all district winners, "whether they be white or Negro teams."[8]

The press jumped on the story when the appearance of an all-Black team in the state tournament seemed imminent. A few weeks before the tournament, the *Greenville News* published an anti-integration letter by a reader named Francis C. Jones of Lexington, South Carolina. He also sent it to the president of the Greenville Junior Chamber of Commerce and the eleven other Little League teams planning to participate in the tournament at nearby Donaldson Air Force Base. It squarely linked the actions of Little League Inc. to the *Brown* decision. Wrote Jones, "This open competition of Negro versus White can and will be used by the integration forces as evidence in the school cases. It is also reasonably expected that those areas represented by teams competing against the Negro team will be flooded with petitions by Negro students seeking admittance to the White schools in those particular areas." He added, "Now, after being properly informed, I realize that this particular tournament could well cause considerable trouble throughout the entire state if the Whites and Negroes compete. In fact, it could resound throughout the entire South as a solid blow for integration."[9]

Ten teams had said they would play if necessary a week before the state tournament. Soon, eight of them dropped out. The teams from Greenville and Walhalla had still been willing to participate in the tournament but finally bowed to pressure a day after Jones's letter was published. With no competition, Cannon Street was declared state champion by Little League Inc. The South Carolina state champion was then supposed to advance to play in the regional qualifier in Rome, Georgia. The winner of that tournament would move on to the Little League World Series in Pennsylvania.[10]

The South Carolina press was not happy with the outcome. In the August 2 edition of the *Charleston News and Courier*, an editorial titled "Agitation and Hate" opined,

> Some Negro adults, knowing that the colored children weren't wanted in the all-white state league, nevertheless decided to force the colored team into the league. As a result the entire state league has been abandoned and the colored team left in an embarrassing position. . . . The case of the South Carolina Little League could well

be cited by sociologists as a textbook example of why racial relations in the South are becoming increasingly difficult. . . . The Northern do-gooders who have needled the Southern race agitators into action may have to answer for the consequences.[11]

The Cannon Street All-Stars were prepared to travel to Georgia, but it was not to be. Tournament organizers had stated that the Cannon Street team would be eligible to play in the competition if it won the South Carolina state tournament. However, they also said that if the team won by forfeit, it would not be allowed to compete, as those were the Little League rules. A team had to win by playing in order to advance. When Cannon Street was declared state champion by forfeit, officials in Rome wrote to Little League president Peter J. McGovern and indicated that they could not accept the team as South Carolina champion. John P. Braud, Region 5 director, said, "There actually is no Little League champion in South Carolina. We do not believe a team can be declared a section winner if it has not won a championship through tournament competition in its own state." No matter what the reason for enforcing them, those were officially the rules in Little League. McGovern had to agree with them. "Because of local difficulties beyond control which prevent holding normal state tournament in Region 5, Section 2, Little League baseball, with extreme reluctance and heartfelt regard for the boys who must now forego the stimulating experience of national tournament associations, regretfully announces there will be no entry from South Carolina in the Regional playoffs," said his official release.[12]

The conflict within South Carolina Little League made news across the country. From New York to California, newspapers ran stories telling the story of the Cannon Street All-Stars. Perhaps because children were involved, most took a sympathetic tone toward the team, even in other southern states. Sports columnist Dick Herbert of Raleigh's *News and Observer* sent a letter to Warren Koon, sports editor of the *Charleston Evening Post,* which Koon included in a column. "What a difference a few miles make," Herbert wrote. "While teams were withdrawing from the South Carolina Little League playoffs because a Negro team from Charleston was entered, a Negro team was playing in the Raleigh Little League championships without dispute or argument." In the *Pittsburgh Courier,* one of the nation's premier Black-owned newspapers, the headline on August 6, 1955, shouted, "Reign of Terror Grips Mississippi; Threaten NAACP Head." Right below it was an article on the Cannon

Street All-Stars. The caption on the accompanying photo was, "These Little Leaguers Were Slapped Down by Ugly Segregation Laws."[13]

Shortly after the Cannon Street All-Stars were declared South Carolina state champions, a similar situation arose in Florida. In district play, organizers of a regional tournament attempted to exclude an all-Black team from Pensacola. Peter McGovern stepped in and told them that any tournament that excluded the Pensacola Jaycees would be ruled illegal. They went on with the tournament and—true to his word—McGovern and Little League declared the results void and named the Pensacola Jaycees the winner of Florida's Northwest Region. This entitled them to advance to the state championship but, like in South Carolina, no one was sure there would be any teams to play. In addition, the Orlando city recreation director had previously said it was the city's policy to forbid interracial competition. Surprisingly, the other three teams that qualified (from St. Petersburg, North Miami, and Orlando) indicated they would participate, and the host city raised no protest after leaders apparently changed their minds. The Pensacola squad traveled to Orlando and on August 9 played the Orlando Kiwanis. The hometown team won, 5–0, but the game was the first time an all-Black and an all-white team had met on the field at such a high level of organized youth play.[14]

Some later articles state that the Cannon Street team was named regional champion because all other state champions refused to play them. This is incorrect. With seven teams, an awkward number for tournament play, the Rome regional went on as scheduled without a South Carolina representative. The seven state champions competing were Gastonia, North Carolina; Paducah, Kentucky; North Miami, Florida; Jackson, Mississippi; Auburn, Alabama; Macon, Georgia; and Jackson, Tennessee. Auburn was the eventual champion and advanced to Williamsport.[15]

Peter McGovern regretted the situation into which the Cannon Street team had been placed. In a letter to Robert Morrison, he acknowledged that the All-Stars were "innocent victims of alien influences that have deprived them of beneficial associations and opportunity to meet and know other boys in Little League Baseball" and invited the team to attend the Little League World Series as his guests. Morrison accepted, and parents and community leaders raised funds for the trip. On a bus owned by local civil rights activist Esau Jenkins, fourteen boys and a group of adults that included Coaches Singleton, Bennett, Graham, and Burke, and YMCA president Morrison made the 740-mile, un-air-conditioned trip to Williamsport. Said Morrison, "We are going to see the game as spectators and we are paying our own way. Our purpose is to inspire the boys to be better citizens."[16]

Though the plan was for the boys to be merely spectators at the event, they all held on to the belief that they would be allowed to play once they got there. Robert Morrison and the coaches tried to negotiate with Little League officials to allow at least one game, but the organization refused. There was no way to fit them into the structure of the tournament and remain fair to the other participants. Even the crowd wanted the boys to play; when the Cannon Street All-Stars were introduced before one game, the chant of "Let them play!" arose from the stands. It was to no avail, however.

Of the trip, John Rivers recalled years later, "We stayed in same college dormitory; we ate in the same dining room; we did everything but play. That was a disappointment because then I realized we were here but were not going to play. Of course, I thought that they didn't want us to play because they were afraid of us. I thought they were afraid because we would whip them, beat them. Are we that good? Were they afraid of us? It was kind of convoluted, but that's the way I saw it. We will never know. But what if?"[17]

Buck Godfrey remembered what it was like to be exposed to a world outside of the Jim Crow South for the first time. "We ate breakfast in the dining hall with the other teams," he said. "For the first time in our short lives, we did not feel the tension of being an all-black team. Some teams were integrated. Others had guys who looked like us but spoke Spanish. We thought to ourselves, the North was different. Black, white, and all others ate together."[18]

On the field at Williamsport, the team from Pennsylvania took the national title. Auburn, Alabama, which had won the regional in which the Cannon Street All-Stars were supposed to have played, finished third. Interestingly, the star player for the runner-up New Jersey team at Williamsport was an African American named Billy Hunter. He went to play college football for Syracuse and in the NFL. Hunter was later a US attorney before serving as executive director of the National Basketball Players' Association for sixteen years.[19]

Other than being a prime example of southern racism (one aimed at kids, at that), perhaps the most important thing about the Cannon Street YMCA incident was what happened afterward. As a result of Little

League Inc. supporting the rights of the Cannon Street team to compete, state Little League commissioner Danny Jones resigned his position, declaring that the national organization's nondiscrimination policy threatened the southern way of life. In his resignation letter he wrote, "Instead of providing recreational opportunities for kids, our state Little League tournament is being used as a vehicle of propaganda in some segments of the Northern press. It may be used as an attempt to overthrow the laws and established customs of South Carolina." He continued, "To use 8 to 12-year-old boys in an attempt to undermine the laws and customs of our people is a dastardly act. I cannot be a party to such an act."[20]

Jones hastily arranged a new tournament in Charleston for white players only, which was put on by a group called the South Carolina Recreational Society. It was not sanctioned by Little League, so there was no opportunity for regional or national play. Stated Peter McGovern, "White teams who compete in a Little Boys tournament sponsored by the South Carolina Recreational Society face disqualification as Little Leaguers and possible loss of their franchises next year." The threat was moot, because Jones decided to start his own youth program, and with Matt Goyak, recreation director of Georgetown County, he founded what was called Little Boys' Baseball Incorporated. It had a charter that was explicitly segregationist. Stated the original rule guide, "The Organizers hereof are of the opinion it is for the best interest of all concerned that this program be on a racially segregated basis; they believe that mixed teams and competition between the races would create regrettable conditions and destroy the harmony and tranquility which now exists."[21]

Given a segregated, southern-controlled organization as an option, Little League programs from across the South began to sever their ties with Williamsport and join Little Boys' Baseball. By 1956, it expanded into seven states and Jones had signed up 122 leagues. Six years later the organization (which became Dixie Youth Baseball in 1962 after Little League Inc. forced it to remove the word "Little" from its name) had enrolled 390 leagues in eight states.[22]

The defection of Little League programs in the Carolinas to segregated Dixie Youth Baseball left youth baseball in something of a quandary in the late 1950s. With Dixie Youth's segregationist policy and no more Little League, Black boys who wanted to play organized baseball were left fewer options: only community programs in cities with larger Black populations or pickup games against each other. With less competition, it was much more difficult for them to advance or improve upon their skills. The repercussions of the secession of southern Little League programs can still be felt. It can be argued that more young Black athletes in the South began to turn to football and basketball because of being excluded from Dixie Youth.

Youth baseball slowly recovered, however, and programs affiliated with Little League Inc. returned and spread. Little League state championships were again played in North Carolina beginning in 1959, though South Carolina lagged behind. Finally, in 1969, a retired African American schoolteacher named Theodore Lester filed a charter with Little League Inc. to begin a league in Florence. Pee Dee Little League was made up of "eight baseball teams of young boys who had been deprived of participation in the Dixie Youth League."[23] From there, Little League slowly expanded across the state to offer an alternative to Dixie Youth, and a state championship tournament was again played in 1971. Little League did not return to Charleston, however, until 1994.

As for Dixie Youth Baseball, it removed the segregation clause from its charter in 1967 and began to admit African American youth. Black major league alumni of the organization include Otis Nixon, who played for Columbus County, North Carolina, in 1971, and Florence, South Carolina's Reggie Sanders, later an all-star and World Series champion. Another notable alumni is basketball superstar Michael Jordan. In 1975, at age twelve, Jordan was named "Mr. Baseball" (essentially the state's best player) by North Carolina's Dixie Youth Association.[24] The organization has made efforts to distance itself from its racist past, including finally removing the Confederate flag from its logo in 1995. However, it annually presents the Danny Jones Sportsmanship Award, named for the man who organized the boycott of the Cannon Street All-Stars.[25]

Fortunately, the story of the Cannon Street All-Stars has not been forgotten. It was first reintroduced to a national audience when it was featured in a 1995 *Sports Illustrated* article titled "Little League's Civil War" written by *Charleston Post and Courier* journalist Gene Sapakoff. That was followed by several events to bring attention to Robert F. Morrison and the players involved. In 1997, the city of Charleston placed a historic marker on the Cannon Street YMCA that told its story. The dedication plaque above it featured a 1955 quote from Morrison: "All I am interested in is the privilege of giving the Negro boys of Charleston the same privilege all boys of the world are allowed under the laws of Little League Inc Williamsport, Pa." In 2002, ten members of the All-Stars were honored guests at the Little League World Series in Williamsport. A dozen years later, five members of the 1955 team—John Rivers, John Bailey, Vermont Brown, Carl Johnson, and Leroy Major—returned to Williamsport as special guests. At Harmon Field, the home playing field of the Cannon Street YMCA, the South Carolina Department of Archives and History dedicated a marker on the sixtieth anniversary of the 1955 Little League World Series.[26]

After the events of 1955, the paths of the members of the Cannon Street All-Stars—which Gene Sapakoff called "the most significant athletic team in South Carolina history"—began to diverge. Some continued to play baseball for a few years, but some never played again. As with all teams, members went on to varying levels of success in their lives. Only one pursued his career in the world of sports: Buck Godfrey played baseball at Delaware State. After graduation he turned to coaching baseball, football, and swimming. He eventually spent thirty seasons at Southwest DeKalb High School near Atlanta, where his football teams went undefeated in the regular season four times and won the 1995 Georgia AAAA state championship. Godfrey was inducted into the Georgia Athletic Coaches Association Hall of Fame in 2014, and in 2015 the Panthersville football stadium in DeKalb County was renamed in his honor. Among the other members of the team, Leroy Major was a marine for twenty-six years before becoming a schoolteacher. John Rivers, John Bailey, and Norman Robinson all became architects. Vernon Gray was a chef, Allen Jackson was a corrections officer, and Vermont Brown pursued a career with Lockheed Aircraft. Several others owned their own businesses. They raised families and went on with normal lives, but all of them—even if eleven or twelve years old and too young to understand at the time—made an important contribution to the story of baseball integration.[27]

Chapter 20
THE CONUNDRUM OF CURT FLOOD

In March 1956, when spring training was underway for professional baseball teams at southern locales, the document known as the "Southern Manifesto," authored by US senator Strom Thurmond of South Carolina, was submitted to Congress. It denounced the 1954 *Brown v. Board of Education* decision as an "unwarranted exercise of power by the court" and a "clear abuse of judicial power." It also referred to anti-segregationists as "agitators and troublemakers invading our States." In all, nineteen senators and seventy-seven members of the House of Representatives signed the document, including Senators Sam Ervin and W. Kerr Scott of North Carolina and Strom Thurmond and Olin Johnston of South Carolina. The only members of Congress from the Carolinas to abstain were North Carolina representatives Thurmond Chatham, Harold Cooley, Charles Deane, and Charles Jonas.[1]

Though the proclamation only amplified racial tensions, Black players were appearing on the rosters of teams in minor league baseball in the South with increasing frequency. In fact, in the Carolina League, only Greensboro and Durham had yet to have Black team members. The 1956 season would see the High Point–Thomasville Hi-Toms, a Cincinnati Reds farm club, field Curt Flood, Orlando Peña, John Ivory Smith, and Bo Bossard. Black players assigned by the New York Giants to the Danville Leafs included Leon Wagner, Willie McCovey, Tony Taylor, and José Pagán. At Winston-Salem, infielder Curtis Hardaway hit .306 with 21 home runs for his Yankees farm club. After a last-place finish in 1955 and poor attendance, the Burlington-Graham franchise moved to Kinston. The team remained a Pittsburgh Pirates farm club, however, and several players made the move with the club. Among them were Cleo Lewright and Frank Washington. They, along with South Carolina–born outfielder Carl Long, were the first African Americans to play for Kinston.[2]

One of the most important primary sources relating to baseball integration in North Carolina is the autobiography of Curt Flood. Published in 1971 when he was just thirty-three years old, *The Way It Is* painted an extremely negative picture of Flood's 1956 season with the Hi-Toms, the first professional team to which he was assigned by the Cincinnati Reds. He wrote of racial abuse from fans, teammates, and the Jim Crow system in general. Though there is doubtless truth to some of his accounts, is has been suspected by some historians that he exaggerated what he wrote and excluded important positive facts. The possible reason was Flood's well-publicized dispute with the professional baseball system at the time he wrote his memoir.[3]

After the 1957 season in Savannah, Flood was traded from the Reds to the St. Louis Cardinals. With that team, Flood established himself as one of the most promising young players in the game. He won his first of seven Gold Glove Awards for outstanding play at center field in 1963 and in 1964 was named to the first of three National League All-Star teams. Flood went on to play 1,759 big-league games over fifteen seasons and had a career .293 batting average. He played a vital role in the Cardinals' World Series titles in 1964 and 1967. Flood is perhaps most famous, however, for challenging baseball's reserve clause, which essentially kept players tied for life to the team that owned their contract. Recalled Flood in the 1994 documentary *Baseball: A Film by Ken Burns*, "In the southern part of the United States, we were marching for civil rights and Dr. King had been assassinated and we'd lost the Kennedys, and to think that merely because I was a professional baseball player, I could ignore what was going on outside the walls of Busch Stadium is truly hypocrisy. And now I find that all of those rights that these great Americans were dying for, I didn't have in my own profession."[4]

In 1969, Flood refused to accept a trade from the Cardinals to the lowly Phillies. He wrote to Bowie Kuhn, commissioner of Major League Baseball, and asked to be declared a free agent. Flood felt his twelve years of service entitled him to some say regarding how and to whom his contract was assigned. Kuhn refused. In protest, Flood sat out the 1970 season. That same year he initiated a lawsuit to gain free agency. In 1972 *Flood v. Kuhn* was finally argued before the US Supreme Court. The court ruled 5–3 in favor of Major League Baseball, a decision that was much criticized. Though he lost, the case did later result in baseball implementing the Curt Flood Rule. It states that when players have played for a team for five straight years and played in the major leagues for a total of ten years, they are able to accept or reject any trade.[5]

Flood's autobiography, released in the midst of his lawsuit, was very bitter toward the business of baseball as a whole. It focuses on Flood's major league career, but it does begin with his first professional season in the Carolina League. Because of the circumstances in which it was written, biographer Stuart Weiss called into question some of Flood's account. In *The Curt Flood Story: The Man behind the Myth*, Weiss wrote, "Flood's experience in High Point, as he describes it in his memoir, was miserable to say the least. But was it? Or to what extent? Was he not in some part a lonely, adolescent victim of his own naïveté? Was his personality such that he perhaps embellished the darker aspects of his 'Adventures in the Bush' [the title of the chapter] and ignored the brighter side, if only to fit his memoir's need when, more than a decade later, he was challenging Major League Baseball?"[6]

In *The Way It Is*, Flood wrote of his time in High Point: "During the early weeks of the season, I used to break into tears as soon as I reached the safety of my room. I felt too young for the ordeal. I wanted to be home. I wanted to talk to someone. I wanted to be free of these animals whose fifty-cent bleacher ticket was a license to curse my color and deny my humanity. I wanted to be free of the imbeciles on the ball team." He added, "My teammates despised and rejected me as subhuman. I would gladly have sent them all to hell. More than once during that horrible season I was tempted to strike out so that our cracker pitcher would lose another game."[7]

It is interesting that Flood professed to be so alone in High Point and felt such animosity toward all his teammates. Undoubtedly, there were players on the team who judged him solely based on race, but during the course of the season, Flood had two African American teammates as well as three Cubans, at least one of whom, Orlando Peña, would have been considered Black by southern social mores of the day. All lived together in the same boardinghouse. When Flood was assigned to High Point, his mother telephoned team general manager George Erath to ask that he be found a nice place to live. Because of his young age, she also hoped he would have "some warm motherly supervision." Erath contacted leading members of the local Black community for suggestions. The result was the boardinghouse in a middle-class neighborhood run by schoolteacher Estelle Nelson. Aware that her tenants could not eat with teammates, Nelson even prepared meals for them after evening games. Surprisingly, Flood never mentioned Nelson in his autobiography. Stuart Weiss wrote that Flood should "have made a point of blessing Mrs. Nelson," but "that would have detracted from his portrait of himself as a victim, which of course in some very real ways he was."[8]

The 1956 High Point–Thomasville Hi-Toms. ***Back row, left to right:*** **general manager George Erath, Nelvin Cooper, Gail Thomas, Woody Rich, Bill Cooke, Amiel Solomon, Haven Schmidt, Jack Taylor, Gus Carmichael, Fred Harrington, and groundskeeper Austin Kearns.** ***Front row:*** **Sergio Garcia, Bo Bossard, René Solis, Bill Ford, manager Bert Haas, Orlando Peña, Curt Flood, Karl Kuehl, and Charlie Brown.** ***Batboys:*** **Raymond Haas (*left*) and Wayne Robbins. Collection of the author.**

Flood's roommate for most of the season was twenty-six-year-old Jack "Bo" Bossard, a native of South Carolina. A 1951 graduate of historically Black Benedict College in Columbia, Bossard had already played two standout seasons in the Reds' organization. He began the 1956 season in Class A Savannah but after 46 games was sent down to High Point. In the June 19 edition of the *High Point Enterprise*, Bossard was featured in a photo with white outfielder Jay Hornsby as the two were introduced as new members of the team. In 72 games for the Hi-Toms, Bossard hit .308 while playing third base and shortstop/third baseman. The other African American member of the Hi-Toms was pitcher John Ivory Smith, a veteran of three minor-league seasons. In 1955, he won 19 games and struck out 320 batters for Daytona Beach, a Florida State League record that still stands. Like Bossard, he was a native southerner, having been raised in Cocoa Beach, Florida. The other minority members of the teams were Cuban pitchers René Solis and Orlando Peña. Catcher Sergio Garcia also spent half of the season with the Hi-Toms.[9]

Perhaps if Flood had sought friendship from Bossard, he would have had an ally in his struggles. Eight years older and college educated, Bossard was a southerner who undoubtedly knew how to live with Jim Crow restrictions. The two played together the following season at Savannah as well, but Flood never mentioned Bossard in his autobiography. Said Stuart Weiss, Flood "for the most part preferred his own company—and perhaps that of a woman—to his fellow Hi-Toms. So, perhaps it is understandable that he was not inclined to discuss his problems with Bossard. But it is curious, and perhaps significant, that in his memoir he did not mention his roommate at all." With regard to the Cubans, perhaps Flood did not feel he could connect with them, even if they likely did have to deal with the same Jim Crow laws and there could have been a language barrier. But Solis, at age thirty, had been playing in the United States for eight years; he spoke English and served as the translator for Peña.[10]

Another reason Flood might have felt shunned by his teammates was his own personality as well as their jealousy about his favored status in the Reds organization. Wrote Weiss, "Flood was cocky and he was earning $800 per month, an amount that greatly exceeded the $350 a month that was average for a Hi-Toms player, and his teammates probably resented the rookie's pay scale." But as the season progressed and Flood powered the team to the Carolina League pennant, it is plausible to think any feelings that he wasn't worth his salary dissipated.[11]

At eighteen, Flood, who grew up in Oakland, was the youngest member of the team. The only other player under the age of twenty was white first baseman Karl Kuehl, who was also from California. Pitcher Woody Rich had made his major league debut for the Red Sox when Flood was just one year old. Even at age forty in 1956, he was still one of the stars of the league with 17 wins for the Hi-Toms. Rich grew up on a farm near Morganton, North Carolina. Interestingly, in an interview at the time of his son's major league debut, Rich's father admitted he knew nothing about baseball. Instead, he said his son had learned the game by playing with "the Negro folk" in the area. There is no way to know Rich's personal feelings toward race relations, but it is apparent the Hi-Toms' veteran leader had not been opposed to sharing the field with Black players in the past.[12]

With regard to his manager, Flood wrote, "The manager, whose name mercifully escapes me, made clear that his life already was sufficiently difficult without contributions from me. I was entirely on my own."[13] That manager was Bert Haas, a native of suburban Chicago and veteran of nine seasons in the major leagues with Brooklyn, Cincinnati, the New York Giants, the Philadelphia Phillies, and the Chicago White Sox. His previous Black teammates included Hank Thompson and Monte Irvin in New York and Minnie Miñoso in Chicago. In 1956, at age forty-two, Haas still played part-time and hit .326 in 67 games for the Hi-Toms. In his assessment of Flood's criticism, biographer Weiss wrote, "It might be wondered why Flood should have expected a manager with many years of major-league experience to pay serious attention to a rookie's contributions."[14]

In his long career, Bert Haas had spent only one other season below the Mason-Dixon Line (1938), so he likely had little experience with Jim Crow laws.[15] They were probably frustrating to him as a manager and caused unwanted complications, particularly with lodging and dining. Perhaps he did not give Flood the attention he wanted and perhaps he did not challenge the social status quo, but Haas was a career baseball professional who would have respected ability above all else. Despite Flood's inability to remember Haas's name, the manager frequently praised his young center fielder. "Curt Flood has certainly come through wonderfully. He's been worth his weight in gold," Haas was quoted in the *High Point Enterprise* (he gave Bo Bossard praise in the same article). He later said that Flood "was invaluable on the base paths and there isn't a better defensive outfielder in Class B ball than that 18 year old kid."[16]

Curt Flood also apparently had no shortage of female companionship during his season in the Carolina League. According to Weiss, "Well before season's end Flood had a fan club in High Point, chiefly white women who passed him (and other players) messages through cracks in the dugout's wood-paneled ceiling." Flood also had numerous admirers among the Black fans, but they were seated farther away in the segregated stands. In a letter to a friend in Oakland, he bragged about the women he dated. They "were always scratching at my door," he wrote. He added, "I expended rage in forbidden beds." Perhaps these were merely the bragging words of a teenager, but regardless of how they are interpreted, they challenge Flood's assertion that he was always alone.[17]

Like all previous Black players in the league, Flood suffered verbal abuse from fans on the road. At home, however, white fans were more accepting, especially after he established himself as the star of the team. He had nothing positive to say about any fans in his autobiography, but during the season, in a letter to his mother, Flood wrote, "The home fans are swell to me." His outstanding play may have made him an even bigger target for racial taunts when on the road. If opposing fans could rattle him, perhaps they could stop him from essentially destroying their team with his bat.[18]

Despite the jeers of road fans toward Curt Flood, the *High Point Enterprise* constantly praised his skills. Interestingly, the newspaper never mentioned his race at any point. This may have been the policy of sports editor Bill Hodges, or maybe it was not deemed a newsworthy fact. Either way, the newspaper was not trying to hide his race, because his photo was often shown. Early in the season Flood was referred to only as a rookie or as a native of California. As the season progressed, his name was often preceded by terms of praise. On June 26, Flood was referred to as a "brilliant youngster" in an article that announced he had taken over the league lead in batting average.[19] The only evidence in the newspaper that Curt Flood's situation was different from any other player's can be found in analysis of the team's off-field publicity events. In May 1956, the team participated in a "Meet the Hi-Toms" promotion at local businesses. The players were divided and sent to make appearances at different businesses that sponsored the team. In the *Enterprise*, business advertisements in the sports section featured a photo and announced which player would be available to meet fans. It was never mentioned that Curt Flood was not involved in the promotion, but neither he nor star pitcher Orlando Peña was featured in any advertisement. The only minority player to participate was René Solis, who was not viewed as Black. It would seem that businesses would have clamored to have the stars of the team make an appearance at their establishment, but this undoubtedly would have had unacceptable social complications. To have white fans turn out at a white-owned business to meet a Black player would have been unheard of, so it was quietly ignored.[20]

In his autobiography, Flood wrote, "What had started as a chance to test my baseball ability in a professional setting had become an obligation to measure myself as a man. As such, it was a matter of life and death. These brutes were trying to destroy me. If they could make me collapse and quit, it would verify their preconceptions. And it would wreck my life."[21] Despite his obstacles, Curt Flood did succeed on the baseball field, and he led the Hi-Toms to the league pennant with a 91–63 record. He averaged .340 with 190 hits, 128 runs batted in, 133 runs scored, 102 walks, 19 stolen bases, and 29 home runs. In the outfield, Flood led the league with 388 putouts, and he was named Most Valuable Player in the Carolina League. Jim Crow laws and racist fans had not defeated Flood, only empowered him to achieve a level of baseball excellence never before seen in the Carolina League.[22]

In the mid-1990s, Kenneth Turan of the *Los Angeles Times* began an autobiographical project with Curt Flood. It was never completed (due to Flood's death in January 1997), but Flood did speak of his time in the Carolina League in the initial interviews. Flood recalled that Jim Crow laws almost prevented him from receiving his league MVP award in 1956. The Hi-Toms had scheduled a banquet to celebrate the end of the season. It was to take place in the city's nicest hotel, which was, of course, segregated. According to general manager George Erath years later, Flood understood the circumstances of the hotel. He decided to accompany the team anyway and boarded the bus wearing a suit. In a test of Jim Crow, Flood disembarked from the bus with his teammates and attempted to enter. He was stopped by the doorman, who, recalled Flood, said, "Hey boy, where are you going? We don't serve no Nigras in here." Flood complained to manager Bert Haas, who told him there was nothing he could do and that he would accept the MVP award for him. Flood stated that he returned to the bus and waited angrily. Soon, a well-dressed white man stuck his head in the bus door and called to him. Flood stated that he snapped, "I'm already at the fucking back of the bus. What else do you want from me?" "No, no, no," said the man to Flood's surprise and identified himself as Tom Finch, one of the wealthy and powerful owners of Thomasville Furniture Company. He had come to get Flood from the bus. Finch apologized for the city's "bad manners" and invited the ballplayer to join him at his table. Flood and Finch entered the hotel—"literally arm in arm"—with no one daring to stop them.[23]

At the banquet Finch was not listed as a speaker, but when it came time to present the MVP award he gave it to Flood himself. "He got up and began reading my stats," recalled Flood later. "Flood he did this, he did that, he won the league's most valuable player trophy." Finch then told the crowd, "He's the first Negro to eat in this goddamn restaurant." Said Flood years later, "I wish I had taped that. God almighty."[24]

Forty years after his season in the Carolina League, Flood spoke of another humiliating example of racism when the Hi-Toms played in Danville, Virginia. Flood claimed that the city had an ordinance that forbade Black and white athletes from sharing the same locker room. Because of it, between games of a doubleheader, he was forced to dress in a tin shack that was attached to the main locker room by only a hole in the wall. After he removed his dirty uniform, he put it through the hole, where a clubhouse boy picked it up with a stick because he was afraid to touch it. He then took it to a Black-owned laundry two blocks away. The rest of the team was already on the field when the uniform was returned, and Flood stated he was humiliated to run on to the field alone. Weiss wrote that, based on Jim Crow laws of the time, "at first glance Flood's story sounds reasonable. . . . But the evidence is to the contrary." Danville had featured the first Black player in the Carolina League in 1951, Bill White had played there in 1953, and the city's team had several Black members in 1956. Weiss stated that Bill White "denies the existence of any ordinance of that kind when he was there. Also, the Danville *Register and Bee* and city officials cannot find the governing ordinance." Those kinds of rules were certainly not unheard of, however, and in 1952 there had been an issue with racial sharing of a locker room in Edenton, North Carolina. That was primarily because the ballpark was on high school property, but professional baseball forced a resolution to be found.[25]

In his book, Stuart Weiss went on to question Flood's story. If it was true, why was he alone in his "hot, separate tin shack"? Orlando Peña and roommate Bo Bossard should have been in the same situation. Catcher Haven Schmidt, who was again Flood's teammate the following season in Savannah, also refuted the story in a 2019 interview. "I don't know why Flood said some of the things he did later, but I will dispute his claim about changing alone and his uniform not being washed in time during a doubleheader," said Schmidt. "I don't know where that came from. We always changed together, and our uniforms were never washed between games of a doubleheader. The only thing we might change was an undershirt."[26]

Flood apparently first told the locker room story to Kenneth Turan of the *Los Angeles Times* in the 1990s. He repeated it to Geoffrey Ward and Ken Burns for their book *Baseball: An Illustrated History*. In that telling, however, he stated it took place in 1957—a season in which he would not have been playing in Danville. It is understandable that so many years later a date could be remembered incorrectly from the middle of a long career, but would that be the case for such a traumatic event in a player's rookie season? Shortly before Flood's death in 1997, his wife, Judy, told the story as well (standing by a dugout, though not in Danville) for a Spike Lee–produced fifteen-minute segment for HBO's *Real Sports*. Biographer Weiss surmised, "That Flood concocted this story of his humiliation in Danville seems apparent." He also questioned why—if it was true—Flood would not have mentioned it his 1971 memoir.[27]

In his 1971 autobiography, Flood wrote about High Point, "I believe I would have quit baseball rather than return there." He certainly faced racism and loneliness, but he also enjoyed a level of celebrity. His photo appeared in the newspaper several times during the course of the season. One large photo on the front page of the sports section showed Flood and Danville outfielder Leon Wagner, who was also Black. It was captioned "They Continue Red Hot Duel Tonight."[28]

The press seems to have had great respect for Flood's abilities, and Flood was always polite when responding to their questions. His popularity extended to the fans. Flood was presented a watch by a local jeweler after being voted winner of the "People's Choice" award, and it was reported that Tom Finch of Thomasville Furniture even anonymously sent him a 1956 Chevrolet to use during his time with the Hi-Toms. After the Carolina League season, Flood was summoned to the big-league club in Cincinnati. Before he left, he told the *High Point Enterprise*, "I've enjoyed the year very much and I'm very happy to be getting this break." It was polite and appropriate, but Flood did not need to say anything nice. With his performance, he was certainly not coming back to High Point. After Flood reported to the Reds, the *Enterprise* kept tabs on his major league appearances that season (5 games, primarily as a pinch runner) in a "local boy makes good" way. Again, possible exaggeration in Flood's writing in 1971 has to be considered.[29]

Haven Schmidt, Flood's former teammate, reflected upon his time in High Point in a 2019 interview:

> I think Curt Flood took it particularly hard. He was a tremendous player, but he was also very young, and I think that was part of the problem. Bo Bossard was older and more used to the situation. He was well educated and a heck of a ballplayer himself. I was with both of them again in '57 at Savannah. At High Point we also had Orlando Peña. He didn't speak much English but was also really good. He had an easy motion with one of the liveliest fastballs I've ever seen.

We never got to eat with any of them as teammates. When we stopped at restaurants, they would have to go to the kitchen to eat, or sometimes we would order food and take it to them on the bus. But the players almost always got along. In High Point, I remember no problems. Actually, the only time I ever remember racial problems amongst the team was in 1960 when I played for Columbia. That season we traveled in small vans rather than buses. On the long ride back after games we would fall asleep, often leaning against each other. I remember there were a couple of white boys from the South who made it clear they did not want to be that close to the black guys on the team. I actually preferred some of the African Americans to many of the white players on the teams. They were guys who just wanted to be good baseball players.[30]

Overall, the Curt Flood story is a complicated one. Much of the writing about him (most of which concerns his struggle for free agency) has a hagiographic tone, and some his exploits—both on the field and off—fall into the category of lore. Regardless, in 1956 he was the brightest star in the Carolina League, and his contributions to the game of baseball are unquestionable.

Several of the other Black players in the Carolina League in 1956 had successful seasons and long baseball careers. High Point–Thomasville's Orlando Peña won 19 games and had an ERA of 2.42. He made his Cincinnati debut in 1958 and went on to pitch in 427 major league games over fourteen seasons. Peña retired after the 1975 season and embarked on another long career as a baseball scout and pitching coach. Danville's Leon Wagner was not far behind Curt Flood in terms of offensive output and hit .330 with 51 home runs and 166 RBIs. He went on to hit 211 big-league home runs over twelve seasons. Wagner's teammate José Pagán played fifteen seasons in the big leagues and won a World Series title with Pittsburgh in 1971. It was Danville's eighteen-year-old outfielder Willie McCovey who found the greatest baseball fame, however. The Alabama native was the National League Rookie of the Year in 1959 and the 1969 National League MVP. A six-time all-star, McCovey played twenty-two seasons with the Giants and Padres and was one of the most-feared sluggers in the game. He retired with 521 home runs and 1,555 runs batted in and was enshrined in the Baseball Hall of Fame in 1986.[31]

As for Curt Flood's roommate Bo Bossard, he advanced up the baseball ladder but, unfortunately, fell just short of making the major leagues; his playing career ended after spending the 1959 season in the Texas League. In 1996, he was named to Benedict College's Athletic Hall of Fame. He died in 2000 but was posthumously named to the Delaware Afro-American Sports Hall of Fame in 2002 for his work with youth baseball programs in that state. Also an avid golfer, Bossard was an "ambassador for the game of golf in the African American community," and in 2000, the Belasco "Jack" Bossard Memorial Golf Tournament was founded in Townsend, Delaware, to raise funds for several community programs.[32]

Chapter 21

SALLY SURVIVES A THREAT

In January 1957, Georgia state senator Leon Butts introduced a bill that would have outlawed the interaction of Black and white players on the baseball field. He stated his bill "was intended to halt use of Negroes in the Sally League." Butts added, "If they [professional baseball teams] can't get away without Negroes, let's do away with baseball."[1] Though it was Georgia legislation, it would have had an effect that went far beyond the four league members (Augusta, Savannah, Columbus, and Macon) from that state. Both Charlotte and Columbia were Sally League members, as were Jacksonville and Knoxville. Passage of the bill would likely have meant the demise of the entire South Atlantic League.

The bill would have affected other leagues as well. By 1957, Major League Baseball no longer accepted racial restrictions on where to place its players (with the exception of the teams in the Southern Association; it disbanded in 1961 rather than integrate). If restrictions were placed on the six teams in the Class D Georgia-Florida League (all members were in Georgia in 1957), the major leagues would likely have looked elsewhere for farm clubs. A few major league clubs also operated spring training camps in southern Georgia for minor league affiliates. In addition, major league clubs often played exhibition games in the state before traveling north for the season. Enactment of a law barring racial mixing on the athletic field would bring an end to all of this. Needless to say, major and minor league baseball executives were vocally opposed to the bill, as were college football administrators. Phil Howser, president of the Charlotte Hornets, had taken his club out of the Tri-State League for its refusal to integrate. He voiced his objections to the bill from a purely baseball standpoint. "Players have to be assigned somewhere, and there are only three Class A loops—the Sally, Eastern and Western. It would put a burden on the majors if they were unable to assign Negroes to the Sally."[2]

The bill unanimously passed in the Georgia Senate, but it never came up for a vote in the Georgia House. With deft political maneuvering, opponents delayed consideration until time ran out. At the end of the last day of the session, lawmakers gave up and voted to adjourn. Butts was disappointed. "I think it's a shame the major league ball clubs and the NAACP have gotten control of the Georgia House," he told reporters.[3]

One of the teams whose continued existence would have been threatened if the proposed Georgia law passed was the Columbia Gems. A farm club of the Kansas City Athletics, the Gems were the only professional baseball team in South Carolina in 1957 and did have Black members. Al Isreal and Fleming Reedy were league veterans and in their second seasons in Columbia. They had both been in the Athletics organization since 1952 and at Savannah in 1953, among the first Black players to integrate the league.[4]

Reedy, an outfielder, had been signed by Athletics scout and former Negro league star Judy Johnson. In 1953, Arthur Ehlers, general manager of the Athletics, had even predicted that Reedy would be the first to break the color line for the club (in Philadelphia at the time). It was not to be, however, and Class A with Columbia, and later Albany, was the highest level he reached.[5]

At league rival Charlotte, the pipeline of talented Cuban players sent by the Washington Senators to their farm club continued to flow. Though likely not considered actually white by fans, none of the Cubans on the 1957 team technically fell into the "Negro" category. There was, however, a Black player on the Charlotte Hornets in 1957: Sam Hill, a native of Birmingham, Alabama. He was the first African American to play for the Charlotte franchise. A veteran of the Chicago American Giants in the Negro American League as a teenager in the late 1940s, Hill was an outfielder in the 1948 East-West All-Star Game at Yankee Stadium. He was signed by the Senators organization after playing independent baseball in Bismarck, North Dakota. Hill appeared in only 12 games for the Hornets, however, before Washington sold his contract to the Chicago White Sox. He was then assigned to Duluth of the Class C Northern League, where he played two seasons before retiring from baseball. Hill's contributions on the field in Charlotte were small, but his presence was a positive sign that the Senators organization was beginning to accept Black players from places other than Cuba.[6]

Chapter 22
THE OTHER JOHN KENNEDY

Of the sixteen players who have the distinction of being the first to integrate each of the major league teams, some—such as Jackie Robinson, Ernie Banks, and Larry Doby—were extremely successful. Others were barely a blip on the radar. One of those players who would have slipped into complete baseball obscurity if not for his brief big-league trial was John Kennedy.

As the 1957 season approached, only three major league teams—the Philadelphia Phillies, the Detroit Tigers, and the Boston Red Sox—had yet to field a player of African heritage. All three of those teams had upper-level minor league affiliates in the Carolina League: High Point-Thomasville was an affiliate of the Phillies, Durham was a member of the Detroit system, and Greensboro was a Boston farm club. High Point-Thomasville had been integrated in 1955 when the team was a member of the Cincinnati Reds organization, but the other two towns had yet to have a Black player on the roster.

In their unhurried efforts to integrate, the Phillies hired former Negro league player Bill Yancey to help them identify suitable prospects. One of the players Yancey recommended was a shortstop from Jacksonville, Florida, named John Irvin Kennedy, who already had some professional experience. Kennedy had played in the independent Mandak (Manitoba-Dakota) League and then one season with St. Cloud, Minnesota, in the Giants farm system in 1953 before being released. He then joined the Negro American League and played for the Birmingham Black Barons and later the Kansas City Monarchs. With Kansas City in 1956, he hit .356, a performance that drew the attention of Bill Yancey. He convinced the Phillies to purchase Kennedy's contract from the financially struggling Monarchs.[1]

After a strong spring training, Kennedy made the Phillies' opening day roster. Just before the season began, however, the Phillies acquired Cuban shortstop Chico Fernández from the Dodgers. The move left Kennedy without a full-time spot on the roster when Fernández was named the starter (though not actually considered Black, Fernández was the first person of any color other than white to play for the Phillies). Kennedy did finally get into a game in late April as a pinch runner. He would appear in 5 games and had no hits in 2 at-bats. A reported shoulder injury also hindered Kennedy, and the Phillies decided he was not a necessary member of the team.[2]

In his book *The Integration of Baseball in Philadelphia*, Christopher Threston wrote that the team did little to develop Kennedy and perhaps played him only to "get the monkey off the Phillies back" with regard to integration.[3] However, it was also discovered during spring training that Kennedy was actually thirty years old instead of twenty-two, which is what the Phillies believed. This is likely one of the reasons the Phillies acquired the twenty-five-year-old Fernández.[4]

Shortly after the Class B Carolina League season began in early May, the Phillies demoted Kennedy to their farm club in High Point–Thomasville. Even then there was confusion as to age and experience. One newspaper in the Philadelphia area erroneously stated that Kennedy was twenty-three years old and in his first season of Organized Baseball after a season with the Kansas City Monarchs. There was no disputing he had had an outstanding spring with the big-league club; in its mention of his reassignment, Raleigh's *News and Observer* referred to him as "rookie shortstop John Kennedy, sensation of the Philadelphia Phillies' spring training camp." Some felt Kennedy did not get a fair trial in Philadelphia, and even Casey Stengel, manager of the New York Yankees, said, "They've been looking everywhere for a shortstop except right under their noses. This fella [Kennedy] does everything."[5]

The Hi-Toms had struggled out of the gate in the Carolina League, and the team's starting shortstop was injured. Kennedy was welcomed to the team, and no mention was made of his race (of course, having a Black player was nothing new in High Point, and not as big news as it was in Philadelphia). "Infielder John Kennedy, considered the top young player in the Phillies' spring camp this year, will come in to take up the slack caused by the injury to regular shortstop Fred Harrington," wrote *High Point Enterprise* sportswriter Bill Hodges. He continued, "Kennedy, who can play third base if needed, comes to the club on direct option from the parent Phillies. He batted .332 against major league competition this spring and the Phillies had originally not planned to send him out." In fact, Kennedy did take over as starting third baseman when Harrington returned. He had a solid season, batting .270 with 19 home runs and a league-leading 23 stolen bases.[6]

John Kennedy was promoted to Tulsa in the Texas League the following season but only batted .225. At Des Moines in 1959, he hit .228.[7] The Phillies apparently no longer considered Kennedy a major league prospect, but they continued to keep him under contract. In 1960 they sent him back to North Carolina to join the Asheville Tourists of the Class A South Atlantic League. In the days before the season opener, the *Citizen-Times* announced that the starting lineup had been decided and Kennedy was named as the third baseman with no mention made of his race. The newspaper also reported that on opening day a breakfast would be held for players, directors, and press at the fourteen-story Battery Park Hotel, one of the city's finest lodging establishments. Its lists of guests over the years had included such celebrities as Babe Ruth, Ty Cobb, F. Scott Fitzgerald, Grace Kelly, Boris Karloff, and Thomas Wolfe. It is unknown whether Kennedy took part in the festivities or quietly avoided them, knowing that it was a segregated facility. If Jim Crow was ignored and he was allowed to attend, the only other Black people in the room would likely have been waitstaff. It would have been yet another example of the loneliness and isolation faced by early baseball integrators. Later on opening day, a parade featuring three bands escorted the Tourists team to the ballpark. Again, it would likely have been an event that included only white people.[8]

In what would prove to be John Kennedy's last full season in professional baseball, he hit .246 for the sixth-place Tourists. He then returned to his hometown, where he played one game for the Jacksonville Jets of the South Atlantic League at the beginning of the 1961 season before retiring. Kennedy continued to play amateur adult baseball, however, until the age of seventy.[9]

It is easy to say race played a role in the briefness of Kennedy's stay in Philadelphia, but a few days after he was sent to High Point–Thomasville, the Phillies traded for African American utility player Chuck Harmon. Perhaps the club made the assessment that, despite a standout training camp, Kennedy's skills were only those of a good minor leaguer rather than a major league starter. His numbers over the seasons after his appearance for Philadelphia tend to support that idea. Perhaps he dealt with nagging injuries that hindered him, or maybe he was simply born a little too early. There is no way to know for sure. What is known is that John Kennedy helped open a door for future Black Phillies (such as Tony Taylor, who was a starter throughout the 1960s) and that his place in baseball history is secure.[10]

Chapter 23
BLACK BULLS

The Detroit Tigers were notoriously slow in their effort at integration. At the time of Jackie Robinson's signing with the Brooklyn Dodgers organization in 1946, the Tigers had stated that they were not opposed to integration, just merely waiting for a player that they felt fit the team. A decade later, they were still waiting. The Tigers' attitudes toward integration were largely a reflection of the personal feelings of team owner Walter Briggs. Briggs himself never commented publicly on racial issues, but his team's actions—or lack thereof—were obvious. George Lerchen, a white outfielder who spent a decade in the Tigers organization, once stated, "It was well known that any scout who signed a colored player would be fired." In 1951, general manager Billy Evans even went so far as to tell the *Michigan Chronicle*, Detroit's African American newspaper, that the Tigers were not interested in signing black players. Attendance was good as things were, and he even doubted that there were suitable Black players available.[1]

Before the 1952 season, Walter Briggs died, though his family continued to run the team. There was some hope for desegregating the Tigers, however, and in late August 1953, the team announced the signing of its first Black player to a minor league contract: outfielder Claude Agee, a high school star from McKeesport, Pennsylvania. In 1956, the Tigers were sold to an investment group led by broadcasting executives John Fetzer and Fred Knorr. It was under their ownership that the major league team finally desegregated.[2]

In 1948, the Durham Bulls became one of twelve teams in the growing Detroit Tigers farm system. It was a strong relationship that would eventually last for fourteen seasons. It also, however, greatly hindered Durham with regard to integration on the baseball field. Despite being a city known for its large Black middle class and very successful Black-owned businesses, Durham had still not fielded a Black player on its Bulls by the end of 1956. Whether the Bulls team had any say in this, however, is up for debate. Most likely they had little. As an affiliate of the

Detroit Tigers, the Bulls relied on that organization to send them players. The Tigers may or may not have supplied them with a full roster, and that could have changed at a moment's notice. If a roster spot was available, it is possible that the Bulls could have filled it themselves, but they would have been responsible for that salary. All players signed by the Tigers were paid by that organization. If the Bulls had an open roster spot and they signed a Black player on their own, they risked the ire of the Tigers, who were essentially their financial lifeline. To the Bulls, it was probably not worth the risk, even if possible.[3]

During spring training for Tigers prospects in 1957, it became apparent that the Bulls would finally be assigned Black players. Sportswriters began to predict which players were ready for which level of the system and who might be sent to the Class B Bulls. When camp broke in mid-April, there were actually three African Americans assigned to Durham: Wycliffe "Bubba" Morton, Ted Richardson, and Wendell Antoine. *Durham Morning Herald* sports columnist Jack Horner gave a preview of the three players in his April 11 column and even predicted Richardson could win 20 games. Horner also commented on the possible positive effect the players could have on attendance. "With the gate going down the last few years, these boys may help give the club a shot in the arm attendance-wise." He concluded his article by stating, "Other Carolina League clubs have used Negroes for several years, but Detroit has just started getting some of the better colored players and they are scattered throughout the Tigers farm system."[4]

In the days before the opening game on April 17, the Durham newspapers made some mention of the fact that Durham would have Black players for the first time, but—since Durham fans had been seeing Black players on visiting teams for five seasons previously—it was not headline news. On opening day, the *Durham Morning Herald* featured a photo of manager Bob Mavis with Ted Richardson, whom he chose as the starting pitcher, and white catcher Jack Feller. It made no mention of race, and the caption merely stated, "Skipper and Tonight's Battery." On the same day, the *Durham Sun* ran a photo of Richardson, Morton, and Antoine. Its caption was "Make Diamond History Here," and it noted that the trio were the "first of their race to play for a Durham team in organized baseball."[5]

Durham lost the opener to the Greensboro Patriots, 4–1, in front of a crowd of 2,993, "about one fourth of them Negroes," reported Jack Horner in the *Durham Morning Herald*. Richardson and Morton both started the game. Stated Horner, "Their presence broke the color line in Durham and also made the turnstiles hum at a pretty merry clip." In his column the next day, Horner reported that the opening day crowd was the largest since 1947: "The big reason for Durham's biggest home opening crowd in 10 years was the presence of Negro players in the Bulls' lineup for the first time in history." He stated that Richardson, Morton, and Antoine were all "topnotch prospects in the Detroit Farm System, but must produce to keep their following." Added Horner, "The trio has a lot of pressure riding on their shoulders. It's almost unfair to these boys. They could do a better job, I'm sure, without the added responsibilities of trying to make the grade against adverse conditions. For the sake of Richardson, Morton and Antoine, I hope they turn out to be stars to lighten the load on their backs."[6]

Of the Black players who appeared for Durham in 1957, outfielder Bubba Morton by far had the biggest impact on the field. Morton grew up in Washington, DC. The third Black player in the Detroit organization, he was signed by the Tigers in 1955 after a stint in the coast guard and a couple years at Howard University. Morton's first assignment was Idaho Falls in the Class C Pioneer League. After a middling season, with a batting average of .247, he was sent to Class D Jamestown, New York, in 1956. His play improved and he earned a midseason promotion to Class B Terre Haute, Indiana. At Durham, Morton's rise continued, and in 126 games, he batted .310, drove in 82 runs batted, hit 18 home runs, and was named to the Carolina League all-star team.[7]

Left-handed pitcher Ted Richardson, a native of Florida, began his career in the final days of the Negro leagues with the Indianapolis Clowns. He was with that team from 1951 through 1955 and was selected to pitch in the 1952 all-star East-West Game in Chicago's Comiskey Park. In 1955, Richardson pitched for the semipro St. Joseph Auscos (Auto Specialties Company), which won the Michigan state championship. His performance with that team caught the attention of the Detroit Tigers, and he signed with them in 1956. Richardson split the next season between Syracuse in the Eastern League and Augusta in the Sally League.[8]

For the 1957 Durham Bulls, Richardson started 13 games and posted a 6–4 record. Midway through the season, the Tigers reassigned him to the Florida State League, where he was 10–9 with a 2.00 ERA for the last-place Orlando Flyers. Richardson pitched one more season in the Tigers organization, split between Lancaster, Pennsylvania, and Idaho Falls,

Bubba Morton's 1963 Topps baseball card. Collection of the author.

and then played a season with an independent team in Canada before giving up on his baseball dream.[9]

Catcher Wendell Antoine was a New Orleans native who had hit .410 his senior year at Grambling College. The *Durham Morning Herald* predicted he might be named starting catcher, but a cold as the season began kept him on the bench. In the meantime, white catcher Jack Feller established himself and secured the job with his strong play. Antoine appeared in only 11 games for the Bulls and was eventually reassigned to the Tigers' Class C affiliate in Idaho Falls, where he became the starting catcher. He would return to Durham in 1960, but—after hitting only .227 in 60 games—he was released by the Detroit Tigers organization. Antoine then signed with the Minnesota Twins in 1961 (the recently relocated Washington Senators) and played for their Class A affiliate in Charlotte for two seasons. He finished his career with the Wilson Tobs in the Carolina League in 1963, having never made it higher than the AAA level.[10]

In 1955, the Black-owned *Detroit Tribune* had speculated that Antoine and Morton were among the top candidates to be the first Black player to make it to the Tigers. Instead, that distinction went to Ozzie Virgil, who had been acquired in trade before the 1958 season. Virgil had been a star in the Carolina League in 1954 with Danville and had appeared in 99 games for the New York Giants, split between the 1956 and 1957 seasons.[11]

Led by Bubba Morton's stellar play, the Bulls finished the 1957 season tied for first with the Hi-Toms. The *Durham Morning Herald* frequently praised Morton's play on the field and prefaced his name only with terms indicating skill, never one indicating race (after the groundbreaking first game of the season). The Bulls eventually prevailed in a playoff that went 7 games to take the Carolina League title.[12]

Bubba Morton continued to climb the baseball ladder the following season and just missed being the first Black player to successfully work his way up through the Tigers' system to Detroit. That distinction went to infielder Jake Wood (a Durham Bull in 1958), who made his Detroit debut April 11, 1961, eight days before Morton. Morton played much of two seasons for Detroit before being traded to the Milwaukee Braves in 1963 and to the California Angels in 1966. All total, Morton played a total of 451 big-league games over seven seasons. He retired from baseball as a player after spending the 1970 season in Japan. In 1972, he was hired as the head baseball coach at the University of Washington, the first Black coach in any sport at the school. Morton remained in the position for five seasons. Upon his death in 2006, an article in the *Seattle Times* included a quote from Morton he had given in the 1990s about his pioneering season in Durham. "[Black players] always had to stay in private homes on the road," he said. "But I'll tell you what kind of teammates I had in Durham—they wouldn't go and eat in a restaurant without me. Somebody would always go in and get sandwiches for everybody; then they'd bring them to the bus and we'd go on our way."[13]

Chapter 24
CHARLESTON

Even if never its physical capital, Charleston, South Carolina, could be considered the spiritual heart of the Confederacy. It is where the Civil War began and the place that perhaps most embodies the lifestyle of the Old South. Common imagination associates the city with big houses, river plantations, Spanish moss, genteel accents, and, of course, slavery.

Charleston was also home to white professional baseball beginning in the latter years of the nineteenth century. Surprisingly, it had no team from 1922 until 1940, when the Spartanburg club of the South Atlantic League relocated to the city in the middle of the 1940 season. Renamed the Rebels as homage to Charleston history, the team lasted until 1953, when—like so many minor league teams at the time—it ceased operations for financial reasons. In 1959, the Class A South Atlantic League expanded from six teams back to eight (where it had been a few season earlier), and a new Charleston team was formed. Named the ChaSox, the club was an affiliate of the Chicago White Sox and owned by local attorney Bill Ackerman. The team played its home games at College Park, a 4,000-seat ballpark located in the corner of Hampton Park, a municipal facility named for a former Confederate general who had been one of the top slaveholders in the South.

The Sally League had been desegregated in 1953 when the first Black players were assigned to clubs in Jacksonville and Savannah. Over the following five seasons, Black players appeared on the rosters of most teams in the league. When Charleston joined the league, there was some speculation as to whether the team would include Black players, but it appears it was more out of curiosity than cause for protest. On March 25, 1959, an article in the *Charleston News and Courier* reported on the makeup of the new team: "So far, the Charleston White Sox appear to be an all-White team. One Negro, Leroy Hicks, is working out with [manager Frank] Scalzi's crew, but he is too inexperienced to make the grade as a Class A ballplayer this season." Two days later, another article stated, "The first indication that Charleston may have a Negro player on the team came to light Thursday. Grover (Deacon) Jones, a 25-year-old third baseman, is working out with the Indianapolis Indians of the Class AAA American Association, may be assigned to Scalzi's squad soon. Jones is a slick fielder and a good hitter but his throwing arm leaves something to be desired."[1]

As it turned out, Deacon Jones was assigned to Lincoln, Nebraska (he did play for Charleston in 1961). Instead, the first Black player assigned to Charleston (on April 10) was pitcher Ollie Brantley. A 6′3″ right-hander, Brantley was from a small town near the Mississippi River in eastern Arkansas. He joined the Memphis Red Sox of the Negro American League out of high school in 1950 and was signed by the White Sox organization two years later. Brantley steadily worked his way up the ladder toward Chicago; he won 22 games at Class B Eugene in 1957 and 15 at Class A Colorado Springs in 1958.[2]

A week after Brantley was assigned to Charleston, he was joined by a second Black player, Sam Hairston. The veteran catcher had been born in a small town in eastern Mississippi and grew up in Alabama. He began playing industrial league baseball as a teenager, which led to a chance to join the Birmingham Black Barons. In 1944, Hairston was traded to the Cincinnati-Indianapolis Clowns of the Negro American League. During several seasons with the Clowns, he developed into one of the top hitters and best catchers in Black baseball.

On July 31, 1950, Hairston—then thirty years old—was the first Black player to sign with the White Sox organization and was assigned to Colorado Springs, the Sox affiliate in the Class A Western League. He earned a promotion to Sacramento in the Pacific Coast League the following season. Injuries at the big-league club led the White Sox to summon Hairston to Chicago in July. With the team five weeks as a backup, he appeared in 4 games, the first Black American to do so (Cuban Minnie Miñoso, who joined the team early in the season, was the first player of African descent to play for the White Sox). Hairston remained in the Chicago farm system for most of the rest of his career but never returned to the major leagues as a player. He spent four more seasons with Colorado Springs and also played in Charleston, West Virginia, and Indianapolis.[3]

In the middle of the 1958 season, Hairston's contract was sold to the San Antonio Missions of the AA Texas League. An Orioles affiliate, the Missions were in need of a starting catcher. Hairston played well in 74 games with San Antonio and was scheduled to move up to Vancouver in the Pacific Coast League in 1959. He was released, however, when

Vancouver made its final cut after spring training. Hairston was due to be sent back to San Antonio, but the White Sox organization repurchased his contract and sent him to Charleston, South Carolina. At thirty-nine years old, not much was expected of Hairston on the field; he was hired primarily to assist manager Frank "Skeeter" Scalzi by working with young pitchers and catchers.

A couple of weeks into the 1959 Sally League season, Hairston and Brantley were joined on the ChaSox by another Black player. Cuban shortstop Chico Terry, who had played in the league for Columbia in 1954, was sent to Charleston after being optioned by Indianapolis. On May 2, one more Black player, outfielder Ernie Johnson, joined the ChaSox. Also a veteran of the Negro American League, the thirty-year-old Johnson had played for the Kansas City Monarchs. He signed with the Baltimore Orioles organization in late 1953 and spent the 1954 season with a Class C team in Canada. In 1955, Johnson joined the Chicago Cubs organization and played part of the season in the Sally League with the Macon Peaches. He was then in Iowa for three seasons (hitting over .300 in all of them) and signed with the White Sox in the spring of 1959.[4]

As far as reports in the two Charleston newspapers, the *Evening Post* and the *News and Courier*, race did not seem to be an issue with regard to the ChaSox. Beyond the initial reports of their signings, the names of the four Black members of the team were not prefaced with the word "Negro" in articles. It even appears that the fact Chico Terry was Cuban was mentioned only once. The true age of Sam Hairston seemed to be of more interest than his ethnicity. Wrote Bill Glance in the *Evening Post*, "Hairston is about 40 years old (nobody but Sam and his mother know his exact age and Sam isn't telling)."[5]

Early in the season, Sam Hairston quietly made history. In the May 14, 1959, game against Jacksonville in Charleston, manager Skeeter Scalzi was ejected in the eighth inning. He appointed Hairston as acting manager in his absence. Though it was for only two innings, there is little doubt it was the first time a person of African descent had been in charge of a team in Organized Baseball in the Carolinas.[6]

On July 21, 1959, the Sally League all-star game took place before a crowd of 3,593 at Charlotte's Griffith Park. It pitted the first-place Gastonia Pirates against a team selected from the other league members. Three Black players were selected for the All-Stars: Knoxville pitcher Jim Proctor (who started the game), Charlotte outfielder Sandy Valdespino, and Charleston's Sam Hairston. "It came as a complete surprise when

Sam Hairston. Collection of the author.

they told me I was an All-Star," Hairston told reporters when he learned of his selection. "I didn't think anybody would vote for an old man."[7]

"Grizzled old veteran" (as the *Charleston Evening Post* called him) or not, Hairston was the hero of the all-star game. With the game tied at 6 at the top of the tenth inning, a man on first and no outs, Hairston came to bat. The hit-and-run sign was on, but Hairston fouled off the first pitch. He then took a called second strike. "I told myself right then, you've shore messed up Sammy boy," he said after the game. "I decided the only thing to do was try to bunt the ball." Hairston did just that; he laid down a perfect bunt and was safe at first without a throw. The next batter walked. The lead runner then scored on a wild pitch, followed by Hairston, who scored on a sacrifice by Sandy Valdespino. Gastonia came back and scored 1 in the bottom half of the inning, but the All-Stars held on to win 8–7. Valdespino hit a single, double, and triple and drove in 2 runs, but it was Hairston's daring bunt that drew the most praise; "Two-Strike Bunt Turning Point" declared the article headline in the *Charlotte Observer*. "He did it on his own," all-star manager Gene Verble of Charlotte said. "I have to thank him breaking up the game."[8]

On the sports page of the *Charlotte Observer*, which included the results of the Sally all-star game, was an article featuring a photo of Cincinnati Reds pitcher Don Newcombe. The pioneering Black star, whose résumé included a Cy Young Award, a National League MVP Award, and a World Series title, had just won his 140th major league game. Also on the page was an Associated Press article with the title "Bosox Recall First Negro." Finally, a dozen years after Jackie Robinson's debut, the last major league team to desegregate was about to have its first Black player.[9]

Surprisingly, Sam Hairston was not named to the South Atlantic League's postseason all-star team, which was voted on by sportswriters around the league. The honor for best catcher went to Knoxville's Bob Rodgers, who batted .287. (Rodgers, later more well known by his nickname, "Buck," went on to a solid big-league playing career and managed in the major leagues for a dozen seasons.) Bob Quincy, sports editor of the *Charlotte News*, was appalled by Hairston's exclusion and even felt he should have been league MVP. "No All-Star group can be perfect and satisfy everyone," he wrote. "Unfortunately, this one has too many glaring omissions. Most obvious, it seems to me, is that of a complete disregard for Sam Hairston, the easy-going ebony backstop of the Charleston White Sox. Sam . . . seemed to me a good bet for the league's most valuable player. He did not even make the team." Despite Hairston's absence, the 1959 Sally all-star team did include three Black players: Asheville first baseman Nate Dickerson (the league batting champ with a .362 average), Sandy Valdespino, and Jim Proctor.[10]

Despite being nearly twice as old as some of his teammates (said Hairston: "I won't tell no man how old I am no matter how many times he asks me, but I can still score from second base on a single like the kids"), Hairston had an impressive season.[11] He batted .330 (second in the league), drove in 63 runs, caught 104 games, and occasionally played in the outfield. On August 26, at Charleston's last home game, Hairston was honored for his performance. Said *Charleston Evening Post* sportswriter Tony Meyer, "Success apparently spoiled Sam Hairston of the ChaSox, the old pro catcher who stands a very good chance of walking away with the Sally League batting championship. Sam was named the most popular player in voting by fans attending ChaSox games this year. He was presented a car and other gifts before last night's game and then failed to get a hit in five appearances." Meyer's article included a photo of Hairston with the caption "Most Popular Player."[12]

Chico Terry had a good season and finished second (to Hairston) on the team in batting with a .276 average. Terry bounced around the minor leagues for a decade. Though always a solid player (career .286 batting average), he never got the call to the major leagues. After playing for Indianapolis in 1960, he finished his career with two seasons in Mexico.[13]

Ernie Johnson turned in a solid performance for Charleston and hit .266 with 10 home runs in 107 games. It was his final season in professional baseball. He returned to Iowa and had a long career working for Armstrong Tire.[14]

For the 1959 ChaSox, Ollie Brantley posted a 12–11 record with a 3.91 ERA. He was back with Charleston in 1960. Brantley was promoted to San Diego during the season, one step from Comiskey Park, but suffered an elbow injury. With the velocity on his fastball gone, he was released by the White Sox the following spring. He signed with the Cincinnati organization and spent part of 1961 back in the Sally League with Columbia. Brantley went on to play several more seasons in the minors, primarily as a relief pitcher, but his days as a prospect were over. He returned to eastern Arkansas where he became a police officer with the Marianna Police Department, working as the only Black officer on the force, and then joined the Lee County Sheriff's Department as the first Black deputy.[15]

Sam Hairston also returned to Charleston in 1960 at age forty. He appeared in 45 games and batted .263 before he decided to retire and pursue a career as a scout for the White Sox. "I've been with the White Sox chain since 1950, my first chance in organized ball," he said. "They've been mighty nice to me. So, I'll try to do whatever job they have for me." In the end, Hairston spent forty-eight years with the White Sox organization. He scouted and coached at several levels and was the bullpen coach in Chicago in 1978. He later spent a dozen seasons on the coaching staff of his hometown Birmingham Barons (including 1994, when NBA superstar Michael Jordan was a member of the team).[16]

Not only did Sam Hairston contribute to baseball personally, but he was also patriarch of one of the game's most successful baseball families. All three sons played professional baseball. Sam Jr. played for the White Sox in the rookie Gulf Coast League but was drafted into the army. He returned from Vietnam with a sore arm that ended his career. Both of Sam Jr.'s brothers, however, made it to the major leagues; John appeared in a few games for the Cubs, and Jerry had a long career, almost all of it with the White Sox. John's two sons, John Jr. and Jason, played Class A professional baseball in the late 1980s and 1990s. Jerry's two sons, Jerry Jr. and Scott, had long major league careers like their father. The Hairstons are one of only three families (the others being the Bells and the Boones) to have been represented in the major leagues by three generations.[17]

In 1961, the year after Sam Hairston retired, the roster of the Charleston White Sox included three Black players: Jim Lynn, Grover "Deacon" Jones, and Don Buford.

Outfielder Jim Lynn was in his second season with Charleston. The North Carolina native was a graduate of segregated Dillard High School in Goldsboro. He enlisted in the navy, and it was there—while stationed on a base in California for three years—that he honed his baseball skills. He caught the eye of a White Sox scout and signed with that organization upon his discharge in 1955. Lynn batted .363 in his first professional season at Dubuque, Iowa. He continued to work his way up and played for Lincoln, Nebraska, before being promoted to Charleston.[18]

First baseman Deacon Jones was from White Plains, New York. In 1951 he led his American Legion team to the national championship. They fell short, but Jones was still named the Legion's Player of the Year. He graduated from White Plains High School in 1952 and enrolled at Ithaca College, where he played both basketball and baseball. In 1955 the Chicago White Sox offered Jones a contract. He signed and was sent to Waterloo, Iowa. Jones won the Midwest League batting title in 1956 with a .409 average, but he missed the next two seasons while on military duty. He returned to baseball in 1959 and was sent to Lincoln, Nebraska.[19]

Outfielder Don Buford grew up in Los Angeles and was a product of the legendary baseball program at the University of Southern California. He had also been a football player at USC and was named All-Pacific Coast in 1958. Buford graduated in 1959 and perhaps because of his size (5′7″) had no professional football offers. Of the four baseball clubs he spoke with, the Chicago White Sox offered the best deal, and he signed that November. Buford began the 1960 season with San Diego in the Pacific Coast League, but after a few games the White Sox assigned him to the Class B Lincoln Chiefs.[20]

In a 2022 interview I had with Buford, he spoke about the 1961 season in Charleston.[21]

In 1961, I think there were three Black players on the Charleston team. Is that correct?

Yes. Me, Deacon Jones, and Jim Lynn. Honestly, we were probably the better players on the ball club. Jim Lynn, he was from the southern states and was more acclimated to what goes on in the South than we were. Deac was from New York, and, of course, I was from California, so a lot of things Jim tolerated, we didn't. We had different backgrounds and said, "Hey, man, we're not doing that. If they're not going to treat us with respect then to heck with them, we're not going to participate."

How were relations with your teammates?

The players were all friendly; we had no difficulties with our fellow teammates at all. One of them, Manly Johnston, was a pitcher, and he lived in the area. He often invited us to his house for dinner, but we didn't go. We were appreciative, but our thought was, "You've got to live in the area. So why make it tough on you and your family when we're just here for the baseball season?"

There were no problems with the managers we had, either. Every time there was a chance to be promoted, the managers wanted us on their ball clubs. We played hard, and they wanted to win. And we didn't let those kinds of racial things interfere with our play on the field.

I went to USC; I was the first Black baseball player at the University of Southern California, and we won the NCAA championship in 1958. Being the only Black on the team, my roommate was white, Bobby Santich. And we got along fine. With all the college hoopla you go through, there was never a negative word, never anything said racial-wise, but Coach [Rod] Dedeaux was a different kind of person, too. I guess that's why he won so many national championships [eleven].

I think the impact of players playing together on the same team and not having any difficulties was very important for racial relations. It's still the same thing today. It's a personal opinion, but you're going to have some people where racism is inbred in their family and you couldn't change it if you turned a quarter over fifty times. That's just the way they grew up, and it's not going to change. Then other people, it's the difference between day and night. I treat people the same as I want to be treated; I am not going to belittle anyone. In fact, if you're a fellow ballplayer, I'm going to try to help you be better. Your success means my success.

Did you have much communication with the White Sox organization in Chicago?
They didn't care much at all at that time.

So they sent you there and left you to deal with it on your own?
[*Laughs*] Very well spoken. It wasn't like, "We're sending you to this place and this is what you'll have to prepare for and look out for." They sent you there and you had to make it. I don't think that the things Black players had to deal with was a consideration at all.

I really didn't know what to expect. In Southern California, racial issues were not part of my growing up. Playing in some of the southern states was really new, and it was tough adjusting to things we couldn't do. I remember one incident when we were traveling on the bus, somewhere in South Carolina. It was afternoon and we stopped for food at a roadside place. I was on the bus when other players were suddenly yelling my name, saying that Deac was being threatened for entering this whites-only place. I ran inside and there was a white man pointing a shotgun at him. He was saying, "Get this n—— out of here or I'll blow his brains out." I grabbed Deac and dragged him out. I said to him, "Man, you know better than that! We don't even get off the bus in some of these places."

The person who brought baseball back to Charleston was owner Bill Ackerman. How were your interactions with him?
Bill Ackerman was outstanding. He rented a house and furnished it for us. We had a couch and an old black-and-white TV. We each had a bedroom, and he furnished it all. Otherwise we had no place to stay. He was good to us. There were no difficulties with him as the owner. He kind of looked out for us.

You know, finding housing was always difficult. My first year was in Lincoln, Nebraska. There were no other African Americans on the team, but there was a Black catcher; he was Cuban. Housing was tough in Lincoln for Blacks as well; it wasn't just the southern states. I stayed with the lady who was the area Aunt Jemima pancake representative. She had a basement apartment and I stayed in her home.

Did you have any problems with fans?

Here's a very true story. One of the first times we went to one of the league cities—I'm not sure which one—there were three gentlemen that had megaphones. One would sit behind third base, one at home plate, one behind first. I was the leadoff hitter. I never dreamed of anything like what was going to happen. The gentleman behind home plate yells out over the megaphone loud, he says, "Don't throw that n—— no fastball!" I stepped back and looked at him, and he says it again, "Don't throw that n—— no fastball!" Boom. Fastball, base hit. "I *told you* don't throw that n—— no fastball!" This was out loud, really loud. I get to first base, and the guy with the megaphone there says, "Watch out, now, that n—— gonna steal. He gonna steal!" I stole a base. "Yonda he go, I *told you* that n—— gonna steal!" I get to second and the guy behind third with the megaphone yells, "Watch out, now, that n—— gonna sco'!" Not "score," "sco'." I scored a run and he yells out on the megaphone, "I *told you* that n—— gonna sco'!" So this would go on for nine innings every night we were there, the same three guys.

They didn't like us much in Macon, either. I remember one game there—we wore those wool uniforms, and it felt like 100 degrees—I was hitting leadoff. I got a fastball and hit a home run. I came back and took the hard hat off, and this guy threw a beer on me from the stands. We didn't have changes, and I had to wear that uniform the whole game. It was the worst smelling game I ever played in [*laughs*]. But those were the two sad incidents I had to deal with [in] regards to fans as a visiting player.

Were you aware of what was going on with civil rights protests?

We were aware, really very aware of it. But we didn't get very much involved in that aspect because we were playing and traveling. So we didn't get to know any of the people who were marching or in that fight. We were at the ballpark, then went home, then back to the ballpark, then traveled, then back to the ballpark. We didn't do very much other than play baseball.

We did actually make some small contributions, I guess. On bus trips, we stayed outside of the city, usually in Black motels. The managers used to go past our motel, go downtown, and all the other players got off the bus. Then the bus driver would drive us back ten, fifteen miles or so to the Black motel. We changed that because finally we had a big discussion—it was kind of vocal—that it wasn't right to treat us that way. Number one, you passed our motel—why go all the way downtown and then have the bus driver bring us back when there are only three Blacks on the ball club? You can let us off at the motel, which takes you five minutes. We had heated discussions with our manager, and they finally changed that. The contribution that we made was that the players and manager and coaches understood our argument that "Hey, we're part of the team, so why treat us differently?"

There was another incident the next year. *[Note: The Charleston ball club—with Buford and Jones—moved to Savannah for the 1962 season.]* There was a luncheon at a Savannah hotel for the league all-star team. Me and Deac were on the team. The hotel said we could come, but we would have to leave as soon as lunch was over. Also, they said our wives couldn't come. I said, "No, you've got to be crazy. I'm not going to a luncheon and all the other all-stars have their wives and families there." We told Mr. Ackerman to tell the league to shove it, that we were not coming, not going and participating in the game. Mr. Ackerman talked to them and said something like, "Listen, they're on your all-star team and you don't want them to play?" That got them to change their minds. They did allow our wives to participate in the luncheon, but we couldn't stay in the hotel. We still had to leave right after the luncheon.

After his time in the South, Don Buford continued to work his way up the professional baseball ladder. He was promoted to AAA Indianapolis in 1963 and received a call-up to Chicago that September. He went on to play four solid seasons with the White Sox, but it was after a 1968 trade to the Baltimore Orioles that he truly established himself as a premier player. The Orioles of the late 1960s–early 1970s (which included former Columbia Reds star Frank Robinson) were one of the best teams in baseball history, and Buford, who was the team's leadoff hitter, was a key member. With Baltimore, Buford won the American League pennant three times and the World Series in 1970. In 1973, he accepted an offer to play in Japan. Buford spent four seasons in Japan, was twice an all-star, and in 1974 was named to the Pacific League's Best Nine team as one of its three outfielders. Buford retired in 1976 but returned to baseball in 1981 when Frank Robinson, who was then managing San Francisco, hired him as his first base coach. Buford was also on Robinson's coaching staff in Baltimore and Washington, served as an assistant coach at his alma mater for a couple of years, and was director of field operations and farm director for the Orioles. Buford also managed in the minor leagues for four seasons. In his seventies, he became director of Major League Baseball's Urban Youth Academy in Los Angeles.[22]

Deacon Jones was always a good hitter (.319 average over eleven years in the minor leagues), but an arm injury hindered him on the field. He did make the major leagues for 40 games, however (three short stints with the White Sox). After his playing days ended in 1969, Jones turned to coaching. He managed one season in the minor leagues and then made it back to the majors as the hitting coach for the Houston Astros from 1976 to 1982. He then spent one season as an instructor in the New York Yankees organization before returning to the big leagues as the San Diego Padres' hitting coach from 1984 to 1987. Jones then went on to spend eighteen seasons as a scout for the Baltimore Orioles.[23]

Jim Lynn appears to have been one of those many players who had the skill to advance but never did. He was a consistent hitter, but perhaps there were better players blocking his path within the White Sox organization. He could also have struggled with injuries. Whatever the reason, he hung up his spikes after spending the 1963 season in Eugene, Oregon.[24]

Despite the best efforts of Buford, Jones, Lynn, and the rest of the team (which included Al Weis and several others who appeared in the major leagues), the 1961 Charleston White Sox finished fifth in the eight-team league with a 70–68 record. Due to poor attendance (fewer than 600 spectators per game), owner Bill Ackerman moved the club to Savannah after the season. Professional baseball did not return to Charleston until 1973.[25]

Chapter 25
JACKIE PAYS A VISIT

Few people can name the first African American to integrate professional football or basketball, but almost everyone knows the name Jackie Robinson. Even nonfans of baseball know why he is famous, and his important story has been told many times. While he is one of the most significant baseball players in the history of the game and the face of its efforts toward integration, Jackie Robinson is not often associated with the sport in the Carolinas. Beyond a few preseason games with the Dodgers and a handful of postseason stops on his barnstorming tours, it is likely that Robinson—who grew up in California and later lived in Connecticut—rarely visited North or South Carolina. He did, however, make one very important visit to Greenville, South Carolina.

When Jackie Robinson retired from baseball at the end of the 1956 season, he became more involved with civil rights and the NAACP. This led to an invitation to address the South Carolina state NAACP conference in Greenville on October 25, 1959. On that day, a group including national NAACP official Gloster Current drove to Greenville Municipal Airport to meet Robinson's arriving flight from New York. In a letter to Robert Carter, general counsel of the NAACP, Current recounted the events that followed:

> We took seats in the main waiting room and shortly after being seated, we were faced with the manager who came over and told the group that we could not occupy seats in that area; that we had to go into the "colored lounge." This is a room which has been specifically set aside, off the main entrance of the airport, for Negroes. It contains seats, telephones and lavatory facilities. We refused to leave the area, although we did arise from our seats and became engaged in conversation with the manager. The manager's name is Mr. O. L. Andrews. He stated that if we attempted to re-seat ourselves, we would be arrested. To emphasize this, he called Officer No. 87, whose name, I learned later, was Woodall. He told the officer to

> arrest us if we attempted to sit down. Several members of the group remonstrated with the manager and told him we had a right to be there; that the airport is federally subsidized; that Mr. Robinson was an interstate passenger and the facilities were rightfully ours to use without discrimination. We made no further protest of the situation at the time and left when the plane was taxiing to the gate. We did not subject Mr. Robinson that morning to the humiliation of the discriminatory treatment indicated by the manager.[1]

Current and his party escorted Robinson to Greenville Memorial Auditorium. There, the retired baseball star spoke before a crowd of nearly 1,700 people. After giving numerous examples of discrimination in his speech, Robinson said, "I don't want my kids to go through this kind of thing, and I don't want yours to go through it either." He urged "complete freedom" with a target date of 1963 and encouraged Black citizens to vote. "I wonder what would happen in Greenville if all of you went down to vote?" he asked the crowd.[2]

After the speech, Robinson left the auditorium to catch a return flight to New York. In an editorial that appeared in the *Baltimore Afro-American*, Robinson stated,

> We arrived at the airport 20 minutes before our plane was due to leave, and I stood while my companions took the only available seats near a television set provided for passenger use. We purposely by-passed a small segregated corner of the terminal which was labeled "Colored Lounge," for we knew that four years ago the Interstate Commerce Commission had ruled that segregation of interstate travelers in public waiting rooms was unlawful.[3]

The manager of the airport, O. L. Andrews, soon arrived and ordered the group out of their seats. They refused, and Andrews summoned a policeman who was on duty in the facility. Wrote Robinson,

> We then informed the officer that we had no desire to create a disturbance, but pointed out that this was a federally-subsidized public facility which came under the rules and regulations of the ICC and we asked under what Greenville law were we being ordered to move. The officer apparently was completely perplexed, for after making a quick telephone call he decided to quit the scene. We stayed on in the main waiting room until our plane arrived. And before we boarded for our flight to New York, we were greatly

heartened by a crowd of well-wishers who entered the terminal as a means of expressing their support for our stand.[4]

There was speculation in newspapers that Robinson's treatment at the airport could lead to a lawsuit. The NAACP's Clarence Mitchell said "it would be up to Robinson to decide whether a private suit will be brought in the case." Mitchell also stated he was aware that Greenville had a "Negro waiting room" but "wasn't asked to use it when I went through there several months ago." Perhaps Robinson's fame did not allow for a violation of segregation policies to be overlooked. As it was, reports of the incident made newspapers regionally in Columbia, Charlotte, and Raleigh as well as in northern cities including Baltimore, New York, and Detroit.[5]

Not all news outlets neutrally reported Robinson's stand against Jim Crow regulations. The editor of South Carolina's *Sumter Daily Item* wrote in his column,

> Robinson expressed his appreciation for the assistance of "a great number of liberal white people." 'Tis pity, 'tis true, 'tis true, 'tis pity but there are some white people right here in our own area who are backing the NAACP and its effort to bring about integration. . . . Jackie Robinson is typical of the agitators being sent out by the NAACP to try to arouse Negroes of the South. So far these agitators haven't met with much success and the series of violent incidents occurring all over the North have served to make the efforts of the agitators harder in the South because the two races have been living together in harmony down here, while there has been much feudin' and fightin' going on elsewhere.[6]

After the Robinson incident drew national attention, it became more widely known that there already was a court case involving discrimination at Greenville Municipal Airport. In late 1958, a Black traveler named Richard Henry had been forced out of the white waiting room in the airport. Henry, a US Air Force public relations employee, had been in town to cover air force maneuvers in the area and was on his way home to Detroit. Backed by the NAACP and a legal team that included Thurgood Marshall, the case was filed in US District Court.[7]

In August 1959, Judge George Bell Timmerman found for the defendants. He stated that Henry "did not go to the waiting room in quest of waiting room facilities, but solely as a volunteer for the purpose of instigating litigation. . . . The Court does not and should not look with favor on volunteer trouble makers or volunteer instigators of strife or litigation."[8] Henry and the NAACP did not give up and took the case to the US Fourth Circuit Court of Appeals. It was awaiting hearing when the Robinson incident occurred.[9]

A suit did not arise from the Jackie Robinson incident. He did consult with Thurgood Marshall about the case, but Marshall felt there was little point in pursuing the matter since it would be essentially the same as the Henry case. Instead, local activists organized a demonstration. On New Year's Day 1960, approximately 1,000 people staged a peaceful march to the airport to protest its policies of segregation. One of the marchers was a young student at the University of Illinois who was home in Greenville for the holiday break. Jesse Jackson would go on to be one of the prominent figures of the civil rights movement as well as a US presidential candidate.[10]

In April 1960, the Fourth Circuit reversed Timmerman's verdict in *Henry v. Greenville Airport Commission* and sent the case back to him to reexamine. He again ruled against the injunction, and again his verdict was appealed. In February 1961, the Fourth Circuit Court reversed Timmerman and ordered him to grant the injunction. It stated that the airport must refrain "from making any distinction based on color." The Henry case officially ended segregation at the Greenville airport, but the influence of Jackie Robinson and the attention he brought to the issue certainly played a large role in helping the case eventually succeed. Robinson's actions in Greenville had no effect on the game of baseball (in fact, the city's Meadowbook Park remained segregated until the Civil Rights Act of 1964), but because of baseball, Robinson was able to help further civil rights in the Carolinas and beyond.[11]

Chapter 26

.400

In 1951, a team in the Western Carolina League, Granite Falls, had been the first in the state to field Black players. It had been a brief experiment, however, and the Granite Falls team went defunct after the season. A year later, the entire league ceased operation for financial reasons. Before the 1960 season, however, it appeared there would be more major league clubs, so the need for low-level minor league affiliates increased. The Western Carolina League was reorganized with clubs representing towns that had been previous members as well as with towns that had been in the neighboring North Carolina State League.[1]

At the same time that plans were being made for the rebirth of the Western Carolina League, the civil rights movement was rapidly gaining traction across the Carolinas. The Greensboro sit-ins began in February 1960, and numerous restaurants and other establishments were picketed for discriminatory practices. Racial tensions were much higher than they had been when a few Black players quietly took the field in the Western Carolina League in 1951.

Teams in the Western Carolina League did field a few Black players in 1960. The most notable was Greensboro native Bill Bethea, who actually began the season with the Winston-Salem Pond Giants, a Black semipro team. After an impressive 8–0 start for the Pond Giants, Bethea was signed by talent scouts for the Continental League and assigned to Lexington. The 6′4″ left-handed pitcher went on to turn in a record of 11–3 and an ERA of 1.35 for the team. He struck out 18 batters in his first game for the team on June 22 and started the all-star game for the East squad on August 14. Unfortunately for Bethea, he was thirty years old at the time; if he had been ten years younger he would have been a serious major league prospect. Instead, he was back in Lexington in 1961.[2]

The beginning of the 1961 baseball season coincided with the first of the Freedom Rides. Mixed racial groups traveled by bus through the

South to challenge segregation on the bus and in bus stations. Jim Crow laws were still being enforced despite being ruled unconstitutional because the buses engaged in interstate commerce.[3]

The first rides, organized by the Congress of Racial Equality, left Washington, DC, on May 4. A few days later the two buses passed through Western Carolina League territory. On May 8, one stopped in Salisbury, North Carolina, and the riders were met with the usual Jim Crow signage that designated separate "Colored" and "White" facilities. The group was able, however, to desegregate the restrooms, and Black riders were served at the "White" lunch counter without incident. The farther south the group traveled, though, the more trouble they faced. Riders were arrested in Charlotte, and in Rock Hill, South Carolina, future congressman John Lewis and others were assaulted. The Freedom Rides continued until December, and many of the participants faced violence, particularly in Alabama.[4]

Despite the social unrest across the region, Black baseball players continued to prove their excellence on the field. In the Western Carolina League, a first baseman named Aaron Pointer turned in what was likely the most impressive performance by a Black baseball player in either North or South Carolina during the Jim Crow era. A native of Oakland, California (and older brother of the singing Pointer Sisters), Pointer attended the University of San Francisco. After two years, however, he decided to pursue a professional baseball career when offered a contract by the expansion Houston organization. He was assigned to the Class D Salisbury Braves.

Pointer dominated league pitchers from opening day. Six weeks into the season, his batting average remained near an unheard-of .500. He maintained his torrid hitting and went into the final game of the season with an average just above the magical .400 number. Salisbury manager Alex Cosmidis offered Pointer a day off to preserve his batting average but he declined; he went 2-for-3 in the game and finished the season at .402. Pointer's other totals were 117 runs scored, 14 triples, 42 stolen bases, and 73 runs batted in. In 418 plate appearances, he struck out only 34 times. No professional baseball player since has batted over .400 in a full season.[5]

In a 2020 interview with me, Aaron Pointer recalled his time in Salisbury.[6]

Members of the 1961 Salisbury Braves included (*left to right*) Dick Loughridge, Tom Murray, Aaron Pointer, and Fred White. Pointer won the batting title with a .402 average and was named the Western Carolina League's Most Valuable Player. Collection of the author.

You signed with the Houston Colt .45s, an expansion club.

Actually, at that time in 1961, they didn't officially have a name, as far as a mascot name. They were not officially in the National League yet. Houston and the New York Mets officially came into the National League in 1963. So, when I signed, it was just with the Houston organization. In 1961 they had just two baseball clubs affiliated with Houston, the Salisbury team where I started out and Houston itself, which was a triple-A minor league team.

When you signed with them, and they told you they were sending you to Salisbury, North Carolina, did you have any expectations of what it would be like going to the Jim Crow South? Did they give you any warning?

I had no idea. I didn't know where I would be assigned. I went to spring training in 1961 in Jacksonville, Florida, and that was my introduction to the South. I'd been to the South as a kid. My parents were from Arkansas, and I remember going back to Arkansas with them during the summer to visit my grandparents, but we never really left the house. We didn't experience the things that were going on in the Jim Crow South at that time. I guess I was nine or ten years old at that time. Getting off the airplane in Jacksonville, Florida, was a shock in itself. It was the first time I had seen open segregation. I got off that plane and there were signs that said Colored Waiting Room and White Waiting Room, and taxicabs were colored cabs and white cabs. I didn't have to get a taxi because someone was there to meet me with the Houston organization to take me to the spring training camp. There were white players staying in one part of Jacksonville and players of color—African Americans and others—staying in another part of town. I remember staying in a motel with four players to a room, no air conditioning, and this was in April. We had to eat at different places. We were never with white players other than being on the field for practice. That was the only time we ever saw them.

It was different, although it was kind of segregated in Oakland, California, where I grew up. My family had white neighbors on either side of the house we lived in. We'd go to school with people of different races, but there in Jacksonville, you'd see the signs that tell you [that you] can't drink at this fountain, you can't go to this park, you can't eat at this restaurant, you can't live at this house. It was not like that in Oakland, although there were unwritten laws and certain places you couldn't go . . . , but you never saw it in writing.

After spring training, I didn't know where I was going. I didn't even realize there was a team in Salisbury, North Carolina. Spring training broke and I was assigned there, and off I went to play the season. That was different because there was no housing available for me. I was there for five months, and I never had a chance to eat at a restaurant in Salisbury, although Salisbury was not that large, 25–30,000 people. Never went to a movie, never went to a park. If it weren't for a historically Black college, Livingstone College in

Salisbury, I probably would not have survived. I didn't have a place to live, so I stayed at a motel outside of town that they had arranged for me. At Livingstone College I had a chance to meet some people and ended [up] renting a house from one of the professors who went away for the summer. That allowed me to stay in Salisbury. So, I bought a car and hung out with the students at Livingstone College. They showed me around and actually help me get seasoned by showing me places where I could and couldn't go. When we had an off day, I would just head to the college and hang out with the students.

At the ballpark—well, they didn't have many African American people coming to games—but they had a section off first base where Black folks could come see the baseball games. That was the only place a Black fan could sit, off first base, at the stadium where we played at the college. I forget the name of the college. *[Note: Salisbury played at Newman Field on the campus of Catawba College.]* But that was the only place where they could sit. But there were very few fans that looked like me at the ball games. In fact, there were times when some of the people in Salisbury would complain to the baseball club—how could they allow me to shower and dress with the white players? Kind of crazy, but that was Salisbury at that time.

In 1961, being naive, I did not know what was going on, even though I was in the middle of some of the civil rights things. At Livingstone College, though I didn't find out until later on, the college was where one of the Freedom Rider buses stopped on the way to Mississippi and Alabama, protesting seating. In fact, on one of those buses was the late John Lewis, I found out. I didn't know what was going on myself, but John Lewis and the other protesters, both African American and Caucasian, were headed south. In fact, the bus that stopped at Livingstone was the bus that was burned and bombed later.

Did fans give you a hard time?

Not really. I heard words from fans. I heard the N-word directed at me or some of the other African American or Latin players on teams we played. I didn't really have a tough time in Salisbury as far as that goes, plus I just ignored it anyway. It's just something I heard even in Oakland. It just wasn't that big of a deal. It didn't bother me that much to hear it. I was bothered at one point during the season by a kid over in center right field that was shooting at me with a BB gun.

They had to get security to take care of that. Later on, I said, "God, what if that wasn't a BB gun? What if that was a .22 or other high caliber gun? I could be dead." It was a real shock.

During the season I never went out to lunch or dinner or any other activity with my teammates. I was just by myself or with the people I met at Livingstone College. I did have one friend in Salisbury, a white boy by the name of Tommy Murray. He played ten years of minor league ball. Tommy was a third baseman on the team. He was from a town in Texas called Marshall. When we'd go on road trips—all of our road trips were by bus because the towns weren't that far apart—I couldn't go in a restaurant. Tommy would ask me if I wanted some food and he would get it. He and I would sit on the bus and eat dinner or whatever after ball games so I wouldn't be alone. Tommy and I became pretty good friends, and when the season ended, I was supposed to report to the Houston baseball team. Since Tommy lived in Texas we rode there together after the season. I'd bought a new car in Salisbury, and Tommy and I drove to Marshall, where I let him off, and I drove on to Houston. I remember on our drive, we drove straight through and didn't stay overnight anyplace. Tommy mentioned to me to "make sure to let me drive during the day because if the police see you driving this car they are going to stop you." So I drove at night. When I got to Houston I parked at the administrative office and got on a plane for Omaha, Nebraska, where the Houston team was playing and finishing the season. . . . After the season, I got my car and went on back to California. *[Note: Pointer appeared in four games for the Houston Buffaloes at the end of the season.]*

That season was a unique experience that I will never forget. Over the years I've had Salisbury contact me and ask me to come back for whatever function they might be having, but I declined. I have no reason to go back to Salisbury. What was memorable there was having a great year in baseball. Between concentrating on baseball and the people I met at Livingstone College, those were the positive things I will never forget that had an effect on me as far as the South was concerned. Even in Houston—it was not great for African Americans anywhere in the South. Not just North Carolina or South Carolina. I remember before the season in 1962 having to get a physical in Houston. I had to go in the back door. My roommate in 1962 was a guy by the name of J. C. Hartman who had played in the Negro professional baseball league. He played for the Kansas City

Monarchs. He and I were roommates in 1962 in Oklahoma City. I remember him saying, "This is the way it is in the South."

How was your relationship with your teammates? I know you were separate from them a lot, but did you get along?
Yeah, I got along with them at the ball field very well, although we stayed in different parts of the town. I never had any problems with any of my teammates.

Even if they were from the South?
It didn't matter if they were from the North or the South at all. Everybody knew what the situation was with accommodations and restaurants and such, but nobody would talk about it or say anything or make a big deal. But you knew the situation because you could see it. But we got along, even though we went separate ways after the ball game. The only problem I ever had with a teammate was in 1968 when I was with Houston. I went to the ballpark for batting practice, and Rusty Staub, who I had played with in the minor leagues at Durham, was sitting around with some of the other players, white players. I walked by them and maybe he didn't see me, but he was telling the other guys he was talking to, "Yeah, Aaron Pointer, he's a good n——." I went up to him and said, "What did you say?" We started to fight right there in the clubhouse. That was actually how I ended up in Tacoma. Two days later I was called in to the administrative office and told I was traded to the Chicago Cubs, which was fine with me. I thought playing in Chicago would be great for me. . . . But Chicago, rather than taking me to the big-league team, sent me out to Tacoma. It was their triple-A club.

Pointer's performance at Salisbury earned him a promotion, and he began the 1962 season in the Carolina League with the Durham Bulls. He played 59 games there before receiving another promotion up the ladder, to Oklahoma City, in the Houston farm system. Pointer would eventually have three short stays with the Houston Astros (40 games total) as well as spend three seasons playing in Japan and winters in Venezuela.

After his baseball career, Pointer began officiating football games in the Tacoma, Washington, area. In the late 1970s, he became the first African American referee in college football's Pacific-10 Conference. Pointer joined the NFL in 1987 as a head linesman and remained in that position until retirement in 2003.[7]

For most of the 1961 Western Carolina League season, the biggest rivals for Pointer and his Salisbury team were twenty-five miles away in the town of Statesville. An affiliate of the expansion Los Angeles Angels, the Statesville Owls finished one game back in the standings. The Owls' roster included four Black players in 1961: Walter Darton, Davey Best, Bob Lucas, and Dick Simpson.

In mid-April, the Angels sent their first group of young prospects to Statesville. Jack Hiatt, Dick Simpson, Glade Cookus, and George Conrad traveled by air to Charlotte and then took a bus to Statesville. When they arrived in the town, the four hungry players entered the first diner they saw. Reportedly, "a cook approached them with a meat cleaver, pointed at Simpson who is black, and said, 'You boys will have to leave, we don't serve their kind here.'"[8]

The discrimination that the Black players in the league faced was stereotypical of all southern towns where Jim Crow was enforced. "The civil rights movement had not yet gained ground in the Western Carolina League cities," wrote Pennsylvania native Russell Buhite, a white player for Rutherford County in 1960. "Racial segregation was pervasive, and the evidence of it was startling to those of us accustomed to a greater degree of racial tolerance."[9]

In a 2011 interview, Best and Darton recalled the team going to movies at the Playhouse Theater in downtown Statesville. "The white players would head around to the front and go in and they sent us to the side to go upstairs," said Best. Added Darton, "And then after a while they would yell up to us, 'Hey did you guys make it in?' and 'What movie are you guys watching up there?'" The outfield wall of the Statesville ballpark featured a sign that offered free breakfast from a local café to any player who could hit the sign and make a double. Recalled Best, "I hit the sign 22 times that year. And I got zero free breakfasts. None of us got a free breakfast."[10]

When the 1961 season ended, Angels farm director Roland Hemond said, "Great things are expected of Simpson, Lucas and Best and the trio look like Angels of the future." Of the group, however, only Dick Simpson made it to the major leagues. The outfielder, who was seventeen years old when the season began, batted .294 for Statesville. He was promoted to San Jose in 1962 and called up to the Angels at the end of the season. The Venice, California, native eventually spent parts of seven seasons in the big league with six different teams.[11]

Davey Best, a second baseman signed out of Florida A&M University, batted .292 at Statesville in 64 games. He was promoted to San Jose in

1962 and eventually spent five seasons in the minor leagues. Best ended his career in his hometown with the Tampa Tarpons of the Class A Florida State League.[12]

Shortstop Bob Lucas, a former teammate of Best's at Florida A&M, joined the Owls in midseason and batted .167 in 32 games. The Angels saw potential, however, and Lucas was promoted in 1962. He went on to play seven seasons of minor league baseball and made it as high as the AAA level but never reached the major leagues. Lucas stayed involved with baseball for many decades; he was a scout for the Atlanta Braves, managed one season in the minors for the same organization, and eventually spent several seasons as the head baseball coach for his alma mater, Florida A&M University. Lucas also had two notable familial baseball connections: his sister was married to Hank Aaron, and his older brother Bill, who also had a minor league playing career, became the first African American major league general manager when hired by the Atlanta Braves in 1976.[13]

Like Dick Simpson, pitcher Walter Darton was a Los Angeles area native. He was on his way to an outstanding season with Statesville in 1961 and had a 5–1 record and an ERA of 2.60 in early June. Unfortunately, an arm injury ended his season. The Angels brought him back to Los Angeles for treatment, but he apparently never completely recovered and was released the following spring.[14]

Despite his short stay, Darton did achieve a footnote to baseball history in 1961. One game that season against Salisbury, the umpires failed to arrive due to car trouble. In order to play, each team selected one player to substitute umpire. Darton, a starting pitcher who had the day off, was chosen by the Owls and assigned to work home plate. The unusual circumstances technically made Walter Darton the first Black umpire in the Western Carolina League and one of the first in minor league history.[15]

Interestingly, Simpson and Best were mentioned in a 1963 article in the Nashville, Tennessee, newspaper that speculated on the upcoming baseball season. If the Angels decided to assign one of the promising prospects to their farm club in the city, they "could become the first Negro players in Nashville history."[16] Neither did go to Nashville, but the article shows that a dozen years after the color line was broken in North Carolina, teams in some of the larger cities in the South had yet to integrate.

Chapter 27
TONY O

In his 1973 autobiography, Tony Oliva wrote, "One thing I never thought about until I arrived in the United States was the color of my skin. In Cuba it never occurred to me that my skin was darker than another person's, that I was black and other Cubans were white."[1]

The double discrimination that had faced the first Spanish-speaking Black players in the Carolinas nearly a decade earlier certainly continued in the 1960s. Jim Crow laws forced them to reside and dine with others of African descent, but the frequent language barrier isolated them even from that group. The pool of talent was deep in Latin America, however, so scouts continued to bring in players from Cuba, Venezuela, Puerto Rico, and elsewhere. In 1961, Joe Cambria—the same Senators/Twins scout who had signed Bobby Estalella decades before—made yet another discovery in Cuba. This time it was an outfielder named Tony Oliva.[2]

Unfortunately, Oliva arrived in Florida near the end of the organization's spring training and had little chance to show his abilities. There were only two Class D teams remaining in camp, Erie of the New York–Pennsylvania League and Fort Walton Beach of the Alabama-Florida League. Oliva hit well in a handful of games, but a lack of fielding skill (and a limited number of available minor league roster spots) led the Twins to release him. Recalled Oliva, "Only Erie could use blacks; in 1961 you couldn't play at Fort Walton Beach if you were black. But Erie's roster was full. So, since I couldn't play in Fort Walton Beach, they had to release me."[3]

Joe Cambria made a phone call to Phil Howser, general manager of the Charlotte Hornets of the Sally League. Howser offered to try to help Oliva and two other unemployed Cuban ballplayers, so Oliva and the others caught a ride north with the Erie team. They were dropped off in North Carolina. Said Howser in 1973, "I remember Tony well because of what later happened. He showed up at the park with one suit and carrying his change of clothes in a straw bag." Howser told the trio he would give them three dollars a day for meal money and pay for their hotel while he tried to find them a job. Recalled Oliva, "There was a hotel for blacks in Charlotte, and we got rooms there, although one of us was white. He wanted to be with us, and since we had to stay there, he stayed there, too."[4]

The stay did not last long for Oliva's two Cuban compatriots. With a paying job on a baseball team uncertain, they decided to go visit relatives in Florida and New York. Fellow Cuban Minnie Mendoza, a minor league veteran who was assigned to Charlotte for the second season, encouraged Oliva to remain awhile before giving up and going home. As the failed Bay of Pigs invasion had just taken place in Cuba, Oliva would likely not have been able to return to the United States if he had gone home.

Phil Howser was intrigued by Oliva's raw abilities and offered to continue the young player's arrangement of paying for meals and a hotel while a solution to his predicament was sought. When the Hornets were home, Oliva was invited to practice with them, so the stay in Charlotte, which lasted six weeks, gave Oliva time to practice his game with no pressure. (Said Minnie Mendoza, "When Tony practiced with us in Charlotte, we could see he wasn't a bad outfielder—he was awful!")[5] But since he was not officially on the roster, he did not travel to road games and was forced to spend considerable time alone. He also had to live in a Black neighborhood, five miles from the ballpark. Because he could not afford a taxi and did not know how to take a bus because he spoke no English, Oliva walked the distance frequently. When the Hornets departed for their first series of road games, Howser reportedly gave Oliva two pieces of paper to show in eating establishments so that he could order food; one read "ham and eggs" and the other "fried chicken." Purchasing food had been a challenge for Oliva. "Because I didn't know English," he said, "I was afraid to take a chance and point at something on the menu. Once I saw a nice chocolate candy bar in a drug store, and I pointed at it and bought it. I took it back to my room to eat that night before I went to bed. Later I unwrapped it and took a bite—and gagged. It was a hunk of chewing tobacco."[6]

Said Phil Howser in 1973, "When the team was on the road, I wanted Tony to have something to do. I wanted him to play catch or whatever with some kids that used to hang around the park. I gave him a brush and had him paint the outfield fences, too. And he cut the grass a few times." Finding Oliva a team was a challenge since the season was

Tony Oliva. Collection of the author.

underway and rosters were full. "I tried to get Tony into the Western Carolina League but three teams refused to take him because he was colored," said Howser over a decade later. Teams were unlikely to sign Black players of their own volition; most of those in the league were assigned by major league clubs. It would have been an unwanted complication to have a player who was Black and spoke only Spanish in small towns where likely no one else did. No team wanted the challenge of trying to help a player like that navigate Jim Crow laws.[7]

"There were two reason I put up with Tony Oliva," said Howser. "First, Minnie Mendoza was my best player and a decent guy, a guy I trusted, and he kept telling me, 'Please find something for him. I'm sure he'll become a good player.' Also, I admired Tony's determination. I don't know what it was, since I couldn't communicate with him—maybe it was the look in his eyes—but I thought to myself, 'This guy really does want to play baseball, he's not here to have fun like so many other players.'" Eventually, Howser, a close friend of the Griffith family (who owned the Senators/Twins organization), was able to convince the Twins to re-sign Oliva and send him to their Class D club in Wytheville, Virginia. The Wytheville Twins played in the short-season Appalachian League and were limited to rookie players. It proved to be a wise move for all involved, because in 61 games, Oliva batted .410 and drove in 81 runs. It was the top batting average in all of professional baseball that season, for which he was awarded a silver bat. The performance also earned Oliva an invitation to Minnesota. Though he was not added to the roster, Oliva worked out with the Twins and met many players who would later be his teammates.[8]

The next season, Tony Oliva's talent allowed him to skip several rungs of the minor league ladder, and he was officially assigned to the Charlotte Hornets. It was a much better situation for Oliva in 1962, and he rented an apartment with fellow Black Cuban Nestor Velazquez, a twenty-two-year-old infielder. (The pair were not the only players of African descent on the Charlotte roster; catcher Wendell Antoine from New Orleans was in his second season with the team.) In his autobiography, Oliva recalled the season:

> The Sally League was another bus[h] league, but it was a good one. The cities . . . were larger, with hotels and restaurants for blacks. So there was no having to sleep in private homes or going to bed hungry because no restaurants were open after night games. . . . Nestor and I didn't do much except go to the ball park for games. There was a lot of racial discrimination in Charlotte, and we tried to avoid incidents. Maybe we were lucky, but Nestor and I didn't have any problems. We sat in any empty seat on buses, even if they weren't in the back. Maybe the whites knew we didn't speak English well, but no one asked us or told us to move to the back. We ate most of our meals in our apartments, and there were some Cuban families in the city who

would invite us to their homes for meals, so we had no problems with restaurants. In fact, we thought Charlotte was a nice city.[9]

On the field, Oliva continued to excel. He batted .350, hit 17 home runs, and had 93 RBIs. By a fraction of a percentage point, Oliva lost the league batting title to another Black player from the Caribbean, Asheville's Elmo Plaskett, but he was named South Atlantic League MVP. He was promoted to Minnesota at the end of the season and made his big-league debut on September 9. Oliva went on to win the American League Rookie of the Year Award in 1964 along with three batting titles and was an eight-time all-star. He played his entire major league career (all 1,676 games) for the Twins and retired at the end of the 1976 season with a .304 career batting average. Oliva was elected to the Baseball Hall of Fame in 2021.[10]

Tony Oliva's biography—written when he was still playing for the Minnesota Twins—is important to the story of integration in the Carolinas because it paints what seems to be a fair picture of the struggles of a Black player in the Jim Crow South in the early 1960s. Unlike some other baseball biographies of the time, it does not ignore racial issues. It addresses discrimination, loneliness, and the added challenge of not speaking English. The book also includes input from teammates and executives who positively contributed to Oliva's story. Oliva seems to have had no motive for writing other than to tell the story—with both ups and downs—of a star baseball player's career.

Chapter 28
SPARTANBURG RETURNS—AND INTEGRATES!

After an eight-year absence, R. E. Littlejohn and Leo Hughes brought baseball back to Spartanburg in 1963 when they bought a franchise in the Western Carolinas League. They also secured a deal to become an affiliate of the Philadelphia Phillies and named the new team after the parent club. Whatever feelings toward integration the owners (or the Spartanburg City Parks Board, on which Littlejohn had placed blame for previous discrimination) might have had, the issue was forced on them by the Philadelphia Phillies. The Phillies had been one of the least progressive clubs in baseball in terms of integration. The team's first Black player, John Kennedy, debuted in April 1957 (a decade after Jackie Robinson had joined the Dodgers), making the Phillies the last team in the National League and the third-to-last team in Major League Baseball to integrate its squad. Despite the hesitancy to integrate, the Phillies were hiring more and more Black players; in 1963 they assigned at least two African American prospects, Silas Jamison and Fred Mason, to Spartanburg during the course of the season.[1]

The Phillies organization began to truly change in 1959, when John Quinn was hired as the general manager. Quinn had spent fourteen seasons with the Boston/Milwaukee Braves. With that franchise he had broken the color line by acquiring Sam Jethroe from the Brooklyn Dodgers after the 1948 season. He then developed Black players such as Hank Aaron, Bill Bruton, Félix Mantilla, Juan Pizarro, and North Carolina native Wes Covington. In Philadelphia, Quinn began signing Black prospects for the minor leagues and trading for others. In 1960, he acquired two Black Cubans, Tony Taylor and Tony González. Both would be Philadelphia starters for several seasons. During spring training in 1962, Quinn was informed that Black and Hispanic members of the Phillies squad would not be allowed to stay in the team hotel in Clearwater, Florida, nor be served meals. His response was to check the entire team out of the facility and move twenty miles to a hotel in Tampa that would provide equal accommodations.[2]

When Phillies prospects arrived in Spartanburg in 1963, area newspapers did not attach much importance to the fact that the town's team was finally integrating. In its game preview before Spartanburg's season opener against the Greenville Braves, the *Greenville News* did point out that the visiting Phillies "have two Negros in their starting lineup" and later prefaced the names of Jamison and Mason with the term "Negro." Otherwise, the newspaper just mentioned hometowns and where the two had played the previous season—like it did for all other players.[3]

Silas Jamison was a Mississippi native who moved to Atlanta as a youth. There, he was a star athlete in both football and baseball at Booker T. Washington High School. He enrolled at Morehouse College but signed with the Phillies in 1960. Jamison's first professional season was spent as an outfielder with Johnson City, Tennessee, in the Class D Appalachian League. He then played at Elmira, New York, in 1961 (with Fred Mason) and spent 1962 in Bakersfield, California. His professional baseball career came to end in midseason when he was given his release after hitting only .225 in 59 games.[4]

Fred Mason, a twenty-seven-year-old first baseman and outfielder from Delaware, joined the Phillies organization in 1961 after two years in the army. His season in Spartanburg was successful; in 121 games he batted .306 with 88 RBIs. Instead of continuing to pursue a baseball career, however, he returned home to Wilmington and decided to play adult softball. In that game he was a star into the 1970s. Mason eventually coached junior college baseball and umpired both baseball and softball at many levels. He was inducted into the Delaware Sports Hall of Fame in 2004.[5]

Hughes and Littlejohn owned the Spartanburg Peaches in the Tri-State League from 1946 to 1955 and the Phillies in the Western Carolinas League (later called the South Atlantic League) from 1963 to 1971. In 2007, the two men (with the reluctance to integrate their first Spartanburg team forgotten) were posthumously elected to the South Atlantic League Hall of Fame. Said the article announcing their induction, "Hughes, locally known as 'Captain Leo,' was a philanthropist who added much to the Spartanburg community. The same can be said of Littlejohn, known as 'Mr. R. E.,' who earned a reputation for his generosity, his concern for his fellow man and his Christian beliefs." Perhaps fittingly, they were inducted with a Black player: Al Oliver, the star of the 1965 Gastonia Pirates.[6]

Chapter 29
KINGS OF THE CAROLINA LEAGUE

The year 1963 was filled with turmoil and tragedy in the United States. In the spring, Martin Luther King Jr. had led mass protests in Birmingham, Alabama. The peaceful demonstrations were met with police dogs and fire hoses, scenes that were broadcast on television; King and hundreds of others were arrested. In May an estimated 1,000 white students marched to protest integration of the University of South Carolina in Columbia. To address the most violent conflicts, President John Kennedy responded by sending troops to bases in the Birmingham area and drafting comprehensive civil rights legislation. In a June address to the nation, Kennedy said, "And this Nation, for all its hopes and all its boasts, will not be fully free until all its citizens are free." He continued, "I shall ask the Congress of the United States to act, to make a commitment it has not fully made in this century to the proposition that race has no place in American life or law."[1]

On the baseball field, the racial situation was resolving itself in a much more peaceful manner. In his book *Baseball Has Done It*, Jackie Robinson wrote, "In 1963 51 Negroes and 24 colored Latins were in the majors, or 15 percent of the total. Among them are five former batting champions, six Rookies of the Year, and six MVPs." The major leagues had come a long way, and in the minors, the Carolina League was not far behind. That same season it included many Black players who would soon join the list of those who made it to "the Show."[2]

On July 21, 1963, the Carolina League all-star game, East vs. West, was held at Kinston, and Black players were prominent on the roster. The starting pitcher for the West squad was Raleigh's Sherman "Roadblock" Jones. Behind him, at second base, was Greensboro's Roy White. In the outfield was Burlington's Lee Green. Later in the game, Burlington's George Pressley and Luis Tiant and Greensboro's Jim Horsford pitched in relief.[3]

Roadblock Jones was from eastern North Carolina. He had attended Calvin Scott Brown High School, the Black high school in Hertford

County, and began playing semipro baseball at age sixteen "for any team in and around his hometown of Winton, NC (population 825) that would pay him the most." Originally a catcher, he switched to pitching in a game against a team of Cuban barnstormers. Said Jones in a later interview, "The guy that was going to pitch had an accident or got hit by a car or something. They were giving me $20, so I said, 'I'll pitch.'" He eventually caught the eye of a scout and signed with the Giants organization in 1953 at age eighteen.[4]

For the 1955 season, the Giants assigned Jones to their Carolina League affiliate in Danville. He worked his way up through the system and made it to the major leagues with the Giants for part of the 1960 season. In 1961 he began the season for Jersey City in the Cincinnati Reds farm system. Promoted at midseason, he appeared in 24 games for the Reds, including Game 5 of the World Series against the New York Yankees. After that season, Jones was selected in the expansion draft by the New York Mets. He was the starting pitcher in the Mets' very first home game in 1962 but after 4 losses was sent to Greenville, South Carolina, the Mets farm club in the South Atlantic League.[5] In 1963, the Mets sent Jones to the Carolina League, where he pitched for the Raleigh Capitals. He pitched well (12–6, 2.10 ERA) and was promoted to AAA the next season, but a shoulder injury ended his attempt to make it back to the big leagues.[6]

After baseball, Sherman Jones went on to play other roles in bringing exposure to African American success. When his pitching career was over, he moved to Kansas, the home state of his wife. After a long career on the Kansas City police force, Jones was elected to the Kansas legislature in 1989, serving in the state House of Representatives and later the Senate until 2001. Jones said in an interview at the time of his election that he lived in "an urban area of blacks and Serbs and Croatians and Czechs and Greeks and Mexicans. Kansas is primarily a rural state, and I think I can represent their interests."[7] During his time in office he chaired the Kansas Legislative Black Caucus and served on the board of the Kansas University Medical Center.[8]

George Pressley was the third pitcher for the West squad. A tall (6′4″), thin right-hander, Pressley was in his second season of professional baseball at nineteen years old. The Cleveland organization signed him in 1962 and sent him to Class D Dubuque, Iowa. There, a 13–7 record and a 3.37 ERA earned the Florida native a promotion. Assigned to Burlington for 1963, Pressley was even better. His 16 wins were one off the league leader, and his ERA (2.96), strikeouts (150), and innings pitched (210) were all among the top ten in the Carolina League. Cleveland apparently saw great potential in Pressley and promoted him to AA Charleston, West Virginia. Unfortunately, injuries seemed to have derailed his career. Pressley spent nearly two months on the injured list in 1965 and won only 2 games. By 1966, at age twenty-two, he was out of baseball.[9]

Pitcher Luis Tiant grew up in Cuba with a baseball pedigree; his father, also named Luis, had been a star pitcher for the New York Cubans of the Negro National League in the 1930s and '40s. In today's world, the younger Luis would have grown up rich because of his father's stardom, but that wasn't the case. Even in the major leagues, very few players made huge salaries; in the Negro leagues, the money was even less. Money was tight in the Tiant household, and the elder Luis worked various jobs in the offseason, including pumping gas at a local filling station. Still, his talented son followed him into a career as a professional baseball player. The younger Luis began his career with Mexico City in 1959 at age eighteen. His performances there caught the attention of the Cleveland Indians, and they purchased his contract in 1961.[10]

Tiant's first season in the United States was spent with the Charleston (West Virginia) Indians of the Eastern League. His performance was mediocre (7–8), but a strong winter season in Puerto Rico resulted in an invitation to big-league spring training. He didn't make the Cleveland roster, but the Indians saw potential and assigned Tiant to their Carolina League affiliate in Burlington.[11]

In Luis Tiant's 2019 autobiography, Barry Levinson, Burlington's second baseman, recalled an event that took place during an early-season game in Raleigh against the Capitals. "Luis wasn't starting that day, so he was coaching first base. One fan called one of our black players a n——, and Luis went right over and vented as best he could to the guy. Our manager [Pat Colgan] came over when the incident was somewhat calmed down, and he said to Luis, 'Stop! They'll kill you.'" Wrote Tiant, "They didn't go that far, but fans were still calling us every name in the book. It was hard to keep my anger in, but like the year before, I tried to channel it into my pitching. I wanted to show them that color had nothing to do with *what* you could do. No matter what our color, or which language we spoke, we could do the same things as everybody else."[12]

Fan abuse drove Tiant to succeed. "Those fans gave me more power to fight back, and *show them*," he said, "so that's what I did. I came there to play baseball, not fight, and if I was good enough I felt I could turn them around." Tiant did just that. His pitching was often phenomenal, and in

May he followed a 4-hit shutout with a no-hitter against Winston-Salem. In the next game he gave up only 1 hit to Rocky Mount. "After that," said Tiant, "the fans filled the park every time I pitched, and they didn't call me anything you wouldn't want a little kid to hear." Tiant was likely the best pitcher in the Carolina League that season. He won 14 games, had an ERA of 2.56 ERA, and led the league in complete games (17), strikeouts (207), and shutouts (6). It was, said Tiant, "one hell of a year."[13]

In his autobiography, Tiant also recalled the struggles he faced with racism off the field during the 1963 season:

> Once in Burlington I went into a store to buy a little toy for my boy—a car that ran on batteries. A white customer was in there too, and when he saw me paying he left all his stuff on the counter and walked right out of the store. He wouldn't buy from any place that sold to me. After I paid I went outside and saw him talking to another white person, and I cussed him with every English word I knew.
>
> Another time, in a fancier department store, I was looking at some of the watches and jewelry they had under the locked glass. I pointed to something, asked the woman behind the counter, "Can I please see that?" and she said, "Well, you know that costs a lot, right?" Just because of my color she assumed I couldn't afford it. So I walked out.[14]

Tiant moved up in the Indians' system to AAA Portland (Oregon) in 1964. There, a 15–1 record with a 2.04 ERA earned him a July call-up to Cleveland. That was the beginning of a storied major league career that spanned nineteen seasons and included three all-star appearances. He led the American League in ERA twice and four times won 20 or more games. From 1972 to 1976, for the Boston Red Sox, Tiant won 96 games and was one of the most dominant pitchers in baseball. Tiant's final big-league appearance came in 1982 at age forty-one, but he pitched one more season in Mexico before officially retiring. He didn't stay away from the game, however, and worked as a scout and minor league pitching coach before becoming head baseball coach for the Savannah College of Art and Design for four seasons. Tiant later worked as a Spanish language broadcaster for the Red Sox. He was inducted into the Red Sox Hall of Fame in 1997.

Luis Tiant's roommate in Burlington was outfielder Lee Green. Arrangements had been made for the pair to live with a family in the African American community, as had been done for other Black players

The 1963 Alamance Indians. *Back row, left to right:* unidentified trainer, Tom Gansauer, June Raines, George Pressley, Willard West, Macon Lowe, Arsenio Sotolongo, and manager Pat Colgan. *Middle row:* Orlando Centellas, Jerry Kelly, Ron Durham, Dick Beres, Larry Patterson, Bob Wolenski, and Lee Green. *Front row:* Luis Tiant, John Parker, Barry Levinson, Tony Paddyfoot, Chuck Kovach, Ken Henderson, and a batboy. Collection of the author.

before. If nothing else, that guaranteed the players some security and comfort when not on the field as well as a place for meals. Despite living together for the whole season, Tiant and Lee likely had little in common except for the color of their skin and a desire to succeed as professional baseball players. Green was born in a small town in northern Louisiana, so—unlike Tiant—he knew what to expect from the Jim Crow system and how to live within its confines. He was also college educated, having attended Southern University in Baton Rouge. There he had been teammates with future Hall of Famer Lou Brock and had been a freshman on the team that won the 1959 National Association of Intercollegiate Athletics National Championship. After a standout junior year, Green had received offers from major league clubs, but his mother convinced him of the value of continuing his education. He did graduate a year later with a degree in business and, on the day he did so, signed a contract with the St. Louis Cardinals.[15]

After splitting the 1962 season between Billings, Montana, and Brunswick, Georgia, in the Cardinals' system, Green was selected by the Cleveland Indians in the minor league draft. The Indians assigned him to Burlington but, not long after the season began, sold his contract to the Baltimore Orioles. At the time, the Orioles had no team at the A level, so they worked out a deal for him to remain with Burlington. In late May, however, the Orioles signed an agreement with Portsmouth, Virginia, and they ordered Green to report there. Green protested and told the Orioles he would rather go home than leave Burlington. The Orioles conceded, and Green stayed with the team for the entire season. It proved to be a fortunate outcome for the Burlington Indians, because Green batted .304 and drove in 65 runs.[16]

Lee Green was promoted to Elmira, New York, in 1964. His career then took him to teams including Rochester and Knoxville. He returned to the Carolina League in 1968 and had a standout season for the league champ Hi-Toms. That led to a two-year stint at the AAA level with Omaha in the Kansas City Royals organization. At the end of the 1970 season he was twenty-eight and playing well but decided the salary of a minor leaguer was not enough on which to raise a family. He returned to Burlington (the hometown of his wife), went back to school, earned an MBA, and embarked on a new career with Western Electric.[17]

Second baseman Roy White was a nineteen-year-old from Compton, California. In 1962, he had turned down college scholarship offers to sign a minor league contract with the Yankees that guaranteed a salary of $6,000. White's career began at Class D Fort Lauderdale, and a strong showing there led to a promotion to Greensboro for the final month of the season. He was back with the Greensboro Yankees in 1963. White batted .309 for the season and led the league with 117 runs scored, was second in hits with 171, and was fifth with 100 bases on balls. The performance earned him a spot on the Carolina League's postseason all-star team.[18]

Roy White made his major league debut in New York at the end of the 1965 season. By the 1968 season he was a fixture in the middle infield for the Yankees and remained so through the 1970s. White played in fifteen seasons for the Yankees, was a two-time all-star, and twice led the American League in plate appearances and once in runs. He totaled more than 1,800 hits, but his career was not over when he hung up his New York uniform; White had three successful seasons in Japan before retiring in 1982 at age thirty-eight.[19]

White's teammate and fellow all-star was Jim Horsford. Born in Puerto Rico, Horsford signed with the New York Yankees as an eighteen-year-old in 1957. As a two-way player who both pitched and played in the outfield, he was a rarity in the game. When the Yankees—who were infamously slow in integrating their organization—assigned Horsford to Greensboro in 1961, he became the first Black player to represent the city in Organized Baseball. That season, as an outfielder, he hit .289 in 83 games. As a pitcher, he was 1–0 in eight games.

Though mostly forgotten by baseball history, Horsford has a claim to fame in addition to being the first to break the color line in a city. In 1962, split between Augusta in the Sally League and Idaho Falls in the Pioneer League, he batted a combined .298 in 105 games and was 12–8 on the mound. That was the last time until Shohei Ohtani in 2021 that a professional player in any league made 300+ plate appearances and pitched 100+ innings in a season. Horsford was back in Greensboro in 1963, and in 36 mound appearances he posted a 12–4 record with an ERA of 1.41. At the plate he hit .294 in 56 games for the league runner-up.[20]

Unfortunately, Jim Horsford's career did not take him to the major leagues. He spent several more seasons in the Yankees system (including 1964, again with Roy White, at Columbus, Georgia, where the team's uniform infamously featured a Confederate flag on the sleeve) and played at the AAA level with Toledo and Syracuse. In 1968, he decided to go to Mexico, where he won the 1968 pitching Triple Crown with Reynosa (14–6, 202 strikeouts, 1.59 ERA). Horsford pitched in Mexico until retiring in 1972 at age thirty-three.[21]

Though the 1963 Carolina League all-star game did feature some of the most talented Black players in the league, several who went on to later fame were not selected. Playing first base for Rocky Mount was Lee May. The twenty-year-old Birmingham native batted .263 with 16 home runs and 80 RBIs in his third professional season. In 1965, May made a brief Cincinnati debut. Two years later, in his first full big-league season, May was named the *Sporting News* Rookie of the Year. He went on to spend a total of eighteen seasons in the majors with the Reds, Astros, Orioles, and Royals and was a three-time all-star. He retired after the 1982 season with 2,013 hits, 354 of them home runs. Three years later, May earned a World Series ring as hitting coach for the champion Kansas City Royals.[22]

Cleon Jones, one of the top prospects in the Mets system, was promoted to Raleigh a few days after the all-star game. Jones, a native of Mobile, Alabama, had been signed out of Alabama A&M College and began his professional career in Auburn, New York. Success there earned him a ticket to Raleigh. In 49 games for the Capitals, he batted .305 and—despite being with the team for only a third of the season—was fifth in the league with 20 stolen bases. On September 14, the Mets called Jones to New York, where he appeared in 6 games.

Jones spent the 1964 season at AAA Buffalo, but he made it back to New York to stay in 1965. In total he played 1,201 games for the Mets over twelve seasons and finished as one of the team's all-time top stars and fan favorites. In 1969, a season in which he was an all-star, Jones memorably caught the final out as the Mets won the World Series. In 1991, Cleon Jones was the sixth player inducted into the Mets Hall of Fame.[23]

Bernie Smith, who split time between outfield and third base for Raleigh, grew up in a small town along the Mississippi River in Louisiana. In 1960, he enrolled at Southern University in Baton Rouge, where he was teammates with Burlington's Lee Green for two seasons as well as future Hall of Famer Lou Brock for one. Smith left college after two years to pursue a baseball career and was signed by the New York Mets at a tryout in Georgia. In his second professional season, he batted .287 for the Raleigh Capitals and finished with 157 hits, tying for sixth in the league with former college teammate Green.[24]

Smith advanced to the AAA level in the Mets system but was traded to the Milwaukee Brewers in 1970. With that organization, he made it to the big leagues for parts of the 1970 and '71 seasons. After the 1972 season at the AAA level with Evansville, Smith retired from playing. The following season, when the Brewers hired him to skipper their Danville (Illinois) affiliate, Smith became the first Black manager in the Midwest League. He eventually returned home to Louisiana, where he was employed as a juvenile officer with the St. James Parish Sheriff's Office for many years.[25]

One of the greatest Black players in the history of the Carolina League joined the Durham Bulls six weeks into the season. Joe Morgan, a nineteen-year-old second baseman, was promoted from Modesto in the California League after 45 games. Morgan was born in North Texas, but his family was part of the Great Migration of African Americans in the late 1940s. They settled in Oakland, California, and there, growing up in the same area that had produced Frank Robinson and Curt Flood, Morgan became a high school baseball star. Though only 5′7″, his speed and agility caught the attention of major league scouts. On November 1, 1962, Bill Wight, a scout for the expansion Houston Colt .45s, signed him for $500 a month and a $3,000 signing bonus. After spending the spring of

1963 at Houston's instructional camp in Moultrie, Georgia, Morgan was assigned to the Modesto Colts.

Durham's manager in 1963 was former big-league batting champ Billy Goodman. The thirty-seven-year-old native of Concord, North Carolina, held Morgan out of his first game with the team. The pressure would have been great on the teenager—the only Black member of the team—who was playing in the South for the first time. Goodman told Morgan to just watch the game and relax. He finally called on him in the ninth inning to pinch-hit. Morgan credited the manager for his approach and "sensing when he could throw me into the game." Wrote Morgan in his autobiography,

> In my first at-bat in the Carolina League, I hit a game-winning home run. Whatever was being said about me in the stands changed immediately to wild cheering, which gave me goosebumps as I circled the bases. In one swing of the bat, I went from being the only black player on the team, n—— this and n—— that, to being just one good player. That one at-bat created another kind of momentum for me. I wound up having a great year at Durham. I hit .332, had 13 homers in just over 300 at-bats, and was, above all, really popular with the hometown fans. The most satisfying part of the whole season was that in the closing days, I finished second in fan balloting for the team's most popular player.[26]

Despite his success on the field, Morgan's life off the field was not as easy in Durham. "I had no social life of any kind," he said. "The organization arranged for me to live with a black family, the Spauldings, who were most kind and generous to me. I spent time with no one, however. . . . I had no girlfriends, didn't spend time with teammates. The Spauldings suggested I might like to keep company with a young friend of theirs, but I declined. I was there for baseball. It was though I had unconsciously put this wall up around myself, as if anything other than baseball would be just too much."[27]

The wall Morgan had put around himself also prevented him from—at first—seeing Jim Crow racism. On the Bulls first road trip, to Winston-Salem, Morgan had a rude awakening.

> When we got to the motel in Winston-Salem, I started to get off the bus with the rest of the players. The bus driver, the only other black person in the organization, called me back.

> "Where do you think you're going?" he said to me.
>
> I pointed and he just smiled. "Come on back," he said. "We don't stay here, we stay somewhere else."
>
> It was strange. Until that moment, I had somehow tricked myself into believing I was just living in another place. Even though I saw the "colored-only" signs at the ballpark and on the streets every day, I had managed to miss them. It had been like standing in the sun and not noticing it was light out.
>
> We went to a motel in the black section of town. There was no air conditioning; the place was run down and gloomy.[28]

Eventually, Morgan felt overwhelmed by the racial situation. He decided to quit baseball and return home. He told the bus driver of his decision. The driver then told Billy Goodman, who called Morgan aside. Morgan recalled the meeting in his autobiography:

> "Joe," he said, "there are people in this world who think this way but your teammates don't."
>
> I had no counter to that because it struck me as true. In the time I had been with the Bulls, there had been no run-ins, no hostility outward or masked, from the other players I could detect. Only baseball. Billy Goodman, in just a few words, reminded me of a home truth I have since never lost. You don't have to like someone to get along with him, to work together as a team.[29]

The following season, Morgan was sent back to the minor leagues but with a promotion to San Antonio (where he was teammates with Aaron Pointer). There, he was named the Most Valuable Player in the Texas League and earned another late-season promotion to Houston. He remained in the majors for over two decades, during which time he won the National League MVP Award twice as a member of Cincinnati's "Big Red Machine" of the mid-1970s and was an all-star ten times. When he retired from the playing field in 1984, Morgan was considered one of the greatest second basemen in the history of baseball. In 1990, the first year of his eligibility, he was elected to the Baseball Hall of Fame. Not content to rest on his laurels as a player, Morgan remained close to the game with a long broadcasting career.[30]

In his autobiography, Morgan mentioned he was the only Black player on the Bulls' roster. That was true for much of the season, but Walt Williams, also a future major leaguer, played 32 games for the team. Like

Morgan, he was nineteen, was born in Texas, and went to high school in the Bay Area of California. Williams also began the 1963 season with Modesto before being promoted to Durham. He made his debut with Houston in 1964 and spent much of ten seasons in the big leagues, most it with the White Sox and the Yankees. Williams also played two seasons in Japan and two in Mexico before retiring. He later returned to the Carolinas as a minor league manager; he was skipper of the Gastonia Rangers in 1992 and the Charleston RiverDogs in 1993 and 1994.[31]

On August 28, 1963, a week and a half before the Carolina League season ended, an estimated 250,000 civil rights supporters took part in the March on Washington. They gathered in front of the Lincoln Memorial, where they heard Martin Luther King Jr.'s now-iconic "I Have a Dream" speech. On September 15, during the league playoffs, a bombing by white supremacists killed four Black girls attending Sunday school at the Sixteenth Street Baptist Church in Birmingham, Alabama. The nation was outraged, but the tragedy did not end there; in late November, President Kennedy was assassinated in Dallas. Shortly after he was sworn in, President Lyndon Johnson said in an address to Congress, "No memorial oration or eulogy could more eloquently honor President Kennedy's memory than the earliest possible passage of the civil rights bill for which he fought so long. We have talked long enough in this country about equal rights. We have talked for one hundred years or more. It is time now to write the next chapter, and to write it in the books of law."[32]

Chapter 30
AMERICAN LEGION, EPISODE IV

The final part of the American Legion baseball story with regard to integration in the Carolinas again involves Gastonia. The city's Legion team had won North Carolina's Area IV titles in 1962 and 1963, but competition was increasing. New post teams had been formed in the area, which diluted the talent pool. Among them was neighboring Belmont, a town that had once supplied the Gastonia team with some of its best players. In 1964, Gastonia Post 23 drew players only from Ashley (formerly Gastonia) High, two-year-old Hunter Huss High, and Dallas High. A solution for the shortage of talent was to turn to still-segregated Highland High.[1]

Before the season began, Lyle Edwards, the city editor of the *Gastonia Gazette* and a member of the Gastonia American Legion post, attended a Highland High baseball practice at Erwin Park, a recreational facility constructed for the city's African American population. Edwards approached two promising players, Elmore "Moe" Hill and Willie Gillispie, and asked them if they would be interested in playing for Post 23. Five weeks before the Civil Rights Act was finally ratified (and two years before Gaston County schools were fully integrated), the teens agreed.[2]

In July, an article appeared in the *Charlotte Observer* that featured an interview with Hill, Gillispie, and Coach Buzz Peeler. Began sportswriter Emil Parker, "Buzz Peeler will cautiously remind anybody who happens to inquire that Gastonia might not be in the current North Carolina American Legion semifinals if it weren't for the two Negro athletes—the first in North Carolina on an American Legion baseball team." Parker went on to ask the athletes about the difference between playing for all-Black Highland High School and the American Legion team. Said Gillispie, "The change doesn't bother me much. On bad nights, when I go hitless or don't play well, it worries me a little because I'm leaving myself open to abuse from the fans. But they've all been pretty understanding and the players, well, they're all fine fellas—all of them." Hill admitted that a few fans had "yelled things from behind the (centerfield) fence a couple of times. But it doesn't bother me. I sort of expect some of that.

The best thing is to let it go. Anywhere you play baseball, the fans will ride you."[3]

In the article, Willie Gillispie made a statement that any Black professional players in the Carolinas during the previous dozen years would have related to. "One night, on the road, the fans rode me pretty good," he said. "But I just took it and went on playing. . . . The main thing here is to play ball." Added Coach Peeler, "Oh, we had a few people tell us we should not have done it. We even had one coach call us and tell us not to bring them when we played in his park. But we took Gillispie and Hill and won easily."[4]

As to reasons why the two players decided to join the American Legion team, both said it was to make them better baseball players. "I want to play pro baseball if I can," said Hill. "I've talked to a few pro scouts. I think playing Legion baseball will help." Gillispie's response was very similar: "I figure it this way, I would rather play here than in a Negro semi-pro league. This league is better organized and the coaching is a little better. It can help me further my career in baseball."[5]

Fifty years later, in another interview, Hill recalled events of that summer and the support of white teammates. "A heckler was yelling at me in the outfield at Hickory, making all sorts of racial insults, and Roddey Edwards and Clyde Brafford ran after him. Roddey told the guy he'd come see him in the parking lot after the game. And I remember him looking all over the place after the game but he couldn't find the guy." Hill also wondered whether the fact that he played for a good team led to increased heckling. "You know, Gastonia had a lot of Legion success in those days, so if another team was yelling at me, was it because I played for Gastonia or because I was black?"[6]

Though there may have been issues with away fans, there were no problems within the team. "The thing I remember is how the whole team just bonded together," said Assistant Coach Don Saine in 2014. "If somebody from another team or town went against Willie or Elmore, they had to go against the whole team. It was the same if you went against one of our white players." Former teammate Leonard Morgan agreed. "There was never anything to it with the guys on the team," he said. "They were on the team, they were our teammates, they were talented players and that was the end of it."[7]

Hill and Gillispie proved to be vital additions to the Post 23 team in 1964 as it won its third straight area title for first-year head coach Buzz Peeler. Gastonia then advanced to regional play but lost 4–3 to Charlotte Post 9 in a best-of-7 Western North Carolina championship series (Charlotte was the eventual national runner-up). As he had hoped, Moe Hill signed a professional contract with the Baltimore Orioles one month after the American Legion season ended. He went on to a fifteen-year career in the minor leagues (in 1999 he was voted the best player in the history of the Class A Midwest League by *Baseball America* magazine) before serving for many years as a coach for several big-league organizations. In 2010, Hill was inducted into the Gaston County Sports Hall of Fame. Gillispie, who was only fifteen in 1964, played for the Post 23 team two more summers and helped Gastonia win two more Area IV titles. After graduation, he enrolled at Raleigh's Shaw University, where he played baseball and football. Gillispie then served in the military before starting a long career with the VA hospital in Salisbury, North Carolina.[8]

After the recruitment of Black players by Gastonia Post 23 in 1964, other segregated posts in the Carolinas eventually followed suit. One notable player is Baseball Hall of Fame member Jim Rice; from 1968 to 1970 he played for previously all-white American Legion Post 14 in Anderson, South Carolina.[9]

Chapter 31
STADIUM SEATS

In the years after baseball teams in the Carolinas began to desegregate, Jim Crow remained strong. Even if everything looked integrated on the field, one glance at the fans would show that the situation was not the same in the stands. African American fans, often by municipal law, were forced to sit in segregated seats at ballparks. Usually it was in uncovered bleachers on one side, far down the foul line, and possibly in a small section at one end of the grandstand. Details on segregated seating, however, are scarce because little was written about it. Said historian Jim Sumner, "The news wouldn't have been that it [the ballpark] was segregated, it would've been if it were integrated. Separate seating was the way it was." A desegregated ballpark in the Carolinas did, in fact, make the news in New York. In a *Wall Street Journal* article on the changes that were taking place in southern baseball, it was mentioned that Ernie Shore Field in Winston-Salem was not segregated. Apparently, when it opened in 1956, it did not limit where African American fans could sit.[1] That report seems contrary to the memories of Durham's Joe Morgan, however, who played against Winston-Salem in 1963. "The first thing I saw was a section of the right-field grandstand fenced in like a cage, the section reserved for black people," he wrote. "The fans in the right-field stands rose and began cheering me as I walked out on to the turf, perhaps wanting me to feel their support and their warmth. But all I could think of was that they were in a cage."[2]

The issue of segregated stadium seating was not often addressed in the 1950s South. It did not garner the same attention as segregation in schools, at lunch counters, or on buses. There were exceptions, however. Wrote prominent Black sportswriter Wendell Smith in 1953, "They call these segregated seats for us, 'separate but equal.' That's the same story they give us about everything in the South that is operated on a segregated basis. They are separate but certainly not equal. . . . We are glad there is a Negro player in the Carolina League. But we aren't so glad we are going to flock to the ball parks and accept segregation. We will continue to sit home until the situation is changed."[3]

In Virginia, the Norfolk Tars had their first Black players in 1953. The team's ballpark, Myers Field, remained segregated, however. Surmised Jonathan Mayo, a writer for MLB.com (Major League Baseball), "The appearance of black players, though, helped give fans the confidence to demand change." A boycott was arranged with the support of the city's Black-owned newspaper, the *Norfolk Journal and Guide*. Stated the weekly paper, "Norfolk's colored baseball fans have been among the league's most faithful home boosters and they deserve better treatment. . . . They've endured inferior accommodations for many years in silence and it appears that they have finally decided to quit supporting Norfolk where it hurts the most—at the box office."[4]

Fans began attending games in nearby Portsmouth, which did not have a segregated ballpark. The Tars won the league in 1953, but the drop in attendance was noticeable in the team's financial bottom line. After meeting with civic leaders in the Black community in an attempt to regain the lost fans, the Tars were told the only thing that would bring them back was an end to segregated seating. The team, which owned the ballpark, conceded. On April 17, 1954, Cal Jacox, editor of the *Journal and Guide*, wrote about the stadium's new integrated seating: "An overflowing throng of an estimated 8,000 fans experienced the simple act of colored and white fans entering the same gate and . . . sitting together in the same sections."[5]

One of the complications with desegregating stadiums was the ownership of the ballpark. A few teams (such as the aforementioned Norfolk Tars) actually owned their stadiums, but most just rented facilities owned by the city. Regardless of what the team ownership thought about segregated seating, they had to follow municipal rules. Of course, if a team did not want to confront the issue (and possibly alienate white fans or lose advertisers), pointing this out was also an easy excuse.

On April 25, 1956, in Wilson, North Carolina, a group of Black fans—led by Dr. G. K. Butterfield, "Negro member of the Wilson City Board of Commissioners"—were denied seating in the grandstand of Wilson Municipal Stadium for a Wilson Tobs game. This was despite the fact that they had season tickets, which were supposed to have no seating restrictions. The group stated that the only seating offered to them "was a bleacher section accommodating about 50." After meeting with the general manager of the team, the group decided to leave. According to a report on the incident in the *Raleigh News and Observer*, "The stadium has no signs to distinguish white and Negro sections. The grandstand, however, is traditionally reserved for white patrons. Negroes are seated in the bleachers."[6] Said Reverend T. A. Watkins, who was a member of Butterfield's group, "Personally, I think it's mighty bad. A city-owned park, a municipal place for recreation, it should be for all citizens. To see a lawmaker not being able to gain entrance looks peculiar. Seating arrangements should not be on the basis of color or race."[7]

The group did not give up on the issue. They attended a city commissioners meeting on May 10 and asked that segregation in the ballpark be ended. The board refused to do so. On September 13, 1956, Watkins and four others filed suit in US District Court against the city, mayor, and city manager to bring about an end to segregated seating at the stadium. However, Wilson city manager Jack Maynard said "he believed the lessee of the ballpark, in this case the Wilson team, set stadium policy." That complicated the issue, since the Wilson Tobs were owned by the Philadelphia Phillies, a team that was still holding out on integration. The incident made newspapers in a few North Carolina locales, but additional news was never reported. It is unknown whether the suit was dropped; possibly the group decided they did not have financial resources to pursue the issue further at that time.[8]

Rather than having anything to do with the Phillies, it is possible the problem was a local one. At the end of the 1956 season, a closed-door meeting took place between the Phillies and the Wilson team. Stated a newspaper article, "It's been rumored that the Phils want to pull out of Wilson, despite a successful season at the gate, because of the city council's reluctance to have Negro ballplayers performing for the Tobs." (Though the Phillies had not integrated at the major league level, the did have some Black minor league players. Apparently they did not want restrictions on where they could assign them to play.) The article continued, "This has been denied by both the Phillies and the Wilson city council." True or not, it showed that the issue of integration was still a hot topic. (Wilson did have a Black player, Ernest Canada, in 1952 when the town was in the Coastal Plain League. There were no reported issues.)[9]

The following season, the issue of segregated seating made news seventy-five miles west in another Carolina League city. The Durham Bulls had not previously fielded any Black players, but in 1957 they had their first; the parent Detroit Tigers assigned three African Americans to the team. The situation with the segregated ballpark was much the same as it was in Wilson. Durham Athletic Park, built in 1939, was owned by the city of Durham. The city leased it for numerous events, including baseball games played by the all-Black semipro Durham Rams, football games in the fall, and even occasional concerts. As was the standard practice in the Jim Crow South, the facility maintained a policy of segregated seating when leased to a group—such as the Durham Bulls—with a primarily white audience. African American fans were allowed to enter only by a separate entrance in right field and were required to sit in the right-field bleachers and a small part of the right-field grandstand.

Thanks to a Black population that included many successful businesses (including North Carolina Mutual Life Insurance, the largest Black-owned business in the country) and an influential Black-owned newspaper, the *Carolina Times*, the issue of segregated seating came to the forefront. On opening day 1957, a group of African American fans attempted to buy tickets at the ballpark's main gate and sit in the grandstand. They were turned away. A small article on the fifth page of the sports section in Raleigh's *News and Observer* reported on the protest: "A delegation of Negroes refused segregated seating for a Carolina League game . . . [and] announce they will fight for equal seating rights in the municipally-owned ballpark. According to [N. B.] White, a leader in Negro civic affairs here, 'more than 150 Negro citizens' attempted to buy tickets to the game between the Durham Bulls and the Greensboro Patriots. They were told, White said, that they would have to enter the park through a segregated entrance and sit in a segregated section of the stands." According to the article, C. R. Wood, Durham's city recreation director, stated that "the city was in no way connected with seating arrangements for games played here by the professional team. He said that those who are granted admission and those who are denied admission is a question for the team management." Charles Allen, president of the Bulls, claimed he knew nothing about the protest and had no comment.[10]

N. B. White, the organizer of the protest, said, "In view of the fact that the Durham Athletic Park is municipally owned, under no circumstances will we accept segregated seating on account of our race. We are fully aware of our rights already well established in legal action taken in the Greensboro golf case and in others, and assure the people of Durham we will pursue these rights." In the golf case, *Simkins v. City of Greensboro*, the judge ruled a city-owned golf course could not be segregated even though it was leased to a private company. The decision was affirmed by the Fourth Circuit Court of Appeals. As White and others realized, the situation in Durham was similar. The city owned Durham Athletic Park but leased it to Durham Sports Enterprises Inc., the company that operated the Bulls.[11]

The *Carolina Times* challenged the Bulls to combine "a little common sense with a little courage" with regard to desegregation of seating. Essentially saying there was no need for white fans to worry about the issue, the newspaper stated, "If the management of the Durham Bulls had had the foresight to go ahead and remove the jim crow [*sic*] signs from the park, 90 percent of the Negro patrons would have, in the very nature of the case, taken seats with members of their own race, as would have the white patrons."[12]

A week later the *Carolina Times* dedicated an editorial to the issue of stadium seating. It stated, "At Negro football and baseball games played at the Durham Athletic Park, white and Negro patrons have been attending for lo these many years and sitting where they desired without even a semblance of trouble or misunderstanding. Occasionally, by reason of mutual desire, white and Negro friends have sat together and enjoyed the games the same as any other American citizens. It is only when the management of such games are in the hands of white persons do Negroes become offensive and are subjected to insults after paying their money." The editorial went on to say that if a lawsuit were brought in federal court, "the management of the Bulls would not have one leg to stand on." It added that "because such a suit would take time and money and most of all only arouse bitterness on both sides," it was hoped the Bulls would "quietly abandon the policy of segregation which now exists." The editorial concluded with the statement that if the team did not change its policy, it "will never receive the patronage of thousands of Negro citizens who are determined that they will not purchase insults at a baseball game merely because one or two Negroes happen to be playing on the same team with white players."[13]

Surprisingly, no litigation arose from the events in Durham in 1957. It is even unknown when the Durham Bulls finally desegregated seating for their games. Aaron Pointer remembered segregated seating with Salisbury, his team in 1961, but had no recollection of it in Durham, his team the following season. "I don't remember it in Durham at all," he said. "I don't remember ever paying attention to whether it was that way. My feeling is that at that time in 1962, things had changed, and African

Americans could sit anywhere in the stands. But not very many African American fans went to baseball games."[14]

Though the seating protests at Durham Athletic Park were unsuccessful in 1957, they possibly inspired another protest in the city that same year. On June 23, 1957, Reverend Douglas Moore, who had attended Boston University with Martin Luther King Jr., led a small group of young members from his congregation at Asbury Temple United Methodist Church to Royal Ice Cream Parlor. They entered through the back door but proceeded to the section reserved for white patrons and asked to be served. When requested to leave, they refused. The police were called, and Moore and the six protesters with him were arrested and fined. With the help of civil rights attorneys, they immediately appealed to the county superior court but lost after a twenty-four-minute deliberation by the all-white jury. The defendants appealed again and the case was heard in the state supreme court in 1958, but the decision of the lower court was upheld.[15]

The Royal Ice Cream protest did not receive much support at the time. According to the Durham County Library, "It provoked controversy not only in the white community; it created a huge uproar among black citizens, many of whose members viewed the protesters not as freedom fighters but as troublemakers led astray by a radical young minister and an outsider."[16] Regardless, the peaceful sit-in became a favored form of protest in the next few years. The most famous of these took place in nearby Greensboro in 1960. In February of that year, four Black students from North Carolina Agricultural and Technical College sat at the lunch counter of Woolworth's and asked to be served. They were not, though the police were not called. The protesters returned the next day with more supporters. The sit-it would eventually last nearly six months and soon spread to other department stores (including Kress, Walgreens, W. T. Grant, and Rose's) and to other southern cities (including Durham, Winston-Salem, and Charlotte). The result was that the Greensboro Woolworth's and many other department stores across the South dropped the segregated seating at their lunch counters.[17]

Despite being the focus of national attention with regard to civil rights in 1960, Greensboro had still not fielded a Black player on its baseball team. Its ballpark, World War Memorial Stadium, like most others, also remained segregated. Reported the *Greensboro News and Record*, "No one can pinpoint when the segregated seating ended. . . . Maybe it tied in with the first African-American player in a Greensboro uniform, believed to be Jim Horsford in 1961." Though exactly when segregation ended is not known, its memory remained strong for decades. In 2004, Harold Cotton, a fan in Greensboro in the 1950s, recalled ushers directing African American fans to segregated seating after they came through the gate. "If anyone tried to sit anywhere else, they would get kicked out and not be able to be with their friends," said Cotton. "No one wanted that." Ken Free, a Greensboro native who was later a Carolina League ballplayer himself, recalled entering World War Memorial Stadium by the front gate, but he and other African American fans were not allowed to walk in front of the grandstand. Instead, they had to turn right and walk down a corridor that took them to segregated bleachers down the right-field line.[18]

As all other Carolina League teams had Black players before Greensboro, African American fans often identified with them rather than with the home team. "Most of the time we were rooting for opposing teams that had black players," said Ken Free. "We had to be careful if we made too much noise, because the white fans would look over at us and be displeased."[19]

The only times World War Memorial Stadium was not segregated was when the local Black semipro team, the Goshen Red Wings (later called the Greensboro Red Birds), used the facility. Most of the stadium was also desegregated when Jackie Robinson's postseason barnstorming tours came to town because organizers of those events knew most spectators would be African American. Before Robinson's appearance in 1949, a story in the *Greensboro Daily News* pointed out that "a special section of box and reserved seats has been set aside for white spectators."[20]

Charlotte's Clark Griffith Park, owned by the Washington Senators organization, was still segregated in 1962. Tony Oliva wrote in his autobiography,

> There was a section in the ball park where the colored had to sit. It was along the left-field line, between third base and the foul pole, separated from the main grandstands. It was odd to see all the blacks sitting in one place; it made me feel funny inside to see them sitting there alone.
>
> Again and again I'd ask Nestor [teammate Velazquez], "Why does it have to be like that?" I could understand blacks wanting it that way, though. If whites don't want you sitting with them, you'd rather sit with blacks, where you feel more comfortable because you're

A 1960s postcard of Charlotte's Clark Griffith Park. The small covered grandstand beyond third base was the section designated for Black fans. Collection of the author.

> wanted. I don't like to have whites stare at me like I'm something they don't want to have next to them. It's too bad they have those feelings—too bad for whites. They're missing out on getting to know some very nice people.[21]

Also in the South Atlantic League, the city-owned ballpark of the Charleston White Sox was segregated. Recalled Don Buford, who played for the team in 1961,

> Segregated ballparks were everywhere in our travels and Charleston wasn't much different in that sense. They talked about segregation of the ballpark and we [*Buford and the team's two other Black players*] told them we were against it as well. We were so few on the ball club; people didn't say very much because we were pretty good players. So no one got on us or anything like that. My wife and Deac's [*teammate Deacon Jones*] wife, they would sit in the stands behind home plate.

They were light complexioned and no one would bother them. They knew they were the players' wives.[22]

While Charleston fans may have turned a blind eye to small violations of the segregated seating policy in Charleston, it was different in 1962 when the franchise relocated to Savannah. After the 1961 season, the owner of the Charleston club, local attorney Bill Ackerman, announced he was relocating his club due to dismal attendance. Its new home was city-owned Grayson Stadium, which was rented for $1,500. It was located in Daffin Park, which also included a white people–only swimming pool.

Tensions with regard to segregated facilities were already running high when the team—now named the Savannah White Sox—arrived. In July 1960, a group of twenty-three African Americans, led by the Reverend Pickens A. Patterson of Butler Presbyterian Church, had petitioned the city recreation director to desegregate Daffin Park, Grayson Stadium, and a few other white people–only facilities. The matter was passed to the city council, which referred it to the city attorney. When no action was taken, protests were organized. In May 1962, picketers, led by local NAACP head W. W. Law, arrived in front of Grayson Stadium. Their protests would continue for more than two months. With the team already struggling for attendance (owner Ackerman stated he needed an average of 1,000 fans per night to stay afloat financially), the picketers had an effect. By early July, Ackerman was already letting it be known he would move the team again.[23]

In 2014, Deacon Jones spoke about realizing during one game in July that his wife, Virginia, and Don Buford's wife, Alescia, had changed seats, moving from the uncovered outfield seats set aside for Black fans to the grandstand. Jones saw the team's general manager, Tom Fleming, pleading with the women to move back. They refused. Recalled Jones, "They said they weren't going to sit in the sun anymore. Tom was asking them to leave, and he said the team was going to lose its advertisements. That's when I got really angry. We went home, and we discussed it. We talked late into the night." The next day, the two women continued their silent protest and returned to the grandstand. It was likely the final straw for baseball in Savannah in 1962; the team moved to Lynchburg in August. There was no professional baseball in Grayson Stadium for the next five years.[24]

Though there were some protests and attention was occasionally brought to the matter, the actual end of segregated seating was rather

Fans watch the New York Yankees play the Philadelphia Phillies in an exhibition game at Capital City Stadium in Columbia on April 6, 1958. The "Colored" grandstand (with an overflow crowd on the roof) is along the left-field line. Courtesy of *The State* Newspaper Photograph Archive, Richland Library, Columbia, SC.

anticlimactic. In most places it seems to have just faded away slowly and without attention. The Civil Rights Act of 1964 officially made segregated seats illegal, but there is evidence that—at least in some ballparks in the region—a few teams had already given up on enforcing it. Whenever it ended, it is likely that fans continued, at least for a while, to sit in the arrangement to which they had been accustomed. Slowly, after years, Black and white fans commingled, and seating in stadiums finally became a nonissue.

Chapter 32
LEGACY

The most important result of the integration of baseball in the Carolinas was not that some exceptional big-league baseball talents were developed but rather that it opened the door—not just for future baseball players, but for participants in all other sports in the region. Countless athletes—professional and amateur, male and female—have now trod on ground that was broken by the sport of baseball.

During the civil rights movement of the 1950s and '60s, integration of schools was always a controversial issue, much more so than the integration of minor league baseball. When the Supreme Court handed down the *Brown v. Board of Education* ruling in May 1954, it spelled the beginning of the end for segregated schools. The court's proclamation that this should happen "with all deliberate speed," however, was largely ignored. While people in parts of the South may have been slowly coming to accept Black and white professional baseball players sharing a field, the idea of children of different races sharing a classroom was another matter altogether. In North Carolina, the first few Black students enrolled in a previously all-white school in the Charlotte school district in 1957. It was 1963 before South Carolina finally began desegregating its public schools. The spread of integrated schools continued through the 1960s but at a slow pace; public schools in both Carolinas were not considered fully integrated until the 1971–72 school year.[1]

After the first integration efforts, it took several years before the first Black students began to appear on high school athletic teams, and it was not in the sport of baseball. The first public high school in the Carolinas to have an integrated athletic team was Brevard High School in western North Carolina. Located in a county (Transylvania) that was only partially integrated, the high school allowed nine African American students to enroll in 1962. The following fall, the school's football coach invited Black students to try out for the football team. Six made the 1963 team, and one of them, Paul Scruggs, also played basketball for the school the following spring.[2] The fall of 1966 saw the integration of the first high school football team in South Carolina, at Belton-Honea Path High School.[3]

Beginning in 1937, the annual Shrine Bowl game pitted the best high school players from North Carolina against the best from South Carolina. Of course, it was not necessarily all of the best, because the game was limited to white players. In 1965, Jimmie Lee Kirkpatrick, a Black star player at Charlotte's recently integrated Myers Park High School, was denied a place in the Shrine Bowl due to his race. Civil rights attorney Julius Chambers filed a lawsuit, demanding that the Shrine Bowl be canceled. It was not, but US district judge Braxton Craven Jr. ordered the directors of the game to submit a desegregation plan by March 1, 1966. They did so, and the following fall, two Black football players, West Charlotte's Titus Ivory and Tommy Love of Sylva-Webster, were selected for the game. Two years later, South Carolina's Shrine Bowl team selected Black players—DeQuincey Davis and LeRoy Thomas—for the first time. In 1970, two-sport star and future Baseball Hall of Famer Jim Rice represented South Carolina in the game.[4]

When previously all-white colleges and universities begin to integrate, it was, like in high schools, often first in the classroom. It was in sports, however, that integration efforts were more visible to the public and the press. Though football and basketball were the most prominent sports at the collegiate level by the 1960s, it was actually the collegiate sports that drew less attention—such as track, tennis, and soccer—that were the first to integrate in the Carolinas. They were followed by football and basketball, so-called revenue sports because they brought in money for universities. The money involved often led to scholarships being offered, which in turn resulted in recruitment of top athletes. Eventually, schools were willing to look beyond race to bring in the best players.

The first instance of athletic integration at the collegiate level in the region occurred when two Black students at North Carolina State University, Irwin Holmes and Manuel Crockett, competed on the freshman track team. In February 1957, both ran the 600-yard race in an indoor meet against the University of North Carolina in what is now known as Dorton Arena in Raleigh. That made them the first African Americans to participate in an Atlantic Coast Conference–sponsored event. The following year, Holmes joined the North Carolina State tennis team. In his first match, he earned a forfeit victory because his opponent's coach did not want his player to face a Black opponent. In some locations he was not even allowed to compete; the team did not take him to road matches against conference foes Clemson and South Carolina. When Holmes was elected co-captain of the tennis team in 1960, he was included in *Sports Illustrated*'s "Faces in the Crowd" feature for becoming the first African American captain of an ACC team.[5]

Smaller institutions also played a role in the early integration of collegiate teams in the region. In 1963, Asheville's Henry Logan enrolled at Western Carolina College to become the first Black basketball player at a predominantly white college in North Carolina. Two years later, basketball player Gene Littles entered High Point College. A Washington, DC, native, Littles went on to be a three-time National Association of Intercollegiate Athletics All-American and was selected in the National Basketball Association and American Basketball Association professional drafts.[6]

At the University of North Carolina, Edwin Okoroma was the university's first Black student athlete. The native of Nigeria played soccer in 1963 and 1964. In 1964, Willie Cooper played on the freshman basketball team as a walk-on. Two years later, Charlie Scott became the first African American scholarship athlete at the university. Recruited by Coach Dean Smith, he went on to be a two-time All-American and a three-time all-Atlantic Coast selection. Scott also led UNC to consecutive NCAA Final Four appearances in 1968 and 1969, played in the 1968 Olympic Games, and had a long professional career. In football, Ricky Lanier was the first Black scholarship athlete at UNC in 1967. The school's baseball team finally had its first Black member in 1969: Joseph "Mickey" Hickerson from Lenoir, North Carolina. After a standout collegiate career, he was drafted by the Chicago White Sox in the second round of the January 1973 draft. Hickerson's professional career, however, only lasted for 37 games with Appleton, Wisconsin.[7]

In 1964, the football team at Wake Forest University saw its first Black players, Robert Grant, Kenneth Henry, and William Smith. Two years later the school recruited its first Black basketball player, Norwood Todmann of New York City. He was joined in 1967 by Charlie Davis and Gil McGregor. The spring of 1966 saw the first Black student athletes to represent Duke University in competition. Jimmy Dorsey was a member of the track team, and C. B. Claiborne played on the freshman basketball team. Claiborne went on to be the first Black varsity basketball player the following season.[8]

At Duke, baseball was behind other sports in terms of integration. This was primarily due to the fact that no scholarships were offered in the sport, so no recruiting took place. In 1975, Larry Doby Jr., son of the former major league star and first Black player in the American League, arrived at Duke. He chose the school because of its academic reputation and the fact that it offered him an opportunity to play both football and baseball with a partial scholarship. Doby eventually earned All-ACC baseball honors in 1978 and 1979.[9] Interestingly, Doby's baseball coach at Duke was former big-league star Enos Slaughter. The North Carolina native had reportedly been one of the opponents of integration while with the St. Louis Cardinals in 1947. Slaughter disputed this, but he is known for aggressively spiking Jackie Robinson when sliding into second base when his team played the Brooklyn Dodgers. "I never had any problem with him," said Doby of Slaughter in a 2022 interview. "I don't know, maybe his views had changed by that point, but he never treated me with anything but respect."[10]

University integration efforts in South Carolina trailed those of North Carolina by only a few years. In 1969, basketball player Craig Mobley and track team member Wayne Jenkins became Clemson's first African American student athletes. That same year saw the first Black student athletes at the University of South Carolina, The Citadel, and Furman University. Football player Carlton Haywood was recruited to South Carolina from Macon, Georgia. He played on the university's 1969 freshman team and earned a varsity letter in 1971. Casey Manning came to South Carolina in 1969 and played freshman basketball. He was later a member of three NCAA Tournament teams. Jackie Brown entered the university on a baseball scholarship in 1969. He switched to football in the fall of 1970, however, and became the first Black starter for South Carolina in football. At Furman, four years after the school's first Black student enrolled, Rodney Acker joined the 1969 freshman football team. He played four years without ever having a Black teammate. Norman Seabrooks was a member of The Citadel's freshman football team in 1969. He earned first-team All-Southern Conference recognition in 1972 and served as the team co-captain.[11]

In an interview with author Barry Jacobs, UNC basketball star Charlie Scott recalled the aftermath of a 1969 game against archrival Duke in which he led a come-from-behind victory with 40 points. "You want to know what I did after I scored the 40 points?" Scott asked Jacobs. "I was by myself. Who am I going to go out with? I was by myself after I did that. We had great fun in the locker room. After that we walked out of the locker room; everybody went one way, and I went another way. I had to celebrate it myself."[12] Duke's C. B. Claiborne could not attend the 1966 postseason basketball banquet held at Durham's Hope Valley Country Club because the private club was segregated and did not even allow Black guests.[13] Stories such as these were common; early Black athletes were often only with their teammates on the court or field.

With a lack of friends and dating options, early Black collegiate athletes sought camaraderie where they could. Much like Aaron Pointer had done at Livingstone College in Salisbury, many turned to nearby historically Black colleges and universities. Charlie Scott and C. B. Claiborne both spent free time at Durham's North Carolina Central College; Claiborne reportedly even had his own meal card at the school.[14] Fortunately for many Black athletes at previously white institutions, there were often nearby HBCUs (there are twelve in North Carolina and eight in South Carolina) where they could temporarily escape some of the pressure of being a racial pioneer and step out of the spotlight.

An important factor to consider when discussing 1950–60s sports was the growing influence of television. For professional baseball as a whole, television had a tremendous effect and was a leading cause for the restructuring of the entire system. It was only major league games that were actually broadcast, however, so for the minor league baseball teams in the region it was not an issue. In 1953, the Atlantic Coast Conference for intercollegiate athletics was created with member schools in North Carolina, South Carolina, Virginia, and Maryland. For the first few years of league competition, no revenue was made from television. That changed in 1957, when the forward-thinking C. D. Chesley Company saw the growing popularity of basketball in the region. It secured the rights to broadcast NCAA Tournament games featuring eventual national champion UNC and convinced three North Carolina stations to carry the games. The broadcasts were so successful that Chesley was able to assure stations that carrying select regular-season games the following season would also be popular; the first was Clemson at UNC on December 7, 1957.[15] From then on, the importance of televised games for fans, schools, and advertisers only increased. In comparison to those early years, the financial landscape of collegiate sports broadcasting today is exponentially different. In 2016, the ACC signed a twenty-year broadcast deal with ESPN. The network pays roughly $240 million annually, meaning each of the fourteen schools receives about $17 million. That is only part of the league's media income, however. For the 2020–21 school year, the ACC set a record with $578 million in total revenue, which resulted in $36.1 million going to each member. That number will likely continue to increase.[16]

In terms of integration, what the increase of televised collegiate games meant was that Black athletes became even more visible and, ultimately, under increased pressure to perform. While it was perhaps easy to ignore newspaper reports of Black players in minor league baseball games, the media spotlight shone bright on players at big universities in the Carolinas beginning in the mid-1960s. If they were fans of collegiate sports, even the staunchest racists would have found it hard to close their eyes to Black players when games were broadcast into their own living rooms.

In the 1950s there were few examples of professional sports other than baseball in the Carolinas, though that eventually changed.[17] Two individual sports that did have professional competitions in the region were auto racing and golf. The first African American to participate in a professional sport other than baseball in the Carolinas is believed to be race car driver Wendell Scott. He began competing in regional races in his native Virginia in the 1950s. In 1961, Scott was granted admission to NASCAR's Grand National Series, and on March 4 of that year he made his debut at Piedmont Interstate Fairgrounds in Spartanburg. That season Scott competed in half the races (23) on the circuit and raced in North Carolina at Hillsborough, Winston-Salem, North Wilkesboro, and Weaverville. In South Carolina, in addition to Spartanburg, he competed in Columbia and Greenville. Scott continued to race through the 1973 season.[18]

A little over a month after Wendell Scott's appearance at a NASCAR race, a Black player appeared on a more established circuit, that of the Professional Golfers' Association. Charlie Sifford, a native of Charlotte, had turned professional in 1947 and played his first PGA tournament in 1954. His golf tournaments took place primarily on the West Coast (where he made his home); his only previous PGA victory had been the Long Beach Open in 1957. In 1961, however, Sifford entered the Greater Greensboro Open. With his participation approved by host Sedgefield County Club and the cosponsoring Greensboro Jaycees, he became the first African American permitted to play in a PGA-sponsored event in the South. Sifford led the tournament after the first round and finished in a tie for fourth. This was an amazing achievement, considering he had never before seen the course at the segregated club, much less practiced on it as most of the white players had. He returned to the Greater Greensboro Open eight more times during his career, though he could not have joined Sedgefield Country Club; it did not allow Black members until 1991.[19]

When interviewed before his first appearance in Greensboro by Jerry Shinn of the *Charlotte Observer*, Sifford stated, "It won't advance me to talk about it—and it won't advance anything else. It's like the schools and all the rest—just something they have to work out for themselves. It's a lot better now than it was. When I first started I had only four or five tournaments I could play." But he recognized the importance of the event, adding, "Sure it means more than the money to me. It should mean more to the whole world."[20]

Tennis was another individual sport that experienced integration during the 1960s, though there were few professional tournaments in the Carolinas. One example, however, was the Charlotte Invitational of 1968. When Arthur Ashe defeated Ron Holmberg in straight sets to win that tournament, the *Charlotte Observer* made no mention of his race. The fact about Ashe that the newspaper found most interesting was that he had taken leave from his service in the military to compete in Charlotte.[21]

After baseball, the next team sport to be played at the professional level in the Carolinas was basketball. The American Basketball Association, an upstart rival of the NBA, was founded in 1967. After two seasons, the unsuccessful Houston Mavericks were sold and relocated to North Carolina. Renamed the Carolina Cougars, the team became a regional franchise. Greensboro Coliseum was the team's primary home, but numerous games were also played in Charlotte and Raleigh.[22]

During the Cougars' first season (1969–70), the team had several Black members. The most notable was point guard and former High Point College star Gene Littles. Littles played six seasons in the ABA and eventually turned to coaching. Among other teams, he led North Carolina A&T at the collegiate level and the Charlotte Hornets in the NBA. Littles's Black teammates during the 1969–70 season for the Carolina Cougars were forward Hank Whitney, who had played at Iowa State, and center George Peeples, who had been a star at the University of Iowa. At shooting guard was Calvin Fowler. He had gained fame as an amateur basketball player and was the captain of the US gold medal team at the 1967 Pan American Games and co-captain of the gold medal team at the 1968 Summer Olympics.[23]

In all fairness, hockey should be mentioned with regard to team sports in the Carolinas in the 1950s and '60s. The Eastern Hockey League was a low-level minor league that had franchises in two Carolina cities: Charlotte (1956–73) and Greensboro (1959–73). The league was officially classified as amateur because it operated under amateur rules, but players were paid salaries. Whether considered amateur or professional, the league likely had no role in the integration process. At the top level of professional hockey, the first Black player, Canadian Willie O'Ree, made his first National Hockey League appearance in 1958. He had two short stints with the Boston Bruins (the second in 1960-61), but it was not until 1974 that another Black player, Mike Marson, appeared in the league. Statistics from the Eastern Hockey League are scarce, but it is very doubtful that a Black player ever appeared for the Charlotte Checkers or Greensboro Generals.[24]

Though the situations differed and all deserve to have their own stories told (and some have been—see for example Barry Jacobs's book *Across the Line: Profiles in Basketball Courage: Tales of the First Black Players in the ACC and SEC*), there are similarities in the experiences of Black baseball players and the racial pioneers in other sports. Beyond the obvious discrimination and harassment, perhaps the most difficult situation to deal with was loneliness and isolation. Whether the only Black golfer in a professional tournament or the only Black player on a collegiate team, athletes were forced to carry the burden of being a de facto representative of their race. It was an incredible weight to put on the shoulders of a person—often a teenager—who just wanted to gain a college education by playing a sport he loved or to make it as a professional athlete. Early Black integrators in other sports were no more equipped to deal with that situation than nineteen-year-old Bill White had been in 1953 or eighteen-year-old Curt Flood in 1956.

Whereas football and basketball have since equaled—or arguably, surpassed—baseball in terms of popularity and essentially became the torchbearers for integration in athletics, those sports and all others in the Carolinas owe a debt to baseball. It was on the diamonds of that sport that the first steps were taken toward racial equality in athletics. It could even be argued that the importance of baseball integration extended well beyond the playing field to other aspects of society. Because of baseball's prominent position in American society, acceptance by fans of Black athletes was immensely significant. They saw that if it was possible for

Black and white players to share the field and achieve success together, then perhaps it was possible for different races to work together in other situations. Overall, the story of integration of baseball in the Carolinas is an important part of a much larger and very complex story about the racial integration of American society.

Acknowledgments

No book is written alone, so I would like to thank all of those who provided me with information, guidance, encouragement, or images. On that list of former players, librarians, historians, and fellow writers are Aaron Pointer, Don Buford, Haven Schmidt, the late Charlie Roach, Lynn Sutter, Ed Di Gangi, David Yount, Ron Green, Marshall Adesman, Anne Keene, the late Robert Gaunt, Larry Doby Jr., Allen Millican, Felton Foushee, Winston Atkins, Kenneth Turan, archivist André Vann at North Carolina Central University, John Horne at the National Baseball Hall of Fame, Jason Tomberlin and Patrick Cullom at Wilson Library at the University of North Carolina at Chapel Hill, Ira King at Duke University's Lilly Library, Virginia Pierce at the South Carolina State Library, Margaret Dunlap at Richland Library in Columbia, and Ehren Foley at the University of South Carolina. The State Archives of North Carolina in Raleigh was also an immense help, as was the microfilm archive of Wilson Library at UNC–Chapel Hill.

This book had its beginnings in the history department at North Carolina Central University. For their guidance, I owe a great deal to three professors in that department, Jerry Gershenhorn, Charles Johnson, and Josh Nadel. I would also like to thank the North Carolina Association of Historians for allowing me to present one of the first chapters at its annual meeting in 2019 and Ernest Dollar at the City of Raleigh Museum for inviting me to speak on the subject long before this book was a reality.

Some of the research for this book was done during the worst of the COVID pandemic. Fortunately, online resources made it possible to continue work. I am so grateful to the North Carolina Digital Heritage Center (digitalnc.org), JSTOR (jstor.org), and newspapers.com.

The website Baseball Reference (baseball-reference.com) is invaluable for statistics. In the not-too-distant past, the only option for researchers to find minor league stats was to track down rare yearly guidebooks. In its digital library, the LA84 Foundation (digital.la84.org) maintains the Sporting News Baseball Player Contract Cards Collection. The more than 172,000 scanned player index cards contain information on contracts signed, hometowns, injuries, and sometimes even race.

A huge thank you goes to Lucas Church at UNC Press for believing in this project, to Julie Bush for her copyediting skills, and to Valerie Burton for pulling it all together. It is an honor to have my book listed among the esteemed titles the press has published over the last century.

Thanks are due most of all to Sue, my wife of more than twenty-five years. I could never have finished this without her support and her ability to keep me on track.

Notes

Author's Note

1. Tygiel, *Baseball's Great Experiment*, 279.

Introduction

1. Wolfe et al., *Code of Laws of South Carolina 1922*, 59.

2. "Jim Crow Laws," Martin Luther King Jr. National Historic Park, National Park Service, last updated April 17, 2018, www.nps.gov/malu/learn/education/jim_crow_laws.htm.

3. Altman with Freedman, *George Altman*, 18.

4. Quoted in J. Robinson, *Baseball Has Done It*, 105.

5. "The History and Function of Minor League Baseball," Minor League Baseball, accessed February 5, 2018, www.milb.com/milb/history/general_history.jsp.

6. Holaday, *Professional Baseball*, 12.

7. "No Average Ball Players," *Negro Digest*, August 1943, 91 (reprinted from *Chicago Daily News*, May 29, 1943); Debono, *Indianapolis ABCs*, 154–60.

8. Bill Plott, "The Southern League of Colored Base Ballists," SABR Research Journals Archive, accessed February 6, 2018, http://research.sabr.org/journals/southern-league.

9. Mitchem, "Wonder Team of the Carolinas," 36.

10. Carroll, "Bubbling Motor of Money," 27; Heaphy. *Negro Leagues*, 78.

11. L. M. Sutter, telephone interview with the author, March 14, 2018.

12. Neither Partlow nor Wright, both pitchers, ever made the major leagues. Both had short stints with Montreal but spent most of the 1946 season—their only one in the Dodgers organization—with Trois-Rivières in the Class C Canadian-American League. They both returned to Negro league teams in 1947.

13. Wendel Smith, "Sports Beat," *Pittsburgh Courier*, February 13, 1954, 14.

14. Adelson, *Brushing Back Jim Crow*, 68.

15. J. Robinson, *I Never Had It Made*, 40.

16. Watkins, "Dave Hoskins."

17. Baseball Reference, accessed November 13, 2019, www.baseball-reference.com; Tiant with Wisnia, *Son of Havana*, 32.

18. Aaron Pointer, telephone interview with the author, April 14, 2020; Tiant with Wisnia, *Son of Havana*, 33.

19. Buhite, *Continental League*, 28.

20. Haven Schmidt, telephone interview with the author, January 16, 2019.

21. Quoted in Kelley, *"I Will Never Forget,"* 5.

22. J. Robinson, *Baseball Has Done It,* 105.

Chapter 1

1. Gene Lawing, "Eastern Final Round Starts Tomorrow," *Charlotte Observer,* August 22, 1934, 27.

2. Membership eligibility in the American Legion has since been expanded to include anyone who served in the US Armed Forces after December 7, 1941. Rumer, *American Legion.*

3. "Founding Value, Long March for Equality," American Legion, June 12, 2020, www.legion.org/news/249252/founding-value-long-march-equality.

4. "History of American Legion Baseball," American Legion, accessed April 12, 2020, www.legion.org/baseball/history. The Carolinas have long been renowned for American Legion baseball. National championships have been won by teams from Gastonia (1935), Spartanburg (1936, 1938), Albemarle (1940), Charlotte (1945), and Charleston (1946). In 2011, Shelby, NC, was designated as the permanent site of the Legion World Series.

5. Diane Broncaccio, "Team Stood Up for Player's Rights," *Greenfield (MA) Recorder,* February 5, 2016, www.recorder.com/Archives/2016/01/MLK-Bunny-GR-011916.

6. Lawing, "Eastern Final Round Starts Tomorrow"; Broncaccio, "Team Stood Up for Player's Rights."

7. Jerry Nason, "Sacrifices Title Chance by Loyalty," *Boston Globe,* August 24, 1934, 18.

8. Nason, "Sacrifices Title Chance by Loyalty"; "Springfield Solons Charge 'Unfairness,' Massachusetts Group Protests to Legion of Discrimination against Negro," *Miami Herald,* August 24, 1934, 9.

9. "Springfield Mayor, Others Protest Gastonia Incident," *Charlotte Observer,* August 24, 1934, 16.

10. Wade Ison, "The Isonglass," *Charlotte News,* August 26, 1934, 15. The Cumberland team that had protested Taliaferro's inclusion in the tournament went on to win in Gastonia and eventually won the national championship in Chicago.

11. Ron Chimelis, "81 Years Later, Gastonia, N.C., and Springfield Shake Hands," MassLive, June 19, 2015, www.masslive.com/news/2015/06/81_years_later_gastonia_nc_and.html.

Chapter 2

1. "Bobby Estalella," Baseball Reference, accessed August 3, 2019, www.baseball-reference.com/register/player.fcgi?id=estale002rob.

2. Jake Wade, "Jake Wade's Sports Parade," *Charlotte Observer,* July 3, 1937, 10.

3. Norman Small, interview with the author, 1995.

4. "Estalella Voted Piedmont's 'Most Valuable,'" *Charlotte Observer*, November 16, 1938, 4.

5. Hulbert, "Bob Estalella," 82.

6. Sandy Grady, "Who Are the All-Time Bees?," *Charlotte News*, June 7, 1951, 23.

7. Box scores from the *Charlotte Observer* between April 7 and May 26, 1951; "Bobby Estalella," Baseball Reference.

8. González Echevarría, *Pride of Havana*, 264.

9. Hulbert, "Bob Estalella," 88.

10. Hulbert, "Bob Estalella," 88.

11. F. Lennox Campello, "Before El Duque There Was Luque and before Robinson There Was Estalella," last revised 2003, http://campello.tripod.com/firstblackinbaseball.html.

12. Hulbert, "Bob Estalella," 88.

13. Bobby Estalella's grandson, also called Bobby Estalella, played major league baseball as a backup catcher for several teams from 1996 to 2004.

Chapter 3

1. *American Legion World Series, 2019 Media Guide and Record Book*, American Legion, 18; accessed September 3, 2020, www.legion.org/baseball/259480/world-series-media-guide; "American Legion Baseball National Champions Since 1926," American Legion, accessed September 3, 2020, www.legion.org/documents/baseball/national_champions.pdf.

2. J. Cullen Fentress, "Down in Front," *California Eagle* (Los Angeles), September 12, 1940, 11.

3. Quoted in Essington, *Integration of the Pacific Coast League*, 47; "Westerners Shatter St. Louis Hopes," *Charlotte News*, August 31, 1940, 3.

4. Fentress, "Down in Front"; E. B. Wesley, "Ritchey and Manuel Make History," *California Eagle*, September 5, 1940, 7.

5. "Westerners Shatter St. Louis Hopes," 3; "Oust Negroes in Little World Series," *Carolina Times* (Durham), September 7, 1940, 1.

6. "Westerners Shatter St. Louis Hopes"; Jake Wade, "Jake Wade's Sports Parade: Two Colored Boys Watch from the Dugout," *Charlotte Observer*, September 4, 1940, 15; John Tudor, "San Diego Tops Albemarle, 6–5," *Raleigh News and Observer*, September 4, 1940, 9.

7. Bill McFayden, "Albemarle Goes Insanely Nuts after Winning World Series," *Charlotte News*, September 9, 1940, 12.

8. "Grateful Gamblers Share Earnings with Kids," *Charlotte News*, September 8, 1940. It would be interesting to know Homer Chaillaux's influence on the situation. In 1939, Chaillaux, the Legion's "national Americanism director," advocated a ten-year curtailment to immigration to "retard the growth of

subversive organizations in this country." One can only surmise that he would have considered those pushing for civil rights as "subversives." He was a staunch anti-communist and died of a heart attack in his forties while delivering a fiery speech. "Chaillaux Asks Ban on Aliens to Halt 'Isms,'" *Edinburg (IN) Daily Courier*, May 23, 1939, 16.

9. Wendell Smith, "Smitty's Sports Spurts," *Pittsburgh Courier*, September 21, 1940, 12; Art Cohn, "Cohn-ing Tower," *Oakland Tribune*, September 27, 1940, 35.

10. "San Diego Wins National American Legion Junior Baseball Title for 1941," *Morning Call* (Allentown, PA), September 8, 1941, 14; Keith D. King, "San Diego Baseball Legend Johnny Ritchey Honored," *San Diego Voice and Viewpoint*, March 2, 2017, https://sdvoice.info/san-diego-baseball-legend-johnny-ritchey-honored; "John Ritchey," Baseball Reference, accessed September 4, 2020, www.baseball-reference.com/players/r/ritchjo01.shtml; Ken Stone, "Padres Grant to Honor San Diego's Version of Jackie Robinson—Johnny Ritchey," *Times of San Diego*, April 15, 2019, 5.

Chapter 4

1. "Carolina Slaughter!," *Brooklyn Daily Eagle*, April 12, 1950, 19; "Diamond Dust–Dodgers in 22–0 Landslide," *New York Daily News*, April 12, 1950, 89.

2. Dick Young, "Rex No Longer a Problem; Brooks Win, 9–8, Anyhow," *New York Daily News*, April 10, 1951, 21C.

3. Barthel, *Baseball Barnstorming*, 240–43; "Jackie Robinson Brings All-Stars to Columbia Soon," *Sumter (SC) Daily Item*, November 2, 1949, 5.

4. Barthel, *Baseball Barnstorming*, 243; James Boyack, "30-Day Tour For Jackie's All-Stars," *Pittsburgh Courier*, October 10, 1953, 14.

Chapter 5

1. "Television," Library of Congress, Moving Image Section, accessed December 8, 2018, https://memory.loc.gov/ammem/awhhtml/awmi10/television.html; Steve Treder, "Dig the 1950s," *Hardball Times* (blog), March 23, 2004, www.fangraphs.com/tht/dig_the_1950s/.

2. Treder, "Dig the 1950s." Major league teams also began to establish radio networks; in 1950, 850 radio stations carried major league games. Surdam, "Television and Minor League Baseball," 65.

3. One of the reasons South Carolina lagged in television is that the FCC placed a freeze on new stations while new channels were created. It was lifted in late 1952, and within a year, stations were on the air in Columbia, Charleston, and Anderson. Patricia G. McNeely, "Television," South Carolina Encyclopedia, June 28, 2016, last updated August 25, 2022, www.scencyclopedia.org/sce/entries/television/; Surdam, "Television and Minor League Baseball," 76.

4. Lester, "History of Air Conditioning."

5. Surdam, "Television and Minor League Baseball," 76.

6. Holaday, *Professional Baseball.*

7. Quoted in Sutter, *New Mexico Baseball,* 78.

8. "Haney To Give Tryout to Negro Players," *Abilene-Reporter-News,* March 12, 1951.

9. Sutter, *New Mexico Baseball,* 79.

10. Sutter, *New Mexico Baseball,* 80.

11. Until recently, Bowman did not receive credit for his groundbreaking season because of confusion over his name. A white player-manager also named Bob Bowman played in the league that season. A former pitcher in the major leagues, Bob Bowman was erroneously credited with the stats of the Black player of the same name. Sutter, *Ball, Bat, and Bitumen,* 94–95.

12. Holaday, *Professional Baseball.*

13. "The 1950 Census of Population," United States Census Bureau, accessed September 19, 2023, www.census.gov/programs-surveys/decennial-census/decade.1950.html.

14. Sumner, *Separating the Men from the Boys,* 18.

15. Michael Hudson, "Breaking a Barrier: Percy Miller Made Baseball History in the Carolina League," *Roanoke Times,* April 12, 1997.

16. Adelson, *Brushing Back Jim Crow,* 41.

17. Sumner, *Separating the Men from the Boys,* 45.

18. "Negro Player Aids Danville," *High Point (NC) Enterprise,* August 11, 1951, 4B; "Leafs Sign First Negro," *Danville (VA) Bee,* August 8, 1951, 5.

19. "Leafs Sign First Negro," *Danville (VA) Bee.*

20. Hudson, "Breaking a Barrier."

21. Hudson, "Breaking a Barrier."

22. "Negro Gets 2-Run Single in Debut," *Danville (VA) Bee,* August 10, 1951.

23. Hudson, "Breaking a Barrier."

24. Quoted in Adelson, *Brushing Back Jim Crow,* 45.

25. Quoted in Adelson, *Brushing Back Jim Crow,* 45.

26. "Miller, Negro Player, Helps Danville Defeat Durham, 5–4," *Norfolk Virginian-Pilot,* August 11, 1951, 15.

27. "Leafs Travel to Durham," *Danville (VA) Bee,* August 16, 1951.

28. "Field Night Programs Set for Monday," *Burlington (NC) Daily Times-News,* August 25, 1951.

29. "1951 Danville Leafs," Baseball Reference, accessed September 9, 2019, www.baseball-reference.com/register/team.cgi?id=54f56a68.

30. "Race Bar in State Baseball Broken," *Carolina Times,* August 15, 1951, 5.

31. "Leafs Release Miller, League's 1st Negro Player," *Danville (VA) Bee,* February 21, 1952.

32. "1952 Danville Leafs," Baseball Reference, accessed September 9, 2019, www.baseball-reference.com/register/team.cgi?id=0336bd31.

Chapter 6

1. "North Carolina: Population of Counties by Decennial Census: 1900 to 1990," United States Census Bureau, accessed September 19, 2023, www.census.gov/programs-surveys/decennial-census/decade.1950.html.

2. "North Carolina: Population of Counties."

3. Holaday, *Professional Baseball*, 64.

4. Browning, *Rocks*, 110.

5. "1951 Western Carolina League," Baseball Reference, accessed December 17, 2022, www.baseball-reference.com/register/league.cgi?id=c38afbec.

6. Holaday, *Professional Baseball*, 71.

7. Browning, *Rocks*, 111–24.

8. "Leo Kantorski," Official Site of Lenoir-Rhyne University Athletics, accessed September 19, 2023, www.lrbears.com/hof.aspx?hof=40.

9. "Leo Kantorksi Pulls Iron Man Stunt with Two Wins; Negroes Make Debut," *Hickory (NC) Daily Record*, August 27, 1951.

10. Browning, *Rocks*, 116.

11. "Rocks Fall to Marion," *Hickory Daily Record*, August 29, 1951.

12. "Negroes Signed in Western Carolina League," *Asheville Citizen-Times*, August 29, 1951, 8.

13. Browning, *Rocks*, 118.

14. Holaday, *Professional Baseball*, 112.

15. "1951 Western Carolina League," *1952 Official Baseball Guide*, 364.

16. David Yount, telephone interview with the author, March 13, 2018.

Chapter 7

1. Moffi and Kronstadt, *Crossing the Line*, 71.

2. Johnson and Wolff, *Encyclopedia*, 416.

3. Gaunt, *We Would Have Played Forever*, 377; Johnson and Wolff, *Encyclopedia*, 416.

4. "The 1950 Census of Population," United States Census Bureau, accessed September 19, 2021, www.census.gov/programs-surveys/decennial-census/decade.1950.html.

5. Charlie Hall, "Local Women Recall Breaking School Color Barrier in 1964," *New Bern (NC) Sun Journal*, May 15, 2018, www.newbernsj.com/news/20180515/local-women-recall-breaking-school-color-barrier-in-1964; Leander Forbes, "Letter: A Life's Lessons on Racism," *New Bern Sun Journal*, July 21, 2016, www.newbernsj.com/opinion/20160721/letter-lifes-lessons-on-racism.

6. Bill Hand, "Baseball: The End of Pro Ball," *New Bern Sun Journal*, November 3, 2012.

7. Charlie Roach, in-person interview with the author, June 8, 1996.

8. Bill Hackney, "Side Line Sorties," *High Point Enterprise*, June 11, 1952, 5B.

9. "First Negro in North Carolina Baseball Hired," *Carolina Times*, June 14, 1952, 1.

10. "1st Negro Plays in Coastal Loop," *Rocky Mount (NC) Evening Telegram*, June 10, 1952, 3B.

11. Johnson and Wolff, *Encyclopedia*, 416.

12. "Bears fall to Eagles, 8–2," *New Bern Sun Journal*, June 11, 1952.

13. Bill Hand, "New Bern Hosted the First Black Player in an All-White League," *New Bern Sun Journal*, November 4, 2012, www.newbernsj.com/article/20121103/Sports/311039813.

14. Gaunt, *We Would Have Played Forever*, 377.

15. Bernard West, "In the Sportlite," *Wilson (NC) Daily Times*, June 12, 1952, 6.

16. "Around the Coastal Plain," *New Bern Sun Journal*, June 13, 1952.

17. Roach interview with the author.

18. "The 1950 Census of Population," United States Census Bureau, accessed September 18, 2023, www.census.gov/programs-surveys/decennial-census/decade.1950.html.

19. Ralph Berger, "Buck Leonard," Society for American Baseball Research, accessed June 3, 2019, https://sabr.org/bioproj/person/231446fd; Buck with Riley, *Buck Leonard*, 230.

20. Howard Criswell Jr., "Sports Talk," *Rocky Mount Evening Telegram*, June 17, 1952, 2B.

21. "Association Spotlight: Black History Month—Charles England," North Carolina High School Athletic Association, February 8, 2013, www.nchsaa.org/news/2013-2-8/association-spotlight-black-history-month-%E2%80%94-charles-england.

22. Criswell, "Sports Talk," June 17, 1952.

23. Johnson and Wolff, *Encyclopedia*, 416.

24. Criswell, "Sports Talk," June 20, 1952, 2B.

25. Criswell, "Sports Talk," June 20, 1952.

26. Howard Criswell Jr., "Sports Talk," *Rocky Mount Evening Telegram*, June 27, 1952, 2B.

27. Bruce Wehrle, "Charlie England Would Have Loved This," *Lexington (NC) Dispatch*, August 13, 2002, www.the-dispatch.com/news/20020813/charlie-england-would-have-loved-this.

28. Howard Criswell Jr., "Sports Talk," *Rocky Mount Evening Telegram*, June 30, 1952, 2B.

29. "Second Negro Pitcher to Start for Leafs Here Tonight," *Rocky Mount Evening Telegram*, July 1, 1952, 2B.

30. Gaunt, *We Would Have Played Forever*, 378.

31. "Stallings Gives Up Nine Hits as Leafs Lose to Eagles," *Rocky Mount Evening Telegram*, July 2, 1952, 2B.

32. Howard Criswell Jr., "Sports Talk," *Rocky Mount Evening Telegram*, July 3, 1952, 2B.

33. R. D. Armstrong, "News about Negroes," *Rocky Mount Evening Telegram*, July 6, 1952, 14A.

34. Armstrong, "News about Negroes."

35. Howard Criswell Jr., "Sports Talk," *Rocky Mount Evening Telegram*, July 8, 1952, 2B.

36. "1950 Census of Population"; Johnson and Wolff, *Encyclopedia*, 416; Drexel Ball, "Five Players Picked for A&T Hall of Fame," *Carolina Times*, September 11, 1982, 6.

37. Bernard West, "In the Sportlite," *Wilson Daily Times*, July 22, 1952, 6.

38. "Negro Player," *Rocky Mount Evening Telegram*, July 22, 1952, 7; "Leafs and Tobs Meet Here Tonight," *Rocky Mount Evening Telegram*, July 23, 1952, 7.

39. "Wilson Signs Colored Player," *Wilson Daily Times*, July 21, 1952, 6; West, "In the Sportlite," July 22, 1952, 6; Bernard West, "In the Sportlite," *Wilson Daily Times*, July 26, 1952, 6.

40. Gaunt, *We Would Have Played Forever*, 379; West, "In the Sportlite," July 26, 1952; "Ernest Canada," Baseball Reference, accessed July 8, 2019, www.baseball-reference.com/register/player.fcgi?id=canada001ern.

41. "Ernest Canada"; "Canada Funeral," *Greensboro News and Record*, October 14, 1991, www.greensboro.com/guilford-county-obituaries/article_c2f83a09-0e42-52e6-9422-28f70811aeec.html; *Jet*, July 9, 1970, 15; Ball, "Five Players Picked for A&T Hall of Fame," 6.

42. Gaunt, *We Would Have Played Forever*, 379.

43. Gaunt, *We Would Have Played Forever*, 379.

44. Gaunt, *We Would Have Played Forever*, 380.

45. Gaunt, *We Would Have Played Forever*, 380.

46. "Wilson Signs Colored Player," 6.

47. "Georgia State League," Baseball Reference, accessed July 8, 2019, www.baseball-reference.com/bullpen/Georgia_State_League.

48. Gaunt, *We Would Have Played Forever*, 377.

49. Gaunt, *We Would Have Played Forever*, 396.

Chapter 8

1. Ronald Jones, "A Revolution Deferred: Racism in Cuba," University of Chicago, Law School International Immersion Program Papers, No. 9 (2015).

2. "Dolf Luque," Baseball Reference, accessed September 3, 2022, www.baseball-reference.com/players/l/luquedo01.shtml.

3. Peter C. Bjarkman, "Martin Dihigo," Society for American Baseball Research, last revised August 22, 2022, https://sabr.org/bioproj/person/dc4b7b28.

4. Miñoso was officially first, though it could be argued that the aforementioned Bobby Estalella deserved that distinction; "Minnie Miñoso," Baseball Reference, accessed September 18, 2022, www.baseball-reference.com/register/player.fcgi?id=minoso001sat.

5. "Juan Delis," Baseball Reference, accessed September 18, 2022, www.baseball-reference.com/register/player.fcgi?id=delis-001jua.

6. Ted Leavengood, "The Clark Griffith Monument," Seamheads.com, June 30, 2011, https://seamheads.com/blog/author/ted-leavengood/.

7. Thom Loverro, "Larry Doby Never Played for Senators, but His Impact Was Still Felt in Washington," *Washington Times*, January 10, 2019, https://apnews.com/article/2c8bc4c84acd1ee7ecea2fca39d9fbca.

8. Quoted in Tygiel, *Baseball's Great Experiment*, 291.

9. Steve Goldman, "Breaking the Barrier: Integrating the Major Leagues One Team at a Time, 1947–1959," SB Nation, April 11, 2013, www.sbnation.com/mlb/2013/4/11/4190990/jackie-robinson-42-integration-baseball-pumpsie-green.

10. Quoted in McGregor, *Calculus of Color*, 149.

11. "Leafs Get Cubans, Infield First Department to Take Shape," *Danville (VA) Bee*, March 24, 1952, 13.

12. "Morrie Aderholt," Baseball Reference, accessed November 13, 2021, www.baseball-reference.com/register/player.fcgi?id=aderho001mor.

13. "Leafs Get Cubans, Infield First Department to Take Shape."

14. "Leafs Get Cubans, Infield First Department to Take Shape."

15. Quoted in Kirkland, *Eddie Neville*, 149.

16. Moffi and Kronstadt, *Crossing the Line*, 116.

17. "Juan Delis," Baseball Reference.

Chapter 9

1. "1952 Rock Hill Chiefs," Baseball Reference, accessed November 8, 2022, www.baseball-reference.com/register/team.cgi?id=548b5f01.

2. Shoals and Stone, *Muscle*, 247.

3. "Baseball Loop Defies Ban on Negro Player," *Arizona Republic* (Phoenix), August 27, 1952, 22; Mobley's age was erroneously reported as being twenty-two in newspaper articles in August 1952.

4. Shoals and Stone, *Muscle*, 249.

5. Utley, "Bobby Hipps," 37–43.

6. "Chiefs Use Negro Despite Request," *Asheville Citizen-Times*, August 27, 1952, 16; "Rock Hill Plays First Negro In Tri-State History," *Greenwood (SC) Index-Journal*, August 27, 1952, 11.

7. Quoted in Shoals and Stone, *Muscle*, 249.

8. Alex Rivera, "Dixie Fans Cheer Player as Owners Force Withdrawal," *Pittsburgh Courier*, September 6, 1952, 14; Bob Quincy, "Hipps Was Put on Spot, but Rock Hill Smashed Old Rumor," *Charlotte News*, August 28, 1952, 12-B.

9. Rivera, "Dixie Fans Cheer Player as Owners Force Withdrawal"; Quincy, "Hipps Was Put on Spot"; "Baseball Loop Defies Ban on Negro Player."

10. Bob Wilson, "Sport Talk," *Knoxville News-Sentinel*, August 31, 1952, B3. In January 1953 the Giants ended their relationship with Knoxville and moved their interests to the Danville club in the Carolina League.

11. Johnson and Wolff, *Encyclopedia*, 369–426.

Chapter 10

1. "More Than Score of Negroes Play for Dixie Minor Clubs," *Indianapolis Recorder*, May 9, 1953, 11; "First Negro Signs," *Burlington Daily Times-News*, May 27, 1953, 10.

2. Sumner, *Separating the Men from the Boys*, 68.

3. Quoted in Marlett, "Leo Durocher."

4. White, *Uppity*, 21.

5. Corbett, "Bill White."

6. Quoted in White, *Uppity*, 29.

7. "Doesn't Want to Go South!," *Pittsburgh Courier*, March 21, 1953, 6.

8. Aaron with Wheeler, *I Had a Hammer*.

9. White, *Uppity*, 31.

10. White, *Uppity*, 32.

11. "Little Giants Again Bow to Caps," *Danville (VA) Bee*, April 20, 1953, 12.

12. Quoted in Michael Hudson, "Breaking a Barrier: Percy Miller Made Baseball History in the Carolina League," *Roanoke Times*, April 12, 1997, 9.

13. White, *Uppity*, 35.

14. White, *Uppity*, 39.

15. White, *Uppity*, 35.

16. White, *Uppity*, 35.

17. White, *Uppity*, 36.

18. White, *Uppity*, 37.

19. White, *Uppity*, 37.

20. Quoted in J. Robinson, *Baseball Has Done It*, 144; Hudson, "Breaking a Barrier," 9.

21. "White Holds Lead as Top Leaf Batter," *Danville (VA) Bee*, June 20, 1953, 10.

22. Sumner, *Separating the Men from the Boys*, 45.

23. "Hot Springs Uses Negro Hurler, Forfeits Game," *Burlington Daily Times-News*, May 21, 1953, 11.

24. "Cotton States and Trautman Revoke Hot Springs Ouster," *Sporting News*, April 22, 1953, 17.

25. Peter Morris, "Jim Tugerson," Society for American Baseball Research, accessed April 12, 2021, https://sabr.org/bioproj/person/402e419d.

26. Sumner, *Separating the Men from the Boys*, 54.

27. Quoted in Dolson, *Beating the Bushes*, 104.

28. Corbett, "Bill White."

Chapter 11

1. Brown v. Board of Education of Topeka, 347 US 483 (1954).

2. Dwight Frady, "In Junior Baseball Here Negroes Will Get a Fair Shake—Sudduth," *Gastonia (NC) Gazette*, May 26, 1954, 9.

3. "Two Negroes Are Dropped from Gastonia Team," *Greenwood Index-Journal*, May 27, 1954, 7; "Crash Davis," Baseball Reference, accessed October 15, 2022, www.baseball-reference.com/players/d/daviscr01.shtml. Cherryville is also in Gaston County, but as it had its own Legion post, it used players from Cherryville High School.

4. Frady, "In Junior Baseball," 9; "Negroes Admitted to Legion Workout," *Sumter Daily Item*, May 26, 1954, 1; "Gaston Negroes in Legon Bid," *Charlotte Observer*, May 27, 1954, 35.

5. Dwight Frady, "Pitching No Weakness for Gastonia Juniors," *Charlotte Observer*, May 30, 1954, 60; Dwight Frady, "Early Showing Has Hefty Costner on Inside Track for Catching Job," *Gastonia Gazette*, May 27, 1954, 9.

6. Dwight Frady, "Ten Juniors Dropped as Work Stepped Up," *Gastonia Gazette*, May 27, 1954, 9; "Six Negro Boys Try Out for N.C. Legion Team," *Greenwood Index-Journal*, May 26, 1954, 1; Dwight Frady, "Gastonia Blues Initiate Season Thursday Night," *Gastonia Gazette*, May 31, 1954, 9.

7. "At Presbyterian Assembly, Church Preparing for Racial Fight," *Gastonia Gazette*, May 28, 1954, 1; "Racial Issue Cloud Primary Picture," *Gastonia Gazette*, May 29, 1954, 1; McKinney, *Greater Freedom*, 73.

8. Dwight Frady, "Blues, Greens Squads," *Gastonia Gazette*, June 1, 1954.

9. Richard Morris, "Juniors Debut Here Tonight," *Charlotte Observer*, June 7, 1954, 21.

10. Dwight Frady, "Two Cut as Blues Host to Kings Mt.," *Gastonia Gazette*, June 9, 1954, 9.

11. Sandy Grady, "The Southern Sportsbeat," *Charlotte News*, July 31, 1954, 17.

12. For the white high schools, the student numbers given are from digitized yearbooks available through the Gaston Library: https://gastonlibrary.libguides.com/digital-gaston-county/yearbooks. In 1950, Highland had an enrollment of 399 and Reid had 194 students. Enrollment was increasing slowly, so the 1955 totals are estimated based on those numbers. "High School Principals' Annual Reports, 1947–1950, Gaston County," North Carolina State Department of Education, accessed September 9, 2022, https://digital.ncdcr.gov/Documents/Detail/high-school-principals-annual-reports-1947-1950-gaston-county/1149619.

13. Norm King, "Jimmie Hall," Society for American Baseball Research, accessed September 10, 2022, https://sabr.org/bioproj/person/jimmie-hall/; Kevin Czerwinski, "Stowe Snags Win without a Pitch," Minor League Baseball, May 11, 2007, www.milb.com/news/charlotte-hornets-lefty-hal-stowe-snags-win-without-throwing-pitch-312465420.

14. Richard Walker, "Gaston County's Last Homegrown Negro League Alumnus Dies," *Gastonia Gazette*, December 23, 2017, www.gastongazette.com/sports/20171223/gaston-countys-last-homegrown-negro-league-alumnus-dies.

15. Pollock, *Barnstorming to Heaven*, 280.

16. "Legion Teams Offer Tryouts for Race Youths," *Carolina Times*, June 5, 1954, 8.

17. While Black American Legion posts did sometimes have their own teams in the Carolinas, the situation was far from equal to that of programs for the white teams. There were far fewer Black Legion posts, which limited competition and left them playing sporadically against whatever competition they could find. "Grays Travel," *Raleigh News and Observer*, June 23, 1946, 12; "Leaders Spit on Negroes Playing SC Legion Ball," *Greenville (SC) News*, May 28, 1954, 21.

Chapter 12

1. Wendell Smith, "Sports Beat," *Pittsburgh Courier*, February 13, 1954, 14.

2. "What Price Prejudice," *Carolina Times*, April 17, 1954, 2.

3. "The 1950 Census of Population," United States Census Bureau, accessed September 18, 2023, www.census.gov/programs-surveys/decennial-census/decade.1950.html.

4. Baseball records give Bush's birth date as November 10, 1930; his tombstone, however, lists his birth year as 1927. "1954 Burlington-Graham Pirates," Baseball Reference, accessed May 12, 2022, www.baseball-reference.com/register/team.cgi?id=ceb499a3.

5. Moffi and Kronstadt, *Crossing the Line*, 120.

6. Bill Hunter, "Bur-Gra Pirates Get 19-Year-Old Negro First Baseman," *Burlington Daily Times-News*, April 12, 1954, 2B.

7. Hunter, "Bur-Gra Pirates."

8. Bill Hunter, "Highlightin' Sports," *Burlington Daily Times-News*, April 13, 1954, 2B; Bill Hunter, "Second Negro Joins Bur-Gra as Team Begins Shaping Up," *Burlington Daily Times-News*, April 14, 1954, 10A.

9. "R. C. Stevens," Baseball Reference, accessed May 12, 2018, www.baseball-reference.com/register/player.fcgi?id=steven001r—; "Herb Bush," Baseball Reference, accessed May 12, 2022, www.baseball-reference.com/register/player.fcgi?id=bush—001her.

10. Alan Cohen, "R. C. Stevens," in *Sweet '60: The 1960 Pittsburgh Pirates*, 187.

11. By comparison, white pitcher Ron Necciai was paid $200 a month at Burlington in 1953. Rickey, Branch, "Branch Rickey Papers: Baseball File, 1906–1971; Scouting reports; 1954," Library of Congress, www.loc.gov/item/mss37820007/.

12. "Bush Injured in Carolina League," *Pittsburgh Courier*, May 8, 1954, 6.

13. Cohen, "R. C. Stevens," 187.

14. Cohen, "R. C. Stevens," 187.

15. "Leafs Host to Luckies Following Sweep of Series at Greensboro," *Danville (VA) Bee*, July 29, 1954, 5.

16. Cohen, "R. C. Stevens," 188.

17. "Herb Bush," Baseball Reference; "Bush, Corbet Heading United Fund Activity," *Burlington Daily Times-News*, September 27, 1966, 8.

18. Rickey, Branch, "Branch Rickey Papers: Baseball File, 1906–1971; Scouting reports; 1956," Library of Congress, www.loc.gov/item/mss37820.05308.

19. "R. C. Stevens," Baseball Reference; "R. C. 'Seaboat' Stevens—Class of 1951," Moultrie Ram Round Up: A Celebration of Colquitt County Georgia Black Schools before 1970, accessed October 17, 2018, www.moultrieramroundup.com/images/R.C.Stevens.html.

20. "1954 Danville Leafs," Baseball Reference, accessed October 17, 2018, www.baseball-reference.com/register/team.cgi?id=700c9ddf.

21. Briley, "In the Tradition of Jackie Robinson," 149; "Ozzie Virgil," Baseball Reference, accessed October 17, 2018, www.baseball-reference.com/register/player.fcgi?id=virgil001osv.

22. "1954 Reidsville Luckies," Baseball Reference, accessed October 17, 2018, www.baseball-reference.com/register/team.cgi?id=04ff6ca1.

23. "Luckies Nip Oak Ridge, 7–6," *Reidsville (NC) Review*, April 5, 1954, 5.

24. "Robinson Scheduled to Pitch Tonight," *Reidsville Review*, April 15, 1954, 5.

25. "Fort Bragg Defeats Luckies, 13–10," *Reidsville Review*, April 16, 1954, 5.

26. "Lose Three Games during Week-End," *Reidsville Review*, May 6, 1954, 5.

27. "No Support for the Bulls Baseball Club," *Carolina Times*, April 24, 1954, 2.

28. Burton Folsom, "The Costs of Segregation to the Detroit Tigers," Foundation for Economic Education, December 1, 2003, accessed December 6, 2018, https://fee.org/articles/the-costs-of-segregation-to-the-detroit-tigers/.

29. "No Support for the Bulls Baseball Club," 2.

Chapter 13

1. W. Rollo Wilson, "Philly Clubs Want Us . . . but We Have to be Good!," *Pittsburg Courier*, March 7, 1953, 15.

2. "Scoreboard," *Spartanburg (SC) Herald*, April 22, 1953, 14.

3. Swaine, *Integration of Major League Baseball*, 158.

4. Van Newman, "Reds Sign Negro Shortstop," *Columbia (SC) Record*, March 30, 1954, 3B.

5. Mac McGrew, "Columbia Reds Again to Have Strong Pitching and Defense," *The State* (Columbia, SC), April 5, 1954, 1B.

6. Ralph Gregory, "First Negro Red Apparently Will Be Welcomed Here If He Can Produce," *Columbia Record*, April 14, 1954, 5B; "Reds Use First Negro Pitcher," *Columbia Record*, April 14, 1954, 5B.

7. F. Robinson with Silverman, *My Life Is Baseball*, 32–33; Vernon Butler, "Robinson Continues Heavyweight Hitting," *Sumter Item*, April 20, 1954.

8. In 2021, June 22 was officially declared "Sarah Mae Flemming Day" in South Carolina. H. 4317, South Carolina General Assembly, 124th Session, 2021–22, www.scstatehouse.gov/sess124_2021-2022/bills/4317.htm.

9. "Woman Sues Bus Company for $25,000," *The State*, July 22, 1954, 3A; Chandler Mack, "Before There Was Rosa, There Was Eastover's Sarah Mae Flemming," WLTX News 19, June 21, 2020, www.wltx.com/article/life/people/comet-buses-reserve-seat-remembering-sarahmae-flemming-civilrights-activist-columbia-southcarolina/101-c6c0a0ef-2606-42de-8b48-ef2900f768cb.

10. "Woman Says Rights Violated in Suit against Bus Company," *The State*, August 11, 1954, 1.

11. Flemming v. South Carolina and Electric Gas Co., 224 F.2d 752 (4th Cir. 1955).

12. Jake Penland, "Reds Blank Braves 11–0; Robinson and Stamey Homer," *The State*, July 22, 1954, D1.

13. Quoted in J. Robinson, *Baseball Has Done It*, 160.

14. Robinson did not mention the name of the player to whom White was referring, but he was likely 6′5″ Al Pinkston. He would later play for Columbia in 1956. F. Robinson with Silverman, *My Life Is Baseball*, 17.

15. F. Robinson with Silverman, *My Life Is Baseball*, 17; "Frank Robinson," Baseball Reference, accessed January 17, 2019, www.baseball-reference.com/register/player.fcgi?id=robins001fra; Johnson and Wolff, *Encyclopedia*, 429.

16. "John Jackson," Baseball Reference, accessed January 17, 2019, www.baseball-reference.com/register/player.fcgi?id=jackso009joh; Al Warden, "Chico Terry to Rejoin Reds," *Ogden (UT) Standard-Examiner*, June 4, 1954; "Chico Terry," Baseball Reference, accessed January 17, 2019, www.baseball-reference.com/register/player.fcgi?id=terry-001laz.

17. F. Robinson with Silverman, *My Life Is Baseball*, 55.

18. F. Robinson with Silverman, *My Life Is Baseball*, 58.

19. "Marvin Williams," Baseball Reference, accessed January 18, 2019, www.baseball-reference.com/register/player.fcgi?id=willia009mar.

20. J. Robinson, *Baseball Has Done It*, 161; F. Robinson with Silverman, *My Life Is Baseball*, 17.

21. F. Robinson with Silverman, *My Life Is Baseball*, 59.

22. F. Robinson with Silverman, *My Life Is Baseball*, 59.

23. "Frank Robinson," Baseball Reference; "Marvin Williams," Baseball Reference.

24. "Frank Robinson," Baseball Reference.

25. "Frank Robinson," Baseball Reference; "Marvin Williams," Baseball Reference.

Chapter 14

1. "1954 Charlotte Hornets," Baseball Reference, accessed February 17, 2019, www.baseball-reference.com/register/team.cgi?id=6bac7dde.

2. Dick Pierce, "Charlotte Club Gets Berth in Sally Circuit," *Charlotte Observer*, November 26, 1953, 4B.

3. Bill Lamb, "Pete Appleton," Society for American Baseball Research, accessed February 17, 2019, https://sabr.org/bioproj/person/366da091.

4. Bob Quincy, "Mullins, Paula Hot in Seventh Bee Win," *Charlotte News*, April 1, 1954; Dick Pierce, "Paula Impressive as Bees Defeat Reading," *Charlotte Observer*, April 1, 1954.

5. "Carlos Paula," Baseball Reference, accessed February 19, 2019, www.baseball-reference.com/register/player.fcgi?id=paula-001car.

6. Brunt, "Carlos Paula, the Man Who Integrated the Washington Senators."

7. Santiago, "Jose Nakamura."

8. Franks, *Asian Pacific Americans*, 154.

9. Shelby moved to the Tar Heel League for the 1953 season. "Jose Nakamura," Baseball Reference, accessed February 19, 2019, www.baseball-reference.com/register/player.fcgi?id=nakamu001jir.

10. Adelson, *Brushing Back Jim Crow*, 181; "Al Isreal," Baseball Reference, accessed February 19, 2019, www.baseball-reference.com/register/player.fcgi?id=isreal001elb.

11. "Catawba College Sports Hall of Fame Announces Six New Members," Catawba College, April 3, 2008, https://catawba.edu/about/news/all-news/archives/catawba-college-sports-hall-of-fame-announces-six-/.

12. Herman Helms, "Vet of 36 Seasons, Hogan Has No Notion of Retiring," *Charlotte Observer*, August 8, 1954.

Chapter 15

1. "Ray Adams Cops Bat Crown of MS League," *Kingsport (TN) Times*, August 3, 1954, 7.

2. Shoals and Stone, *Muscle*, 283; "Smokies Sign Shoals and Negro Player," *Asheville Citizen-Times*, July 24, 1954, 8.

3. Shoals and Stone, *Muscle*, 285; "Scores Prevail," *Greenville News*, July 27, 1954, 10.

4. Shoals and Stone, *Muscle*, 285–86.

5. Mal Malette, "Aldo Salvent Affair Made Phones Jangle," *Asheville Citizen-Times*, August 5, 1954, 18.

6. Irwin Cohen, "Major League Baseball's Integration: A Short History," *Detroit Jewish News*, August 3, 2020, https://thejewishnews.com/2020/08/03/major-league-baseballs-integration-a-short-history/.

7. "Hank Greenberg Bans Games Where Negro Players Barred," *Sporting News*, April 8, 1953, 31; "Brooks Lawrence," Baseball Reference, accessed November 19, 2019, www.baseball-reference.com/register/player.fcgi?id=lawren001bro; "Billy Harrell," Baseball Reference, accessed November 19, 2019, www.baseball-reference.com/register/player.fcgi?id=harrel001wil; Joseph Wancho, "Mudcat Grant," Society for American Baseball Research, accessed November 19, 2019, https://sabr.org/bioproj/person/mudcat-grant/.

8. Malette, "Aldo Salvent Affair Made Phones Jangle"; Shoals and Stone, *Muscle*, 285.

9. "Knoxville Backtracks, All Tri-State Clubs to Finish Season, Salvent Not Play," *Greenville News*, August 4, 1954, 11.

10. Malette, "Aldo Salvent Affair Made Phones Jangle."

11. Bob Terrell, "Salvent a Victim of Circumstances," *Asheville Citizen-Times*, August 6, 1954, 8.

12. Johnson and Wolff, *Encyclopedia*, 430.

13. "Spartanburg Plans to Keep Pro Baseball Team In '55," *Greenville News*, August 24, 1954, 8.

14. "Aldo Salvent," Baseball Reference, accessed November 20, 2019, www.baseball-reference.com/register/player.fcgi?id=salven001ald.

Chapter 16

1. Warren Corbett, "Tom Alston," Society for American Baseball Research, accessed July 2, 2019, https://sabr.org/bioproj/person/3c1c76e0.

2. *Ayantee* [1949 yearbook], Agricultural and Technical College of North Carolina, Greensboro, 62; "Black History Month: Tom Alston," *Redbird Rants* (blog), February 13, 2010, https://redbirdrants.com/2010/02/13/black-history-month-tom-alston/.

3. "Tom Alston," Baseball Reference, accessed July 2, 2019, www.baseball-reference.com/players/a/alstoto01.shtml; "Tom Alston," Western Canada Baseball, accessed July 8, 2019, www.attheplate.com/wcbl/profile_alston_tom.html.

4. Scott Pitoniak, "Voice from a Tormented Past," *Rochester (NY) Democrat and Chronicle*, April 7, 1991, 9E.

5. Harry Grayson, "St. Louis Cardinal Recruits Flop, So It's Same Old Cast," *Gastonia Gazette*, March 27, 1956, 9.

6. Corbett, "Tom Alston."

7. Lorraine Key, "When Gussie Busch Bought the Cardinals in 1953, He Asked, 'Where Are Our Negro Ballplayers?,'" *St. Louis Post-Dispatch*, April 13, 2021, www.stltoday.com/sports/baseball/professional/when-gussie-busch-bought-the-cardinals-in-1953-he-asked-where-are-our-negro-ballplayers/article_bb3d28a2-98df-5327-b647-bc9fda8fc8a3.html.

8. Pitoniak, "Voice from a Tormented Past."

9. Corbett, "Tom Alston."

10. Marilyn Green, "St. Louis Cardinals Blast from the Past—Bill Greason," Cardinal Nation, June 15, 2020, https://thecardinalnation.com/st-louis-cardinals-blast-from-the-past-bill-greason/.

Chapter 17

1. Eddie Lopez, "Lewright's Climb Was Not So Easy," *Bakersfield Californian*, March 25, 1949, 27.

2. "George Handy," Baseball Reference, accessed October 19, 2018, www.baseball-reference.com/register/player.fcgi?id=handy-001geo.

3. Bill Hodges, "By Bill Hodges," *High Point Enterprise*, April 17, 1955, 4B.

4. "A Problem in Comparative Linguistics," *High Point Enterprise*, April 22, 1955, 7B.

5. Bill Hodges, "Bron Ayon to Start on Hill for Locals," *High Point Enterprise*, April 22, 1955, 7B.

6. This is based on viewing *High Point Enterprise* sports pages from April through June 1955.

7. Morejon did have a few other Cuban teammates for parts of the season, including Juan Visteur and future big-league coach Tony Pacheco. "Jesus Ayon," Baseball Reference, accessed October 2, 2020, www.baseball-reference.com/register/player.fcgi?id=ayon—001jes.

8. "All-Star Team Is Selected," *Dunn (NC) Daily Record*, July 8, 1955, 5.

9. "League Departmental Marks In '55," *Danville (VA) Bee*, October 20, 1955.

10. "Bob Schmidt Is Barely Beaten Out; Hi-Toms' Morejon 'Player of Year,'" *Danville (VA) Bee*, September 7, 1955; "Flood Is Chosen as Most Popular," *High Point Enterprise*, September 5, 1956, 12.

11. Figueredo, *Who's Who in Cuban Baseball*, 175–76.

12. "Danny Morejon," Baseball Reference, accessed October 2, 2020, www.baseball-reference.com/register/player.Fcgi?Id=Morejo001dan; "Cuban Baseball Hall of Fame," Cuba Béisbol, accessed October 4, 2020, https://cubanbeisbol.com/Cuban-Baseball-Hall-of-Fame.

13. "Resolution Approving Naming Baseball Field No. 4 at Tropical Park as 'The Daniel Morejon Field,'" Miami-Dade Legislative Item File Number: 092788, miamidade.gov, December 1, 2009, www.miamidade.gov/govaction/matter.asp?matter=092788.

Chapter 18

1. "Satchel Paige Hurls Tonight for Patriots," *Greensboro Daily News*, August 17, 1955, 5.

2. Marshall Adesman, email correspondence with the author, October 31, 2018.

3. "Trautman Rules Paige Ineligible," *Greensboro Daily News*, August 18, 1955, 5.

4. Ribowsky, *Don't Look Back*, 118.

5. Craig, *Herb Pennock*, 197.

6. "Minor League Heads Discuss Woes in Session at Columbia," *Greensboro Daily News*, August 18, 1955, 5.

7. Adesman correspondence with the author.

8. Mike Holtzclaw, "The Day Satchel Paige Pitched on the Peninsula," *Norfolk (VA) Daily Press*, August 21, 1994.

Chapter 19

1. Simkins v. City of Greensboro, 246 F.2d 425 (4th Cir. 1957); Wolfe v. North Carolina, 364 US 177 (1960).

2. "1955 South Atlantic League Batting Leaders," Baseball Reference, accessed April 2, 2021, www.baseball-reference.com/register/leader.cgi?type=bat&id=03594981.

3. "History of Little League," Little League, accessed April 2, 2021, www.littleleague.org/who-we-are/history/.

4. Ramon Jackson, "Baseball Dreams Deferred: The Story of the Cannon Street Y.M.C.A. All Stars," *Sport in American History* (blog), September 1, 2014, https://ussporthistory.com/2014/09/01/baseball-dreams-deferred-the-story-of-the-cannon-street-y-m-c-a-all-stars-part-two/.

5. Godfrey, *Team Nobody Would Play*, 24.

6. "LL Continues to Be a 'Football,'" *Binghamton (NY) Press and Sun-Bulletin*, August 9, 1955, 23.

7. Quoted in Godfrey, *Team Nobody Would Play*, 26.

8. "Little League Tournament Set," *Raleigh News and Observer*, July 14, 1955, 23.

9. "Lexington Man Urges No Little League Play Here," *Greenville News*, July 25, 1955, 9.

10. "Negro Entry Champ of Little League," *Greenville News*, July 27, 1955, 1.

11. Quoted in Stan Grossfeld, "Justice Delayed," *Boston Globe*, August 20, 2002, E6.

12. "Can't Play," *Raleigh News and Observer*, July 26, 1955, 25; Gene Sapakoff, "Little League's Civil War: In '55 a Black All-Star Team Was Sidelined by a Racial Boycott in South Carolina," *Sports Illustrated*, October 30, 1995, 83,

25–26; Jackson, "Baseball Dreams Deferred"; "Cannon Street Team Can Not Enter Meet," *Sumter Item*, July 28, 1955, 8.

13. Warren Koon, "State's Little League Tourney Race Question Resolved as White Teams Plan to Withdraw—Negro Team May Get Title Recognition," *Charleston Evening Post*, July 7, 1955; "Reigh of Terror Grips Mississippi; Threaten NAACP Head," *Pittsburgh Courier*, August 6, 1955; "Champs Not Champs," *Pittsburgh Courier*, August 6, 1955, 1.

14. "Controversy," *Raleigh News and Observer*, August 8, 1955, 13; Troy Moon, "Pensacola Little League Team's Historic Game Is Subject of New Documentary," *Pensacola News Journal*, May 22, 2018, 1; Albert J. Dunmore, "Little League Champs Overcome Opposition to Reach Title Tourney," *Pittsburgh Courier*, August 27, 1955, 16.

15. Douglas E. Abrams, "The Little League Champions Benched by Jim Crow in 1955: Resistance and Reform after *Brown v. Board of Education*," *Journal of Supreme Court History* 51 (2013), https://scholarship.law.missouri.edu/facpubs/735.

16. "LL Continues to Be a 'Football'"; Sapakoff, "Little League's Civil War"; Bart Wright, "They Were Just a Bunch of Kids Who Wanted to Play Baseball," *Greenville News*, August 17, 2005, 1C.

17. Quoted in Godfrey, *Team Nobody Would Play*, 56.

18. Quoted in Godfrey, *Team Nobody Would Play*, 56.

19. "Meet the African American Members of the Little League Hall of Excellence," Little League, February 6, 2020, www.littleleague.org/news/meet-the-african-american-members-of-the-little-league-hall-of-excellence/.

20. "Jones Resigns Little League Post; Fires Propaganda Charge at Press," *Greenwood Index-Journal*, July 25, 1955, 6.

21. Matt Goyak, one of the original incorporators of Dixie Youth Baseball, served as its president from 1955 until 2005. "Color Barrier Causes S.C. Ban in LL," *New York Daily News*, July 30, 1955, 44; Sapakoff, "Cannon Street All-Stars," 162; Dan Friedell, "Despite a Racist Past, Dixie Youth League Still Dominates Southern Baseball," *Fatherly*, April 26, 2018, www.fatherly.com/play/dixie-league-baseball-history-south/.

22. Gene Sapakoff, "1955 Snub Still Echoes in S.C. Baseball; Segregation Began with Cannon St. All-Stars," *Charleston Post and Courier*, June 2, 2013, 11.

23. Carl Reynolds, "Little League Park Improvements Eyed," *Florence (SC) Morning News*, March 30, 1969, 19.

24. "The Greatest Ever?," *Washington Post*, January 13, 1999, www.washingtonpost.com/archive/sports/1999/01/13/the-greatest-ever/91382648-f143-462a-9aaa-17ea3cd2288a/; Jiggs Powers, "Sports Corn," *Whiteville (NC) News-Reporter*, August 16, 1982, 1.

25. Carey Freeman, "Baseball Team Must Stay Focused," *Tampa Bay Times*, July 27, 2001, 12.

26. "Cannon Street Y," Historical Marker Project, accessed April 2, 2021, https://historicalmarkerproject.com/markers/HM1JGX_back-to-HM1JGX.html; "Little League International Remembers Cannon Street YMCA Little Leaguer Carl Johnson," Little League, March 2, 2015, www.littleleague.org/news/little-league-international-remembers-cannon-street-ymca-little-leaguer-carl-johnson/.

27. Sapakoff, "Cannon Street All-Stars," 162; Travis Hudgons, "Beyond the Field: William 'Buck' Godfrey Inducted into Georgia Athletic Coaches Hall of Fame," *Decatur (GA) Champion* (Decatur, GA), June 4, 2014, 9; Godfrey, *Team Nobody Would Play*.

Chapter 20

1. Day, *Southern Manifesto*, 88–110.

2. Sumner, *Separating the Men from the Boys*, 62; David Dalimonte, "Kinston Has a Rich Tradition in Baseball," The Official Site of the Down East Wood Ducks, accessed February 5, 2018, www.milb.com/down-east.

3. Flood with Carter, *Way It Is*, 37–41.

4. Terry Sloope, "Curt Flood," Society for Americana Baseball Research, accessed June 12, 2019, https://sabr.org/bioproj/person/23a120cb; "Inning 8: A Whole New Ballgame (1960 to 1970)," episode 8 of *Baseball: A Film by Ken Burns*, dir. and prod. Ken Burns, Turner Home Entertainment, 1994.

5. "Inning 8: A Whole New Ballgame."

6. Weiss, *Curt Flood Story*, 33.

7. Flood with Carter, *Way It Is*, 38–39.

8. Weiss, *Curt Flood Story*, 34.

9. "Newcomers to Finch Field Scene," *High Point Enterprise*, June 19, 1955, 5B; "Jack Bossard," Baseball Reference, accessed November 23, 2018, www.baseball-reference.com/register/player.fcgi?id=bossar001bel; "1956 High Point–Thomasville Hi-Toms," Baseball Reference, accessed November 25, 2018, www.baseball-reference.com/register/team.cgi?id=858026b6.

10. Weiss, *Curt Flood Story*, 35; "René Solis," Baseball Reference, accessed November 29, 2018, www.baseball-reference.com/register/player.fcgi?id=solis-001ren; John Cathey, "Pena Not 'Pooped' after Gem," *High Point Enterprise*, April 25, 1956, 3B.

11. Weiss, *Curt Flood Story*, 37.

12. Weiss, *Curt Flood Story*, 37; "1956 High Point–Thomasville Hi-Toms"; Mark Armour, "Woody Rich," Society for American Baseball Research, accessed November 25, 2018, https://sabr.org/bioproj/person/4f306bcc.

13. Flood with Carter, *Way It Is*, 38.

14. "Bert Haas," Baseball Reference, accessed November 28, 2018, www.baseball-reference.com/register/player.fcgi?id=haas—002ber; Weiss, *Curt Flood Story*, 37.

15. Weiss, *Curt Flood Story*, 37.

16. John Cathey, "We Have a Great Team, Say Pennant-Winning Pilot Haas," *High Point Enterprise*, August 31, 1956, 3B; Weiss, *Curt Flood Story*, 38.

17. Weiss, *Curt Flood Story*, 36.

18. Weiss, *Curt Flood Story*, 36.

19. This was determined by reading descriptions of Curt Flood in the *High Point Enterprise* from throughout the 1956 season. "Flood Takes Over CL Batting Lead," *High Point Enterprise*, June 26, 1956, 3B.

20. The *High Point Enterprise* featured advertisements for "Meet the Hi-Toms" on several Saturdays in April and May 1956.

21. Flood with Carter, *Way It Is*, 38.

22. "Flood Is Chosen as Most Popular," *High Point Enterprise*, September 5, 1956, 12; "Curt Flood," Baseball Reference, accessed December 4, 2018, www.baseball-reference.com/players/f/floodcu01.shtml; Weiss, *Curt Flood Story*, 38.

23. Kenneth Turan, email correspondence with the author, January 16, 2022. Turan gave transcripts of his interviews to Flood's family, who shared them with Stuart Weiss. Weiss, *Curt Flood Story*, 39.

24. Weiss, *Curt Flood Story*, 39–40.

25. Weiss, *Curt Flood Story*, 40.

26. Haven Schmidt, telephone interview with the author, January 16, 2019.

27. Ward and Burns, *Baseball*, 339.

28. "Leon Wagner Challenges Curt Flood," *High Point Enterprise*, August 12, 1956, 7B.

29. Weiss, *Curt Flood Story*, 40; "They Continue Red Hot Duel Tonight," *High Point Enterprise*, August 28, 1956, 4B; "Flood Is Chosen as Most Popular," 12; "Reds Recall Flood for Rest of Season," *High Point Enterprise*, September 7, 1956, 7B.

30. Schmidt interview with the author. Haven Schmidt played in the minor leagues from 1953 to 1960, with teams including Savannah, Nashville, Albuquerque, and Columbia.

31. Joel Rippel, "Orlando Peña," Society for American Baseball Research, accessed December 12, 2018, https://sabr.org/bioproj/person/35708aec; "Leon Wagner," Baseball Reference, accessed December 12, 2018, www.baseball-reference.com/players/w/wagnele01.shtml; "José Pagán," Baseball Reference, accessed December 12, 2018, www.baseball-reference.com/players/p/paganjo01.shtml; "Willie McCovey," Baseball Reference, accessed December 12, 2018, www.baseball-reference.com/players/m/mccovwi01.shtml.

32. "Jack Bossard," Baseball Reference; "Belasco J. Bossard," Official Website of the Benedict College Tigers, accessed November 23, 2018, https://benedicttigers.com/hof.aspx?hof=79; "Belasco 'Jack' Bossard Memorial Golf Tournament," Psi Iota Chapter, accessed September 21, 2023, www.psiiota.org/the-24th-annual-belasco-jack-bossard-memorial-golf-tournament/.

Chapter 21

1. "Bill Sought to Bar Negroes in Sally," *Charlotte Observer*, January 23, 1957, 22.

2. "Bill Sought to Bar Negroes in Sally."

3. Quoted in Martin, *Benching Jim Crow*, 83.

4. The Columbia club became an affiliate of the Athletics before the 1956 season and changed its name from the Reds to the Gems. "Al Isreal," Baseball Reference, accessed May 2, 2019, www.baseball-reference.com/register/player.fcgi?id=isreal001elb.

5. W. Rollo Wilson, "Philly Clubs Want Us . . . but We Have to Be Good!," *Pittsburg Courier*, March 7, 1953, 15.

6. "Sam Hill," Baseball Reference, accessed August 20, 2019, www.baseball-reference.com/register/player.fcgi?id=hill—005sam; Lester, *Black Baseball's National Showcase*, 321; "Corner Chatter," *Austin (MN) Daily Herald*, May 28, 1957, 10.

Chapter 22

1. Threston, *Integration of Baseball*, 89.

2. Bob Lemke, "Phillies' Pioneer John Kennedy Now Has a Card," *Bob Lemke's Blog*, September 12, 2012, http://boblemke.blogspot.com/2012/09/phillies-pioneer-john-kennedy-now-has.html.

3. Threston, *Integration of Baseball*, 89.

4. Mark Dent, "The Story of John Kennedy, the Phillies' Forgotten First Black Player," Billy Penn at WHYY, February 1, 2017, accessed May 15, 2018, https://billypenn.com/2017/02/01/the-story-of-john-kennedy-the-phillies-forgotten-first-black-player/.

5. "Phils Send Kennedy to Carolina League," *Wilmington (DE) News Journal*, May 6, 1957, 28; "Kennedy Optioned," *Raleigh News and Observer*, May 6, 1957, 16; "Phillies Ship John Kennedy to Farm Club," *Alabama Tribune* (Montgomery), May 31, 1957, 7.

6. A more successful African American on the 1957 Hi-Toms was outfielder Eddie Logan. He won the Carolina League batting title with a .327 average. Logan and Kennedy played together again in 1958 at Tulsa; Bill Hodges, "Hi-Toms Battle W-S; More Help on Way," *High Point Enterprise*, May 7, 1957, 9.

7. "John Kennedy," Baseball Reference, accessed May 15, 2019, www.baseball-reference.com/register/player.fcgi?id=kenned003joh.

8. The Battery Park Hotel was also the scene of an infamous murder in 1936 for which a Black janitor was found guilty of killing of a white female college student. The verdict was protested by the NAACP, but the janitor was fast -tracked through the system and executed five months later. David Krajicek, "NYU Student's Killer Rushed to Execution in Just 5 Months in 1936," *New York Daily News*, July 30, 2017, www.nydailynews.com/news/crime/nyu -student-killer-rushed-execution-5-months-1936-article-1.3368737; Bob Terrell, "Tourists Host Smokies in '60 Opener Tonight," *Asheville Citizen-Times*, April 18, 1960, 14.

9. "John Kennedy," Baseball Reference; Dent, "The Story of John Kennedy, the Phillies' Forgotten First Black Player."

10. By comparison, Chico Fernández batted .262 in 1957 as the Phillies starting shortstop. He eventually played 856 games over eight seasons for four big-league teams. "Chico Fernández," Baseball Reference, accessed October 12, 2020, www.baseball-reference.com/players/f/fernach01.shtml; "1957 Philadelphia Phillies," Baseball Reference, accessed October 13, 2021, www .baseball-reference.com/teams/PHI/1957.shtml.

Chapter 23

1. Quoted in Briley, "In the Tradition of Jackie Robinson," 143–44.

2. "Negro Signed by Tigers," *Detroit Free Press*, August 27, 1953, 39. Agee played with three teams (none in the South) over two seasons in the Tigers' system; "Claude Agee," Baseball Reference, accessed December 2, 2021, www .baseball-reference.com/register/player.fcgi?id=agee—001cla.

3. Johnson and Wolff, *Encyclopedia*, 416.

4. Jack Horner, "Jack Horner's Sports Corner," *Durham Morning Herald*, April 11, 1957, D1.

5. "Skipper and Tonight's Battery," *Durham Morning Herald*, April 17, 1957, B2; "Make Diamond History Here," *Durham Sun*, April 17, 1957, B2.

6. Jack Horner, "Patriots Topple Bull in Opener, 4–1, before 2,993 Fans," *Durham Morning Herald*, April 18, 1957, D1; Jack Horner, "Jack Horner's Sports Corner," *Durham Morning Herald*, April 19, 1957, D1.

7. "Bubba Morton," Baseball Reference, accessed October 13, 2018, www .baseball-reference.com/register/player.fcgi?id=morton001wyc.

8. "The Negro League/Cuban Connection," Western Canada Baseball, accessed October 19, 2019, www.attheplate.com/wcbl/negro.html; "Ted Richardson," Baseball Reference, accessed December 13, 2019, www.baseball -reference.com/register/player.fcgi?id=richar001the.

9. "Ted Richardson," Baseball Reference.

10. "Patriots Topple Bull in Opener, 4–1"; "Wendell Antoine," Baseball Reference, accessed December 13, 2019, www.baseball-reference.com/register /player.fcgi?id=antoin001wen.

11. "Sixth Tan Player Enters Tiger Farm-Den," *Detroit Tribune*, August 20, 1955, 5; "Ozzie Virgil," Baseball Reference, accessed December 11, 2019, www.baseball-reference.com/register/player.fcgi?id=virgil001osv.

12. This was determined by examining game reports in the 1957 *Durham Morning Herald* in which the only terms used for Morton were superlatives, such as "slugging" or "speedy."

13. "Jake Wood," Baseball Reference, accessed January 13, 2020, www.baseball-reference.com/register/player.fcgi?id=wood—001jac; "Bubba Morton," Baseball Reference; Larry Stone, "Former UW Coach Morton Dies at 74," *Seattle Times*, January 18, 2006, http://old.seattletimes.com/html/huskies/2002746128_morton18.html.

Chapter 24

1. Indianapolis was the next step up in the Chicago White Sox farm system; Doug Donehue, "Chasox Squad Not Yet Known," *Charleston News and Courier*, March, 25, 1959, 14; "Deacon Jones," Sporting News Player Contract Cards, LA 84 Foundation: Digital Library Collections, accessed March 23, 2019, https://digital.la84.org/digital/collection/p17103coll3/id/43682/rec/2; "Chasox Training Report," *Charleston News and Courier*, March, 27, 1959, 14.

2. "Ollie Brantley," Sporting News Player Contract Cards, LA 84 Foundation: Digital Library Collections, accessed March 23, 2019, https://digital.la84.org/digital/collection/p17103coll3/id/9034/rec/1; "Ollie Brantley," Baseball Reference, accessed April 1, 2019, www.baseball-reference.com/register/player.fcgi?id=brantl001oll.

3. It is often reported that Bob Boyd was the first African American signed by the White Sox organization, but newspapers of the time state that Hairston was first. Boyd's signing, from the Memphis Red Sox of the Negro American League, was reported August 4. He soon joined Hairston in Colorado Springs. "Sox Farm Signs First Negro Player," *Chicago Sun Times*, August 1, 1950, 9; "White Sox Sign 1st Negro Star," *Lafayette (IN) Journal and Courier*, August 1, 1950, 11; "White Sox Sending Negro to Sky Sox," *Sioux City Journal*, August 1, 1950, 14; Rory Costello, "Sam Hairston," Society for American Baseball Research, accessed April 3, 2019, https://sabr.org/bioproj/person/sam-hairston/.

4. "Ernest Dunbar Johnson," Sporting News Player Contract Cards, LA 84 Foundation: Digital Library Collections, accessed April 9, 2019, https://digital.la84.org/digital/collection/p17103coll3/id/92575/rec/9; "Ernie Johnson," Baseball Reference, accessed April 9, 2019, www.baseball-reference.com/bullpen/Ernie_Johnson_(Negro_Leagues).

5. Bill Glance, "Beeniks Beatnik 'Beat' Generation of Chasox," *Charleston Evening Post*, April 23, 1960, 5A.

6. Warren Koon, "Sibby Out-Guessed Locals," *Charleston Evening Post*, May 15, 1959, 12.

7. On July 6, the Columbus, Georgia, team moved to Gastonia in search of better attendance. Due to the poor condition of the facilities in Gastonia, the league decided to hold the all-star game in Charlotte. "Facilities Terrible; Sally President Blasts Gastonia," *Charleston News and Courier*, July 15, 1959, 13; "'Surprised,' Say All-Star Catcher," *Knoxville News-Sentinel*, July 15, 1959, 29.

8. Bob Quincy, "Sam's Hunch Pays Off: The Bunt Was a Beaut," *Charleston Evening Post*, July 22, 1959, 9; Herman Helms, "Two-Strike Bunt Turning Point," *Charlotte Observer*, July 22, 1959, 16.

9. "Bosox Recall First Negro," *Charlotte Observer*, July 22, 1959, 16.

10. Bob Quincy, "Disagree on Picks of Stars," *Charlotte News*, August 27, 1959, 22. Nate Dickerson, from Pennsylvania, also won a batting title in 1958 with the Olean Oilers in the New York–Penn League. He was drafted into the army after the 1959 season and never returned to professional baseball. Sandy Valdespino played for six teams over seven seasons in the major leagues, often as a reserve outfielder or pinch hitter. Jim Proctor, 15–5 with a 2.19 ERA for Knoxville, earned a September call-up to Detroit. He appeared in 2 games. Proctor played in the minors three more seasons but never made it back to the major leagues.

11. Helms, "Two-Strike Bunt Turning Point."

12. "Sam Hairston," Baseball Reference, accessed April 11, 2019, www.baseball-reference.com/players/h/hairssa01.shtml; "Hairston Wins Most Popular Chasox Award," *Charleston News and Courier*, August 27, 1959, 13; Tony Meyer, "Sox End Season Same Way They Started: With Loss," *Charleston Evening Post*, August 27, 1959, 37; "Charleston Fans Gift Negro Star," *Las Vegas Review and Journal*, August 28, 1959.

13. "Chico Terry," Baseball Reference, accessed April 11, 2019, www.baseball-reference.com/register/player.fcgi?id=terry-001laz.

14. "Ernest Johnson," Negro Leagues Baseball Museum, accessed April 12, 2019, https://nlbemuseum.com/history/players/johnsone.html.

15. Nick Diunte, "Ollie Brantley, Former Negro League Pitcher, Dies at 87," *Forbes*, April 14, 2020, www.forbes.com/sites/nickdiunte/2020/04/14/ollie-brantley-former-negro-league-pitcher-dies-at-87.

16. In its June 1967 issue, *Ebony* magazine noted that Hairston was one of eight full-time Black scouts in the majors; "'Surprised,' Say All-Star Catcher."

17. Phil Hersh, "Jerry Hairston: A Nice Guy Who Has Finished 1st," *Chicago Tribune*, August 3, 1986, 17.

18. John O'Donnell, "Twin Streak Sports Chats," *Quad City Times* (Davenport, IA), May 10, 1958, 10.

19. Richard Walker, "1951 ALWS Player of the Year and a Hall of Fame Trivia Answer," American Legion, September 21, 2020, www.legion.org/baseball/250367/1951-alws-player-year-and-hall-fame-trivia-answer.

20. Mark Armour, "Don Buford," Society for American Baseball Research, accessed April 14, 2019, https://sabr.org/bioproj/person/Don-Buford/.

21. Don Buford, telephone interview with the author, July 21, 2022.

22. Bill Dwyre, "Buford Keeps the Dream Alive," *Los Angeles Times*, January 22, 2013; Mark Fitzhenry, "Buford Where He Wants to Be," *Washington Post*, July 17, 1993.

23. "Deacon Jones," Baseball Reference, accessed March 11, 2020, www.baseball-reference.com/players/j/jonesde02.shtml.

24. "Jim Lynn," Baseball Reference, accessed March 11, 2020, www.baseball-reference.com/register/player.fcgi?id=lynn—003jam.

25. Johnson and Wolff, *Encyclopedia*, 470.

Chapter 25

1. Quoted in Long, *First Class Citizenship*, 75.

2. Gil Rowland, "Jackie Robinson Refuses to Use Negro Waiting Room Here: 'Complete Freedom' Urged," *Greenville News*, October 26, 1959, 3.

3. Jackie Robinson, untitled newspaper column, *Baltimore Afro-American*, November 10, 1959, 8.

4. J. Robinson, untitled newspaper column.

5. Wes Hayden, "Protest Is Talked in Airport Case," *Greenville News*, October 27, 1959, 20; "Jackie Ignores 'Jim Crow,'" *Detroit Free Press*, October 27, 1959, 32; "Jackie Robinson Uses White Waiting Room," *Columbia Record*, October 26, 1959, 7.

6. H. D. Osteen, "Greenville and Spartanburg Counties Are Given Warning," *Sumter Daily Item*, October 27, 1959, 6.

7. "U.S. Judge Denies Airport Injunction," *Greenville News*, July 21, 1959, 1; Bill Priestley, "Jackie Robinson and the Civil Rights Movement in Greenville, South Carolina," unpublished paper for independent study class under Dr. Lloyd Johnson, Campbell University, July 31, 2012, https://billpriestley.files.wordpress.com/2012/08/jackie-robinson-paper.pdf.

8. Henry v. Greenville Airport Commission, 191 F. Supp. 146 (D.S.C. 1961).

9. "Greenville, S.C. Airport Lawsuit Is Now Pending in Federal Court," *Alabama Tribune*, November 6, 1959, 4.

10. Priestley, "Jackie Robinson and the Civil Rights Movement in Greenville, South Carolina"; "CORE Plans March on South Carolina Airport," *Detroit Tribune*, October 31, 1959, 1.

11. Ted Shelton, "Airport Injunction Filed; Timmerman Takes Exception to Ruling," *Greenville News*, February 21, 1961, 1.

Chapter 26

1. The reborn Western Carolina League was originally intended to be affiliated with the Continental League, Branch Rickey's proposed third major league. It was scheduled to begin play in 1961 but folded in 1960 when the existing major leagues decided to allow expansion and admitted some of the

proposed Continental League entries, including Houston and a second New York team. Buhite, *Continental League.*

2. In 1960, Bethea told the *Winston-Salem Journal* his age was twenty-five, but the writer doubted this and called it his "baseball age." On Bethea's official contract card, he listed his birth year as 1931, but the date on his tombstone is 1929. Bob Cole, "Strikeout Artist Bethea Fits into Setting," *Winston-Salem Journal,* August 11, 1960, 13; Jerry Josey, "East All-Stars Edge West in WCL Tilt," *Statesville (NC) Record and Landmark,* August 15, 1960, 5; "William Homer Bethea," Sporting News Player Contract Cards, LA 84 Foundation: Digital Library Collections, accessed June 9, 2020, https://digital.la84.org/digital/collection/p17103coll3/id/17057/rec/7.

3. Sarah Keys v. Carolina Coach Company, 64 MCC 769 (1955).

4. Arsenault, *Freedom Riders,* 78–80.

5. A batting average of .400 has been achieved by a few players in short-season, rookie-level professional baseball. The most notable is Gary Redus, who batted .462 for the Billings Mustangs of the Pioneer League in 1978. Doug Williams, "In '78, Redus Hit .462, a Season for the Ages," ESPN.com, April 16, 2013, www.espn.com/blog/playbook/fandom/post/_/id/20959/in-78-redus-hit-462-season-for-the-ages; "Aaron Pointer," Baseball Reference, accessed June 9, 2020, www.baseball-reference.com/register/player.fcgi?id=pointe001aar; "Pointer Pacing WCL Hit Race," *Statesville Record and Landmark,* June 5, 1961, 9; www.espn.com/blog/playbook/fandom/post/id/20959; Greg Bishop, "Aaron Pointer Is a Man for All Seasons," *Seattle Times,* April 16, 2006, 16.

6. Aaron Pointer, telephone interview with the author, April 14, 2020.

7. Tom Verducci, "The Hard, Historic Roads That Lead to Baseball's Magic Number: .400," *Sports Illustrated,* July 29, 2019.

8. Stephen C. Smith, "The Statesville Owls Meet the Tempe Angels," *FutureAngels.com* (blog), September 28, 2009, https://mlblogsfutureangels.wordpress.com/2009/09/28/the-statesville-owls-meet-the-tempe-angels/.

9. Buhite, *Continental League,* 120.

10. Jim McNally, "1961 Owls Relive Days on the Field," *Statesville Record and Landmark,* June 19, 2011.

11. Brad Pye, "L.A. Angels Farm Clubs Have Several Big League Prospects," *Alabama Tribune,* September 8, 1961, 7; "Dick Simpson," Sporting News Player Contract Cards, LA 84 Foundation: Digital Library Collections, accessed April 17, 2020, https://digital.la84.org/digital/collection/p17103coll3/id/80541/rec/2; "Dick Simpson," Baseball Reference, accessed April 18, 2020, www.baseball-reference.com/register/player.fcgi?id=simpso001ric.

12. "David Best," Sporting News Player Contract Cards, LA 84 Foundation: Digital Library Collections, accessed April 17, 2020, https://digital.la84.org/digital/collection/p17103coll3/id/7173/rec/1.

13. "Robert Lucas," Sporting News Player Contract Cards, LA 84 Foundation: Digital Library Collections, accessed April 17, 2020, https://digital.la84.org/digital/collection/p17103coll3/id/142965/rec/7; "Lucas Named Head Baseball Coach at FAMU," Onnidan.com HBCU Sports, August 2, 2007, https://onnidan.com/07-08/news/august/famu0802.htm.

14. Pye, "L.A. Angels Farm Clubs Have Several Big League Prospects"; "Walter Darton," Sporting News Player Contract Cards, LA 84 Foundation: Digital Library Collections, accessed April 19, 2020, https://digital.la84.org/digital/collection/p17103coll3/id/54008/rec/1.

15. McNally, "1961 Owls Relive Days on the Field."

16. "8 Youthful Angels Potential Vols," *Tennessean* (Nashville), March 3, 1963.

Chapter 27

1. Oliva with Fowler, *Tony O!*, 9.

2. The list of Cambria's Cuban signings include major leaguers Camilo Pascual, Sandy Consuegra, Mike Fornieles, and Zoilo Versalles, among others.

3. Oliva with Fowler, *Tony O!*, 12.

4. Oliva with Fowler, *Tony O!*, 14.

5. Quoted in Oliva with Fowler, *Tony O!*, 19.

6. Oliva with Fowler, *Tony O!*, 17.

7. Quoted in Oliva with Fowler, *Tony O!*, 16.

8. Quoted in Oliva with Fowler, *Tony O!*, 19; Peter Bjarkman, "Tony Oliva," Society for American Baseball Research, accessed May 11, 2020, https://sabr.org/bioproj/person/tony-oliva/; Henninger, *Tony Oliva*, 30.

9. After their playing careers, both Nestor Velazquez and Minnie Mendoza made their permanent homes in Charlotte. Oliva with Fowler, *Tony O!* 32.

10. Bjarkman, "Tony Oliva."

Chapter 28

1. "1963 Spartanburg Phillies," Baseball Reference, accessed June 1, 2020, www.baseball-reference.com/register/team.cgi?id=0627b973.

2. Rhiannon Walker, "The Day the Philadelphia Phillies Left a Hotel That Wouldn't Accommodate Black and Latino Players," Andscape, March 8, 2017, https://theundefeated.com/features/the-day-the-philadelphia-phillies-left-a-hotel-that-wouldnt-accommodate-black-and-latino-players/.

3. Frank Ballenger, "Braves Open Western Carolinas Slate Here," *Greenville News*, April 24, 1963, 10.

4. "Silas Samuel Jamison," Sporting News Player Contract Cards, LA 84 Foundation: Digital Library Collections, accessed June 2, 2020, https://digital.la84.org/digital/collection/p17103coll3/id/102029/rec/20.

5. "Fred A. Mason," Delaware Sports Museum and Hall of Fame: 2004 Inductees, accessed June 3, 2020, www.desports.org/inductees/2004/.

6. "Sally League Announces Hall of Fame Class of 2007," *Ballpark Digest*, June 8, 2007, www.ballparkdigest.com/20070609574/major-league-baseball/news/archives-june-3-9-2007.

Chapter 29

1. John F. Kennedy, "Radio and Television Report to the American People on Civil Rights, June 11, 1963," John F. Kennedy Presidential Library and Museum, www.jfklibrary.org/archives/other-resources/john-f-kennedy-speeches/civil-rights-radio-and-television-report-19630611.

2. J. Robinson, *Baseball Has Done It*, 109.

3. "Carolina League All-Star Test Hopes to Draw 3,000 Today," *Newport News (VA) Daily Press*, July 21, 1963, 3C.

4. John Hanna, "Roadblock Jones Makes a Pitch for Politics," *St. Louis Post-Dispatch*, November 27, 1988, 31.

5. George Vecsey, "Roadblock Jones Wins One," *New York Times*, November 13, 1988, 2H.

6. "Sherman Jones," Baseball Reference, accessed May 12, 2020, www.baseball-reference.com/register/player.fcgi?id=jones-002she.

7. Vecsey, "Roadblock Jones Wins One."

8. Dennis Moore, "Tribute to the Late State Senator Sherman Jones," *Congressional Record* 153, no. 35, March 1, 2007, www.congress.gov/congressional-record/2007/03/01/extensions-of-remarks-section/article/E443-3.

9. "George Pressley," Baseball Reference, accessed May 13, 2020, www.baseball-reference.com/register/player.fcgi?id=pressl001geo; "George Charles Pressley," Sporting News Player Contract Cards, LA 84 Foundation: Digital Library Collections, accessed May 13, 2020, https://digital.la84.org/digital/collection/p17103coll3/id/85779/rec/2.

10. Luis Eleuterio Tiant was the full name of the elder, while the younger is Luis Clemente Tiant. Tiant with Wisnia, *Son of Havana*, 18.

11. In his 2019 autobiography, Tiant mistakenly wrote that he played for Charleston, South Carolina, in 1962. In actuality, he played for Charleston, West Virginia. Tiant also said it was his "introduction to the American South," and he wrote of verbal harassment ("They called us n——s, saying they were going to send us back to Africa or hang us. How we looked like monkeys"). He repeated the same story that so many Black players in the South from that time told: that they had to eat on the bus while white teammates went inside and couldn't stay in the same hotels with teammates. While West Virginia did have Jim Crow laws, the other teams in the Eastern League were located in Massachusetts, New York, and Pennsylvania. Though there was certainly discrimination in these places, it was not at the level of the South, so it is possible he confused memories with ones from Burlington in 1963.

12. Tiant with Wisnia, *Son of Havana*, 31.

13. Tiant with Wisnia, *Son of Havana*, 32; Tiant and Fitzgerald, *El Tiante*, 34.

14. Tiant with Wisnia, *Son of Havana*, 33.

15. Ron Green, telephone interview with the author, September 10, 2021.

16. Bill Hunter, "Lee Green (He's Back) Sparks Tribe over Tides," *Burlington Daily Times-News*, May 24, 1963, 2B.

17. Lee Green batted .306 in 1968 and led the league with 106 runs scored. Johnson and Wolff, *Encyclopedia*, 501.

18. James Lincoln Ray, "Roy White," Society for American Baseball Research, accessed May 13, 2020, https://sabr.org/bioproj/person/roy-white/.

19. "Roy White," Baseball Reference, accessed May 13, 2020, www.baseball-reference.com/register/player.fcgi?id=white-003roy.

20. "James Horsford," Baseball Reference, accessed May 13, 2020, www.baseball-reference.com/register/player.fcgi?id=horsfo001jam; "Shohei Ohtani," Baseball Reference, accessed May 13, 2020, www.baseball-reference.com/players/o/ohtansh01.shtml.

21. "James Horsford," Baseball Reference; J. Gordon Hylton, "Was There Really a Professional Baseball Team Called the Confederate Yankees?," *Marquette University Law School Faculty Blog*, July 11, 2011, https://law.marquette.edu/facultyblog/2011/07/was-there-really-a-professional-baseball-team-called-the-confederate-yankees/.

22. Eric Aron, "Lee May," Society for American Baseball Research, accessed May 14, 2020, https://sabr.org/bioproj/person/lee-may/. Lee May's grandson also has a Carolina connection. A star player for Coastal Carolina University, he was drafted by the Chicago White Sox. As he worked his way up in the system, he played for Kannapolis, Winston-Salem, and Charlotte. May made it to Chicago for a brief stint in 2017. "Jacob May," Baseball Reference, accessed May 14, 2020, www.baseball-reference.com/register/player.fcgi.

23. Fred Worth, "Cleon Jones," Society for American Baseball Research, accessed May 14, 2020, https://sabr.org/bioproj/person/cleon-jones/.

24. "Bernie Smith," Baseball Reference, accessed May 14, 2020, www.baseball-reference.com/register/player.fcgi?id=smith-003cal; Douglas Gladstone, "As Black History Month Is Celebrated, Former Brewer Bernie Smith Is without an MLB Pension," *Sports Daily*, February 26, 2013.

25. Gladstone, "As Black History Month Is Celebrated, Former Brewer Bernie Smith Is without an MLB Pension."

26. Playing only 95 games, Morgan scored 74 runs and was sixth in the league with 91 bases on balls. Walks and runs scored were statistics for which he later became known. Morgan and Falkner, *Joe Morgan*, 50–51.

27. Morgan and Falkner, *Joe Morgan*, 51.

28. Morgan and Falkner, *Joe Morgan*, 51. The bus driver was likely Fred McNeill. He had been in the 1962 team photo.

29. Morgan and Falkner, *Joe Morgan*, 53.

30. Charles F. Faber, "Joe Morgan," Society for American Baseball Research, accessed October 13, 2019, https://sabr.org/bioproj/person/joe-morgan/.

31. "Walt Williams," Baseball Reference, accessed October 13, 2019, www.baseball-reference.com/register/player.fcgi?id=willia009wal.

32. Lyndon B. Johnson, "President Lyndon B. Johnson's Address to a Joint Session of Congress, November 27, 1963," National Archives, www.archives.gov/legislative/features/civil-rights-1964/lbj-address.html.

Chapter 30

1. Richard Walker, "Post 23 Pioneers: Gastonia's Gillispie and Hill Broke N.C. Legion Baseball Color Line 50 Years Ago," *Gastonia Gazette*, August 9, 2014, 5.

2. Walker, "Post 23 Pioneers."

3. Emil Parker, "Main Thing Is Baseball Say Negro Legion Stars," *Charlotte Observer*, July 26, 1964, 1D.

4. Parker, "Main Thing Is Baseball Say Negro Legion Stars."

5. Parker, "Main Thing Is Baseball Say Negro Legion Stars."

6. Walker, "Post 23 Pioneers."

7. Walker, "Post 23 Pioneers."

8. Adam Houston, "Legion Baseball: 50 Years after Breaking Color Barrier, Gillispie Going to Hall of Fame," *Salisbury (NC) Post*, January 20, 2015, www.salisburypost.com/2015/01/20/legion-baseball-50-years-after-breaking-color-barrier-gillespie-going-to-hall-of-fame/; "Moe Hill," Baseball Reference, accessed August 3, 2020, www.baseball-reference.com/register/player.fcgi?id=hill—002elm; Richard Walker, "Elmore Hill Was a Pioneer in Gastonia and a Minor League Baseball Star Who Made It to the Majors as a Hitting Instructor," *Carolinas Sports Hub* (blog), February 5, 2021, https://carolinassportshub.com/elmore-hill-was-a-pioneer-in-gastonia-and-later-a-minor-league-baseball-star-before-making-it-to-the-majors-as-a-hitting-instructor.

9. Earl Gault, "Anderson Has Win Habit," *Greenville News*, June 22, 1969, 36.

Chapter 31

1. Quoted in Jonathan Mayo, "Integration Spread from Field to Stands," milb.com, January 15, 2020, www.milb.com/somerset/news/integration-spread-from-field-to-stands-in-durham-312445042; Paul Lancaster, "Sports Segregation Slips in the South, Though Many Barriers Remain," *Wall Street Journal*, March 18, 1958, 1.

2. Morgan and Falkner, *Joe Morgan*, 52.

3. Wendell Smith, "Wendell Smith's Sport Beat," *Pittsburgh Courier*, July 11, 1953, 16.

4. Mayo, "Integration Spread from Field to Stands."

5. Mayo, "Integration Spread from Field to Stands"; Cal Jacox, "From the Press Box," *Norfolk (VA) Journal and Guide*, April 17, 1954, 18.

6. Dr. G. K. Butterfield was the father of G. K. Butterfield Jr., a civil rights attorney who went on to represent eastern North Carolina for nine terms in the US Congress; Wilson Municipal Stadium is today known as Fleming Stadium. It is home to the North Carolina Baseball Museum. "Wilson Negroes Sue for Ballpark Rights," *Asheville Citizen-Times*, September 14, 1956, 18; "Wilson Negroes Denied Admittance to Grandstand," *Raleigh News and Observer*, April 27, 1956, 1.

7. "Negroes Seek Grandstand Seating," *Rocky Mount Telegram*, April 27, 1956, 11.

8. The Tobs were the only team in the Carolina League owned outright by a major league club. "Wilson Negroes Sue for Ballpark Rights"; "Negroes Seek Grandstand Seating."

9. Bill Hodges, "Hi-Toms Open Playoffs against Scots Here," *High Point Enterprise*, September 4, 1956, 10.

10. "Segregated Seats Refused by 150 at Durham Game," *Raleigh News and Observer*, April 18, 1957, 21.

11. Simkins v. City of Greensboro, 246 F.2d 425 (4th Cir. 1957); Mayo, "Integration Spread from Field to Stands."

12. "Race Players Force Issue of Park Seating," *Carolina Times*, April 20, 1957, 1.

13. "A Costly and Unnecessary Blunder," *Carolina Times*, April 27, 1957, 2.

14. Aaron Pointer, telephone interview with the author, April 14, 2020.

15. Gershenhorn, *Louis Austin*, 149–50.

16. "Royal Ice Cream Sit-In, 1957," Durham County Library, September 18, 2020, https://durhamcountylibrary.org/exhibits/dcrhp/events/royal_ice_cream_sit_in_1957/.

17. Chafe, *Civilities and Civil Rights*, 71–101; Carlton Harrell, "Evans Seeks Negotiations," *Durham Sun*, February 9, 1960, 1. The former Woolworth building in which the Greensboro sit-ins took place now houses the International Civil Rights Center and Museum.

18. Bill Hass, "Segregated Seats: Black Fans Remember Stadium's Special Seats, Robinson," *Greensboro News and Record*, August 24, 2004, www.greensboro.com/sports_professional/baseball/segregated-seats/article_374e5c50-7140-556f-b546-a734ccb68879.html.

19. Hass, "Segregated Seats." Ken Free was one of the first Black players for the Raleigh Capitals in 1961. He later served for many years as commissioner of the Mid-East Athletic Conference, which comprised historically Black institutions. In 1987, he became the first African American appointed to the NCAA Division I Men's Basketball Selection Committee. Steven J. Gaither, "Ken Free, Former MEAC Commish, Passes Away," HBCU Gameday, December 31,

2021, https://hbcugameday.com/2021/12/31/ken-free-former-meac-commish-passes-away/.

20. Hass, "Segregated Seats"; "Robinson, Newcombe, Doby, Campanella Set For Contest," *Greensboro News and Record*, October 14, 1949, 33.

21. Oliva with Fowler, *Tony O!*, 31–32.

22. Don Buford, telephone interview with the author, July 21, 2022.

23. "Negroes Petition for Desegregated Recreational Facilities," *Savannah Tribune*, July 30, 1960, 1; "Savannah Loses Franchise unless Attendance Picks Up," *Macon Telegraph*, July 3, 1962, 6.

24. Quoted in Ben Cates, "The Summer the White Sox Came to Lynchburg," *Lynchburg (VA) News and Advance*, September 13, 2014. Savannah recreational facilities were desegregated in October 1963, nine months ahead of the national Civil Rights Act. Eric Curl, "City Pools One Example of Savannah's Racial Split," *Savannah Morning News*, August 31, 2013.

Chapter 32

1. Michael Graff, "This Picture Signaled an End to Segregation. Why Has So Little Changed?," *The Guardian*, September 17, 2018, www.theguardian.com/us-news/2018/sep/17/dorothy-counts-north-carolina-school-segregation-racism; Adam Harris, "The Persistence of Segregation in South Carolina," *The Atlantic*, September 29, 2020, www.theatlantic.com/education/archive/2020/09/firsts-school-segregation-south-carolina/616492/.

2. *Brevardier* 1964 (yearbook), Brevard County High School, North Carolina, https://archive.org/details/transylvaniacountylibrary; "Football Team Was Integral to Integration," *Transylvania County Library Blog*, September 15, 2014, http://nchistoryroom.blogspot.com/2014/09/transylvania-county-schools-integration.html.

3. "Sports Led the Way: Integration at Belton-Honea Path High School, South Carolina," Museum on Main Street, Smithsonian Institution Traveling Exhibition Services, 2016, https://museumonmainstreet.org/content/sports-led-way-integration-belton-honea-path-high-school-south-carolina.

4. Jalon Hill, "Decades after a Shrine Bowl Snub, Jimmie Lee Kirkpatrick Gets His Recognition," Qcitymetro, October 11, 2021, https://qcitymetro.com/2021/10/11/decades-after-a-shrine-bowl-snub-jimmie-lee-kirkpatrick-gets-his-honor/; Tom Bradbury, "Shrine Bowl Board Oks Negro Players," *Charlotte News*, February 25, 1966, 1; Larry Tarleton, "2 Negro Players Picked on N.C. Shrine Team," *Charlotte Observer*, October, 27, 1966, 32A; "Shrine Bowl Player Sees No Problem," *High Point Enterprise*, December 4, 1968, 27.

5. Matt Shipman, "10 North Carolina Sports Legends," North Carolina State University, September 28, 2018, https://news.ncsu.edu/2018/09/ten-north-carolina-sports-legends/; "Faces in the Crowd," *Sports Illustrated*, April 18, 1960, https://vault.si.com/vault/1960/04/18/faces-in-the-crowd.

6. Shipman, "10 North Carolina Sports Legends."

7. Turner Walston, "Tar Heel Trailblazer: Ricky Lanier," GoHeels.com, February 6, 2014, https://goheels.com/news/2014/2/6/209397974; Pat James, "Tar Heel Trailblazer: Willie Cooper," GoHeels.com, February 15, 2020, https://goheels.com/news/2020/2/15/mens-basketball-tar-heel-trailblazer-willie-cooper.aspx; Turner Walston, "Tar Heel Trailblazer: Charlie Scott," GoHeels.com, February 13, 2014, https://goheels.com/news/2014/2/13/209405060; "Joseph Hickerson," Baseball Reference, accessed December 3, 2022, www.baseball-reference.com/register/player.fcgi?id=hicker001jos.

8. Les Johns, "Nothing Fancy, Just Charlie," Wake Forest Athletics, February 15, 2021, https://godeacs.com/news/2021/2/15/mens-basketball-nothing-fancy-just-charlie; "African-American Firsts at Duke University," Duke University, accessed December 3, 2022, https://spotlight.duke.edu/50years/african-american-firsts-at-duke-university/.

9. Larry Doby Jr., telephone interview with the author, December 3, 2022; "1978 Baseball," Duke University, accessed December 4, 2022, https://static.goduke.com/custompages/stats/baseball/baseball-1978.pdf.

10. Doby interview with the author.

11. "Clemson Athletics Black History: Craig Mobley," Clemson Tigers, February 1, 2021, https://clemsontigers.com/black-history-month-craig-mobley/; "Gamecocks Celebrate First African American Student-Athletes," Gamecocksonline.com, November 18, 2013, https://gamecocksonline.com/news/2013/11/18/gamecocks-celebrate-first-african-american-student-athletes/; Mandrallius Robinson, "Furman's Football Pioneer Still Pushes Integration," *Greenville News*, April 18, 2015, 9; Diane Knich, "Seabrook's Time at Citadel 'Complicated,'" *Charleston Post and Courier*, November 9, 2010, 7.

12. Jacobs, *Across the Line*, 102.

13. Jacobs, *Across the Line*, 64. Duke students picketed Hope Valley Country Club (which also did not allow Jewish or Asian members), and in April 1967, Black students signed an open letter that protested the continued membership of university administrators and professors in the club. President Douglas Knight, athletic director Eddie Cameron, and basketball coach Vic Bubas were members. Knight eventually resigned his club membership. "Negroes Sign Protest Letter," *Duke Chronicle*, April 25, 1967, 1.

14. Greg Veis, "C. B. Claiborne B.S.E. '69, Breaking Down Barriers," *Duke Magazine*, January–February 2006, 36.

15. Daniel Haygood, "Through Parts of Seven Decades, from C. D. Chesley to Raycom Sports, ACC Basketball Has Gained TV Exposure through Partnerships, Distribution, Innovation," *ACC Sports Journal*, Spring 2013, 12–15.

16. Brian Murphey, "Big Ten Signs Huge New TV Deals, Increasing Revenue Gap with ACC," WRAL SportsFan, August 18, 2022, www.wralsportsfan.com/big-ten-signs-huge-new-tv-deals-increasing-revenue-gap-with-acc/20422465/.

17. Professional boxing was popular in the United States, but matches were rarely held in the Carolinas due to the association with illegal gambling. The states have produced prominent fighters, though they pursued their sports elsewhere. World heavyweight champion boxer Floyd Patterson was a native of North Carolina; however, his family moved to New York when he was a child. All of his 64 professional fights between 1952 and 1972 took place outside of his home state. Boxer Jack Wilson, winner of the silver medal at the 1936 Berlin Olympics and a longtime professional, was also born in North Carolina, but his family relocated to California. Most of his fights took place in that state, where he was the first African American boxer to fight a main event at the Hollywood Legion Stadium in 1940. "Floyd Patterson," BoxRec, accessed September 2, 2022, https://boxrec.com/en/box-pro/9038; "Jack Wilson," BoxRec, accessed September 2, 2022, https://boxrec.com/en/box-pro/24429; Jim Sumner, "Sports in the 1920s," NCPedia, January 1, 2004, www.ncpedia.org/sports/golden-age-sports.

18. Tom Jenson, "The Pioneering Career of Wendell Scott," NASCAR Hall of Fame, August 28, 2020, www.nascarhall.com/blog/pioneer-wendell-scott.

19. "Golf's Jackie Robinson, Says Sifford," *Raleigh News and Observer*, April 14, 1961, 19; Jack Horner, "Sports Corner: Sifford Could Take It All," *Durham Herald-Sun*, April 14, 1961, D1; Mary Beth Reed and Sherry Teal, "Historic Structures Survey Report for the Replacement of Bridge No. 402 on SR 1376 (Mecklenburg Road) over Reddicks Creek in Sedgefield, Guilford County, North Carolina," prepared for North Carolina Department of Transportation, August 27, 2021, New South Associates Technical Report 4179, https://files.nc.gov/ncdcr/historic-preservation-office/PDFs/ER_21-2174.pdf.

20. Jerry Shinn, "For Sifford, Between Puffs, 'It Means More Than Money,'" *Charlotte Observer*, April 14, 1961, 45.

21. Ashe competed as an amateur to maintain Davis Cup eligibility. "Ashe Blasts Holmberg for Tennis Title," *Charlotte Observer*, April 22, 1968, 4C.

22. Pluto, *Loose Balls*, 248–49.

23. "1969–70 Carolina Cougars Roster and Stats," Basketball Reference, accessed September 3, 2022, www.basketball-reference.com/teams/CAR/1970.html.

24. "Constitution and Bylaws, Eastern Hockey League, 1961," The EHL: The Eastern Hockey League (1954–1973), Documents, accessed September 3, 2022, www.theehl.com; "Willie O'Ree—Builder Category," Hockey Hall of Fame, June 26, 2018, www.hhof.com/induction_archives/ind18ORee.shtml.

Bibliography

PRIMARY SOURCES

Books

Aaron, Hank, with Lonnie Wheeler. *I Had a Hammer: The Hank Aaron Story.* New York: HarperCollins, 1991.

Altman, George, with Lew Freedman. *George Altman: My Baseball Journey from the Negro Leagues to the Majors and Beyond.* Jefferson, NC: McFarland, 2013.

Flood, Curt, with Richard Carter. *The Way It Is.* New York: Trident Press, 1971.

Godfrey, Buck. *The Team Nobody Would Play.* Pittsburgh: Dorrance, 2008.

Kelley, Brent. *"I Will Never Forget": Interviews with 39 Former Negro League Players.* Jefferson, NC: McFarland, 2003.

Leonard, Buck, with James Riley. *Buck Leonard: The Black Lou Gehrig.* New York: Carroll and Graf, 1995.

Long, Michael G., ed. *First Class Citizenship, The Civil Rights Letters of Jackie Robinson.* New York: Holt, 2008.

Morgan, Joe, and David Falkner. *Joe Morgan: A Life in Baseball.* New York: W. W. Norton, 1993.

1952 Official Baseball Guide. St. Louis: Charles C. Spink and Son, 1952.

Oliva, Tony, with Bob Fowler. *Tony O! The Trials and Triumphs of Tony Oliva.* New York: Hawthorn Books, 1973.

Robinson, Frank, with Al Silverman. *My Life Is Baseball.* Garden City, NY: Doubleday, 1968.

Robinson, Jackie. *Baseball Has Done It.* Philadelphia: J. B. Lippincott, 1964.

———. *I Never Had It Made.* New York: G. P. Putnam's Sons, 1972.

Shoals, Leo "Muscle," and George Stone. *Muscle: A Minor League Legend.* Haverford, PA: Infinity Publishing, 2003.

Tiant, Luis, and Joe Fitzgerald. *El Tiante: The Luis Tiant Story.* New York: Doubleday, 1976.

Tiant, Luis, with Saul Wisnia. *Son of Havana: A Baseball Journey from Cuba to the Big Leagues and Back.* New York: Diversion Books, 2019.

White, Bill. *Uppity: My Untold Story about the Games People Play.* New York: Grand Central Publishing, 2011.

Interviews and Correspondence

Adesman, Marshall. Email correspondence with the author, October 31, 2018. Emails in the author's possession.

Buford, Don. Telephone interview with the author, July 21, 2022. Notes in the author's possession.

Doby, Larry, Jr. Telephone interview with the author, December 3, 2022. Notes in the author's possession.

Green, Ron. Telephone interview with the author, September 10, 2021. Notes in the author's possession.

Pointer, Aaron. Telephone interview with the author, April 14, 2020. Notes in the author's possession.

Roach, Charlie. In-person interview with the author. June 8, 1996. Recording in the author's possession.

Schmidt, Haven. Telephone interview with the author, January 16, 2019. Notes in the author's possession.

Small, Norman. In-person interview with the author. September 1995. Recording donated to the National Baseball Hall of Fame, Cooperstown, NY.

Sutter, L. M. Telephone interview with the author, March 14, 2018. Notes in the author's possession.

Yount, David. Telephone interview with the author, March 13, 2018. Notes in the author's possession.

Newspapers and Magazines

ACC Sports Journal
Alabama Tribune (Montgomery)
Allentown (PA) Morning Call
Arizona Republic (Phoenix)
Asheville Citizen-Times
Austin (MN) Daily Herald
Bakersfield Californian
Baltimore Afro-American
Binghamton (NY) Press and Sun-Bulletin
Boston Globe
Brooklyn Daily Eagle
Burlington (NC) Daily Times-News
California Eagle (Los Angeles)
Carolina Times (Durham)
Charleston Evening Post
Charleston News and Courier
Charleston Post and Courier
Charlotte News
Charlotte Observer
Chicago Sun Times
Chicago Tribune
Columbia (SC) Record
Danville (VA) Bee
Decatur (GA) Champion
Detroit Free Press
Detroit Jewish News
Detroit Tribune
Dunn (NC) Daily Record
Durham Herald-Sun
Durham Morning Herald
Durham Sun
Ebony
Edinburg (IN) Daily Courier
Fayetteville Observer
Florence (SC) Morning News
Forbes
Gastonia (NC) Gazette
Greenfield (MA) Recorder
Greensboro Daily News
Greensboro News and Record
Greenville (SC) News
Greenwood (SC) Index-Journal
Hickory (NC) Daily Record
High Point (NC) Enterprise
Indianapolis Recorder
Jet
Kingsport (TN) Times

Knoxville News-Sentinel
Lafayette (IN) Journal and Courier
Las Vegas Review and Journal
Lexington (NC) Dispatch
Los Angeles Times
Lynchburg (VA) News and Advance
Macon Telegraph
Miami Herald
Negro Digest
New Bern (NC) Sun Journal
Newport News (VA) Daily Press
New York Daily News
New York Times
Norfolk (VA) Daily Press
Norfolk Journal and Guide
Norfolk Virginian-Pilot
Oakland Tribune
Ogden (UT) Standard-Examiner
Pensacola News Journal
Pittsburgh Courier
Quad City Times (Davenport, IA)
Raleigh News and Observer
Reidsville (NC) Review
Roanoke Times
Rochester (NY) Democrat and Chronicle
Rocky Mount (NC) Evening Telegram
Salisbury (NC) Post
San Diego Voice and Viewpoint
Savannah Morning News
Savannah Tribune
Seattle Times
Sioux City Journal
Spartanburg (SC) Herald
Sporting News
Sports Daily
Sports Illustrated
The State (Columbia, SC)
Statesville (NC) Record and Landmark
St. Louis Post-Dispatch
Sumter (SC) Daily Item
Tampa Bay Times
Tennessean (Nashville)
Times of San Diego
Wall Street Journal
Washington Post
Washington Times
Whiteville (NC) News-Reporter
Wilmington (DE) News Journal
Wilson (NC) Daily Times
Winston-Salem Journal

SECONDARY SOURCES

Adelson, Bruce. *Brushing Back Jim Crow: The Integration of Minor League Baseball in the American South.* Charlottesville: University Press of Virginia, 1999.

Arsenault, Raymond. *Freedom Riders: 1961 and the Struggle for Racial Justice.* New York: Oxford University Press, 2006.

Barthel, Thomas. *Baseball Barnstorming and Exhibition Games, 1901–1962.* Jefferson, NC: McFarland, 2007.

Bayne, Bijan. "Black Professional Baseball in North Carolina between World War I and the Depression." In *Baseball in the Carolinas,* edited by Chris Holaday, 123–54. Jefferson, NC: McFarland, 2002.

Bjarkman, Peter C. "Tony Oliva." In *A Pennant for the Twin Cities: The 1965 Minnesota Twins,* edited by Gregory H. Wolf, 180–89. Phoenix: Society for American Baseball Research, 2015.

Briley, Ron. "In the Tradition of Jackie Robinson: Ozzie Virgil and the Integration of the Detroit Tigers." In *The Cooperstown Symposium on Baseball and American Culture, 2002*, edited by William M. Simons, 137–53. Jefferson, NC: McFarland, 2002.

Browning, Wilt. *The Rocks: The True Story of the Worst Team in Baseball History*. Asheboro, NC: Down Home Press, 1992.

Brunt, Larry. "Carlos Paula, the Man Who Integrated the Washington Senators." National Baseball Hall of Fame. Accessed September 18, 2023. https://baseballhall.org/discover-more/stories/going-deep/carlos-paula-integrated-washington-senators.

Buhite, Russell. *The Continental League*. Lincoln: University of Nebraska Press, 2014.

———. "The Continental League and Its Western Carolina League Affiliate: Branch Rickey's Second Finest Hour." *North Carolina Historical Review* 81, no. 4 (2004): 426–60.

Chafe, William H. *Civilities and Civil Rights: Greensboro, North Carolina and Black Struggle for Freedom*. New York: Oxford University Press, 1981.

Chibbaro, Mike. *Voices from Meadowbrook Park: Memories of Greenville, South Carolina's Historic Ballpark, 1938–1972*. Greenville, SC: Thirty-Seven Publishing, 2022.

Cohen, Alan. "R. C. Stevens." In *Sweet '60: The 1960 Pittsburgh Pirates*, edited by Clifton Blue Parker, 187–91. Phoenix: Society for American Baseball Research, 2013.

Corbett, Warren. "Bill White." Society for American Baseball Research. Last revised January 28, 2022. https://sabr.org/bioproj/person/c3eea582.

Craig, Keith. *Herb Pennock: Baseball's Faultless Pitcher*. Lanham, MD: Rowman and Littlefield, 2016.

Cryan, Mark. *Cradle of the Game: Baseball and Ballparks in North Carolina*. Madison, WI: August Publication, 2008.

Day, John Kyle. *The Southern Manifesto: Massive Resistance and the Fight to Preserve Segregation*. Jackson: University Press of Mississippi, 2015.

Debono, Paul. *The Indianapolis ABCs: History of a Premier Team in the Negro Leagues*. Jefferson, NC: McFarland, 1997.

Dolson, Frank. *Beating the Bushes: Life in the Minor Leagues*. South Bend, IN: Icarus Press, 1982.

Essington, Amy. *The Integration of the Pacific Coast League: Race and Baseball on the West Coast*. Lincoln: University of Nebraska Press, 2018.

Figueredo, Jorge S. *Who's Who in Cuban Baseball, 1878–1961*. Jefferson, NC: McFarland, 2003.

Franks, Joel S. *Asian Pacific Americans and Baseball*. Jefferson, NC: McFarland, 2003.

Gaunt, Robert. *We Would Have Played Forever: The Story of the Coastal Plain Baseball League.* Durham: Baseball America, 1997.

Gershenhorn, Jerry. *Louis Austin and the Carolina Times, A Life in the Long Black Freedom Struggle.* Chapel Hill: The University of North Carolina Press, 2018.

González Echevarría, Roberto. *The Pride of Havana, A History of Cuban Baseball.* New York: Oxford University Press, 2001.

Heaphy, Leslie A. *The Negro Leagues.* Jefferson, NC: McFarland, 2003.

Henninger, Thom. *Tony Oliva: The Life and Times of a Minnesota Legend.* Minneapolis: University of Minnesota Press, 2015.

Holaday, J. Chris. *Professional Baseball in North Carolina: An Illustrated City-by-City History, 1901–1996.* Jefferson, NC: McFarland, 1998.

Hulbert, Joanne. "Bob Estalella." In *Van Lingle Mungo: The Man, The Song, The Players,* edited by Bill Nowlin, 124–28. Phoenix: Society for American Baseball Research, 2014.

Jacobs, Barry. *Across the Line: Profiles in Basketball Courage: Tales of the First Black Players in the ACC and SEC.* Guilford, CT: Lyons Press, 2007.

Johnson, Lloyd, and Miles Wolff, eds. *The Encyclopedia of Minor League Baseball.* Durham: Baseball America, 2007.

Kirkland, Bill. *Eddie Neville of the Durham Bulls.* Jefferson, NC: McFarland, 1993.

Land, Kenneth C., Walter R. Davis, and Judith R. Blau. "Organizing the Boys of Summer: The Evolution of U.S. Minor-League Baseball, 1883–1990." *American Journal of Sociology* 100, no. 3 (November 1994): 781–813.

Lester, Larry. *Black Baseball's National Showcase: The East-West All-Star Game, 1933–1953.* Lincoln: University of Nebraska Press, 2002.

Lester, Paul. "History of Air Conditioning." Energy.gov, July 20, 2015. www.energy.gov/articles/history-air-conditioning.

Marlett, Jeffrey. "Leo Durocher." Society for American Baseball Research. Accessed September 18, 2021. https://sabr.org/bioproj/person/35d925c7.

Martin, Charles H. *Benching Jim Crow: The Rise and Fall of the Color Line in Southern College Sports, 1890–1980.* Urbana: University of Illinois Press, 2010.

McGregor, Robert Kuhh. *A Calculus of Color: The Integration of Baseball's American League.* Jefferson, NC: McFarland, 2015.

McKinney, Charles W. *Greater Freedom: The Evolution of the Civil Rights Struggle in Wilson, North Carolina.* Lanham, MD: University Press of America, 2010.

Mitchem, Pamela. "Wonder Team of the Carolinas: C. L. Moore and the Asheville Blues." *Black Ball: A Negro Leagues Journal* 5, no. 1 (Spring 2012): 33–51.

Moffi, Larry, and Jonathan Kronstadt. *Crossing the Line: Black Major Leaguers, 1947–1959*. Iowa City: University of Iowa Press, 1994.

Plott, William J. *The Negro Southern League: A Baseball History, 1920–1951*. Jefferson, NC: McFarland, 2015.

Pluto, Terry. *Loose Balls: The Short, Wild Life of the American Basketball Association*. New York: Simon and Schuster, 2007.

Pollock, Alan J. *Barnstorming to Heaven: Syd Pollock and His Great Black Teams*. Tuscaloosa: University of Alabama Press, 2006.

Ribowsky, Mark. *Don't Look Back: Satchel Paige in the Shadows of Baseball*. New York: Simon and Schuster, 1994.

Riley, James A. *The Biographical Encyclopedia of the Negro Baseball Leagues*. New York: Carroll and Graf, 1994.

Rumer, Thomas A. *The American Legion: An Official History, 1919–1989*. New York: M. Evans, 1990.

Santiago, Chiori. "Jose Nakamura: The First Nikkei in American Baseball." *Discover Nikkei*, October 9, 2009. www.discovernikkei.org/en/journal/2009/10/9/nikkei-heritage/.

Sapakoff, Gene. "The Cannon Street All-Stars." In *Baseball in the Carolinas*, edited by Chris Holaday, 162. Jefferson, NC: McFarland, 2002.

Sullivan, Neil J. *The Minors: The Struggle and Triumph of Baseball's Poorer Relation from 1876 to the Present*. New York: St. Martin's Press, 1991.

Sumner, Jim L. *Separating the Men from the Boys: The First Half Century of the Carolina League*. Winston-Salem, NC: John F. Blair, 1994.

Surdam, David G. "Television and Minor League Baseball: Changing Patterns of Leisure in Postwar America." *Journal of Sports Economics* 6, no. 1 (February 2005): 61–77.

Sutter, L. M. *Ball, Bat, and Bitumen: A History of Coalfield Baseball in the Appalachian South*. Jefferson, NC: McFarland, 2009.

———. *New Mexico Baseball: Miners, Outlaws, Indians and Isotopes, 1880 to the Present*. Jefferson, NC: McFarland, 2010.

Swaine, Rick. *The Integration of Major League Baseball: A Team by Team History*. Jefferson, NC: McFarland, 2009.

Terrell, Bob. *The Old Ball Yard: McCormick Field, Home of Memories*. Asheville, NC: WorldComm, 1997.

Threston, Christopher. *The Integration of Baseball in Philadelphia*. Jefferson, NC: McFarland, 2003.

Tuck, Stephen. "A City Too Dignified to Hate: Civic Pride, Civil Rights, and Savannah in Comparative Perspective." *Georgia Historical Quarterly* 79, no. 3 (Fall 1995): 539–59.

Tygiel, Jules. *Baseball's Great Experiment: Jackie Robinson and His Legacy*. New York: Oxford University Press, 1983.

Utley, Hank. "Bobby Hipps." In *Baseball in the Carolinas*, edited by Chris Holaday, 37–43. Jefferson, NC: McFarland, 2002.

Ward, Geoffrey C., and Ken Burns. *Baseball: An Illustrated History*. New York: Knopf, 2010.

Watkins, John J. "Dave Hoskins." Society for American Baseball Research. Last updated March 2023. http://sabr.org/bioproj/person/ecodf53d.

Weiss, Stuart. *The Curt Flood Story: The Man behind the Myth*. Columbia: University of Missouri, 2007.

Wiggins, David K. "Wendell Smith, the *Pittsburgh Courier-Journal* and the Campaign to Include Blacks in Organized Baseball, 1933–1945." *Journal of Sport History* 10, no. 2 (Summer 1983): 5–29.

Wolfe, Samuel Marion et al. *Code of Laws of South Carolina 1922, Vol. 2*. Columbia: R. L. Bryan Co. and the State Co., 1922.

Index

Page numbers in italics refer to illustrations.